Gordon Welchman

Bletchley Park's Architect of
Ultra Intelligence

Joel Greenberg

With a Foreword by
Rosamond Welchman

FRONTLINE BOOKS
LONDON

Gordon Welchman:
Bletchley Park's Architect of Ultra Intelligence

This edition first printed in 2014 and reprinted in 2016 by
Frontline Books
an imprint of Pen & Sword Books Ltd
47 Church Street
Barnsley, South Yorkshire
S70 2AS

www.frontline-books.com

HB ISBN: 978-1-84832-752-8
TPB ISBN: 978-1-47388-525-7

Printed and bound in Malta by Gutenberg Press Ltd

Typeset in 11/13.9pt Minion Pro

For more information on our books, please visit
www.frontline-books.com, email info@frontline-books.com
or write to us at the above address.

Contents

Plates

Plate 10: 'Cobra' high speed four-wheel bombe attachments; bombes under construction at BTM's Letchworth factory. (*both Crown © reproduced by kind permission of Director GCHQ*)

Plate 11: The British Typex cipher machine, modified to replicate an Enigma machine; prototype of the RM-26, designed by Welchman as a replacement for the Typex; a four-wheel bombe. (*all Crown © reproduced by kind permission of Director GCHQ*)

Plate 12: British, American and Canadian participants in the secret J.A.C. Conference held on 13 March 1944 at Arlington Hall, Virginia. (*Author's collection*)

Plate 13: GW while manager of Ferranti Electric Inc. *circa* 1957 (*Author's collection*); GW with his second wife, Fannie Hillsmith (*Welchman family*); GW while visiting his daughter Ros in Paris in 1972 (*Welchman family*); GW with his third wife Teeny and her son Tom in 1972. (*Welchman family*)

Plate 14: Bletchley Park in the early 1970s (*The Times*); Diana Lucy. (*Author's collection*)

Plate 15: GW with MITRE colleagues Bobbie Statkus and Bob Coltman. (*picture used with the permission of the MITRE Corporation. Copyright © The MITRE Corporation. All Rights Reserved*); GW with former BP colleague William Bundy. (*picture used with the permission of William Adams*)

Plate 16: GW on holiday with Teeny in the Virgin Islands at the end of March 1985 (*Welchman family*); GW's son Nick in 2011. (*Author's collection*)

Foreword

Unlike my brother Nicholas Welchman, my sister Susanna Griffith and I were born too late to have any direct memory of my father's work at Bletchley Park. During my childhood Dad's war work was a mere rumour in our family – a hint that he had done something important during the war that we couldn't talk about. I was a sceptical child and did not totally believe this. When the secret was let out and Dad wrote his book, *The Hut Six Story*, it was a revelation to me, and something of a surprise. I was very fortunate to help Dad in his last year of life with his final paper on his codebreaking experience, which made those years more real to me. In 2001 I visited Bletchley Park – not nearly as developed then as it is now – with my son Daniel Tischler. We were lucky to hear John Herivel give a talk on the occasion of the opening of an exhibit about the 'Herivel Tip'. Both of us were surprised and delighted to find that the talk was largely about Dad's leadership role at Bletchley Park. It was the first time that I had heard in detail of Dad's work in words other than his own. I was also surprised to find myself and my son being identified as part of a sort of Bletchley Park 'family', a child and a grandchild. That must now be rather a large family!

Dad's war work and the secrecy about it for many years afterwards had a significant impact on our family life. I think it was difficult for Dad to settle down after the excitement and creativity of the war years, and we moved frequently, three times across the Atlantic. I never stayed in one school for more than two years, and often felt myself to be an outsider, too English in the United States, and too American in England. However, there are benefits to being an outsider, and I was very lucky to land up in some very interesting schools.

Dad was a charming person, quite the gentleman. His inclination was to enjoy life, and I remember him most with a twinkle in his eye and a subtle smile. I was occasionally startled, after he had met some slightly disreputable friend of mine, to hear of his disapproval because in their presence he was so polite and accepting. The friend would have no clue of Dad's disapproval. However he was capable of changing his opinion later, and often did. He was always in control of himself, in my memory at least. If displeased, or perhaps a bit intoxicated, he would withdraw to his study to 'write a letter'. We always wondered if in fact all of that time was spent writing letters, but judging by the piles of letters that remain, a lot of it was!

Dad had several personal characteristics that I believe were related to his work during the war. When something interested him, he threw himself into it. He loved music, and amassed an enormous collection of records, all of which he seemed to know quite well, and played quite often. There was a time when he took up gardening, and performed Olympian feats in transforming an unpromising rocky slope into a lush and colourful garden. He claimed that his close reading of *Aku-Aku* (Thor Hyerdahl's book about the Easter Island statues) taught him how to move the ridiculously large stones. He was always curious and loved to read and learn about new ideas. When he was bed-ridden in his last months I remember him musing about a mobile of little sailing ships that floated about in the breeze above his bed, and wondering how one could tell just when they would all be in a straight line.

Dad had methodical habits. For example I remember that when leaving the house he had a system for counting off tasks that should be done on his fingers (turn out the lights, turn off the gas, lock the door, things like that). In his bachelor days after his first divorce he learned one recipe (a pot roast cooked in an electric frying pan) that I believe he served to me every time I visited during that period. It was always done in exactly the same way – quite delicious, by the way! He paid close attention to detail, for example recording even minuscule household expenses. He kept meticulous records of his tape recordings of music that he assembled into concerts he offered in a local nursing home. When calculating a tip in a restaurant, he insisted on doing long multiplication with paper and pencil, rather than estimating, which could be a bit embarrassing for his guests.

Dad's world shifted considerably during his lifetime. He took time to change in some respects but he certainly did change eventually both in attitudes and tastes. When his children were young Dad was sometimes distant as perhaps many English fathers of his generation were. He told me in the context of my own children that he didn't really know what to do with small children until he could read them a book. I remember being a little embarrassed by his attempts to produce appropriate Southern United

States accents when reading Uncle Remus folk stories aloud to us as children. However, I believe that at times he was able to do special things with each of us children as individuals, for example birding with my sister Susanna, and fishing with me. Hiking and camping were some of the best memories that I have of family activities. I inherited a collection of Dad's favourite photos, and several that clearly meant a lot to him were of my sister Susanna and me on a mountaintop in northern Vermont, where we used to go for summers.

I believe that Dad always considered himself to be English at heart. He applied for United States citizenship for reasons of security in his work, but he loved to return to visit his family and friends in England. It was sad that for so much of his life he did not get recognition for his work at Bletchley Park, but he told me that he felt his career had been interesting and rewarding regardless. My brother, my sister and I were enthusiastic when Joel Greenberg told us of his intention to write a book about our father. When Joel visited Nick and me in 2011 (sadly, less than a year before Nick's death) it gave us a wonderful opportunity to revisit old memories together. We found that we had a good collection of documents to offer Joel, and were pleased by his excitement about the boxes of Dad's papers that had been stashed in Nick's attic, forgotten. I also had a number of photos and items of memorabilia that I was given by Dad's third wife, Teeny. I am sure that Dad would have been very pleased to know of Joel's project and the considerable interest in his many achievements.

Rosamond Welchman

Preface

Along with the general public, I first became aware of the story of Bletchley Park (BP) and the codebreaking activities which took place there during the Second World War when Frederick Winterbotham published his book *The Ultra Secret* in November 1974. I had been awarded a PhD in Numerical Mathematics by the University of Manchester several months earlier and was aware of the contributions of both Max Newman and Alan Turing to the developments in computing which had taken place there in the 1950s. I of course knew nothing of their work at Bletchley Park and was keen to find out how it had influenced their post-war work in Manchester. Much to my disappointment, Winterbotham's book contained no technical detail. To get official approval for the book, he had restricted himself to describing how intelligence produced at BP was processed and distributed to Allied commanders in complete secrecy. In any event, he had neither access to official records nor direct knowledge of the actual techniques which produced it. British authorities continued to oppose the release of any information about the methods which were used to obtain the intelligence. Thus, subsequent books, such as Anthony Cave Brown's *Bodyguard of Lies* in 1975 and Ronald Lewin's *Ultra Goes to War* in 1978, also had little technical detail as those whom these authors interviewed were bound by the Official Secrets Act. R. V. Jones, who had become Assistant Director of Intelligence (Science) in the Air Ministry during the war, published his personal memoir, *Most Secret War* in 1978. His book told the story of the rise of scientific intelligence during the Second World War from his perspective. I eagerly purchased a copy but again was frustrated because, like Winterbotham, Jones was restricted both by what he could say about how intelligence was produced and by the fact that he was also not directly involved in the process. However, before the end of the decade, some details of the Enigma encryption machine and how it was broken were revealed in French and Polish publications.

In 1982, I came across a book published first in the United States and then in Britain, which provided a detailed description of how encrypted German communications sent over wireless networks had been intercepted by Britain's 'Y' Service and subsequently read by the codebreakers at BP. Here at last was a book that I and other mathematicians, technologists and historians could get our teeth into. Unfortunately, the British and American governments didn't feel the same way. The book, *The Hut Six Story*, caused quite a stir in both Britain's Government Communications Headquarters (GCHQ) and its American counterpart, the National Security Agency (NSA). It was written by an insider who had first-hand knowledge of how the Enigma machine operated and how messages encrypted by it had been read on an industrial scale. Its author was Gordon Welchman, the man who had produced the blueprint for the BP 'codebreaking factory' and who had personally led the attack against the German Air Force and Army's communications networks. With the publication of Winterbotham's book, Welchman had felt that he was at last released from his wartime pledge of secrecy. He had always been scrupulous in protecting the secret of his wartime activities and had avoided all conversation about the war itself, other than with those in the know. This was not a position that he felt comfortable with, as he revealed to the BBC in one of several interviews which were included in their *Secret War* series, broadcast in 1977:

> One was terrified that somehow or other one would reveal a bit of information that one had learned from an Ultra decode rather than from a newspaper . . . I had really had enough of this awful responsibility by the end of the war when I was very glad to drop it, and after the war, for years and years, I didn't even read the histories of the war because I was afraid that somehow or other I might reveal something that I had learned from Ultra.

I was certainly puzzled by Welchman's book because earlier works had given little indication of how important his contribution had been. Yet reading *The Hut Six Story* and working through the technical detail provided, it seemed to me that he must have been a key figure at BP.

Welchman subsequently became an individual of some concern to both GCHQ and the NSA until his untimely death in 1985. He was interviewed several times by American Federal Agents following publication of his book and received aggressive communications from both GCHQ and NSA senior staff. Under threat of prosecution by the US Government, he was prevented from promoting his book.

He had been at BP throughout the war, arriving on 4 September 1939, the same day as the only BP veteran widely known to the general public, Alan Turing. His remarkable contribution to cryptography was achieved without any previous experience of it apart from a brief course that he attended in the spring of 1939 at the request of Alastair Denniston, the head of MI6's cryptography section, the Government Code and Cipher School (GC&CS). He was in fact a lecturer in algebraic geometry at Sidney Sussex College, Cambridge, and had been writing a book on the subject for five years. In the early years of the Second World War he was transformed into a key figure in the triumph of BP. Within two months of his arrival, he had independently reinvented a key part of the pre-war work of Polish cryptographers and laid the foundations for Sixta, a fusion of signals intelligence and cryptography. After a further month he had made three fundamental contributions to the ultimate success of BP: he was one of the first to recognize the need for a rapid expansion of BP's infrastructure for the decryption and analysis of intercepted Enigma traffic; he drew up an organizational plan which would enable BP to achieve such an expansion; he invented a device which would transform Turing's design for the bombe into a workable machine. Along with Alan Turing, he had in effect developed a radically new production-orientated approach to machine cryptanalysis. BP then turned to Welchman to put his plan in place and he took on the leadership of the group which would ultimately decrypt over one million German Air Force and Army signals. In 1943 he was given responsibility for all 'machine' developments at BP and while he was not directly involved in its creation, the world's first electronic computer, Colossus, was designed and built on his 'watch'. The role also included technical liaison with American cryptographic agencies.

In 1948 he decided to emigrate to the United States and initially played a key role in Project Whirlwind, an ambitious project at MIT which would, for the first time, apply computers to air traffic control and air security. Once again his insightful mind recognized the need for original work on the problems of computer applications. He also gave the first course of lectures on programming for a digital computer at MIT for the electrical engineering department. After working for several companies in the fledgling American computer industry, he joined the MITRE Corporation in 1962. MITRE had been tasked with the development and integration of digital computers to monitor US airspace, detect potential threats, and co-ordinate tactical responses. His work with MITRE led to numerous classified publications and several inventions which now lie at the heart of

American air defence systems. While his work at BP contributed to the birth of the digital age, his post-war career helped nurture it through its infancy.

After reading Welchman's book I became intrigued by BP and when I joined the Open University in 1977, I was delighted to discover that it was only a few miles away. I subsequently took every opportunity to snoop around the place, read books about it and take my children there when it opened to the public in the 1990s. After leaving the Open University in 2010, I joined BP as a volunteer supporter, historian, and later as a part-time member of the management team. I quickly realized that colleagues who had been researching BP for many years held Welchman in the highest esteem. Soon I started to think about writing his biography and, after getting the support of the Welchman family, I began researching this book.

Today, BP is a Museum and Heritage Site which receives thousands of visitors weekly from around the world. A number of the wartime huts and buildings remain, although many are in need of urgent repair. The story of GC&CS's wartime activities is told through guided tours, demonstrations of some of the technologies developed there, such as the bombes and Colossus and numerous displays. While visitors marvel at the achievements of those who worked there, most are hearing the names of the story's key players for the first time. Only two, Alan Turing and Dilly Knox, have inspired serious biographies. Yet they, along with Alastair Denniston, Edward Travis, John Tiltman, Bill Tutte, Tommy Flowers and Gordon Welchman, remain unknown to the general public. Each, in his own way, made BP's achievements possible but, like Turing's, Welchman's contribution is seen by many historians and former BP colleagues as being fundamental to its ultimate success.

As Welchman's BP colleague Sir Stuart Milner-Barry wrote in his obituary in 1985:

> It was indeed a classic example of the hour producing the man. Without the fire in his belly, without the vision which again and again proved his intuition correct, and his capacity for inspiring others with his confidence, I do not believe that the task of converting the original break-through into an effective organization for the production of up-to-date intelligence could have been achieved.

Joel Greenberg

Acknowledgements

When I first started to think about writing this book, I approached the Bletchley Park Trust to seek their support. I am grateful to Simon Greenish, the Trust's former CEO, for offering it unreservedly. Simon introduced me to Mark Baldwin, whom I would like to thank for putting me in touch with the Welchman family. Nick Welchman's loft held a treasure trove of his father's letters and documents, which he had faithfully kept safe since his father's death in 1985. Sadly, Nick passed away before this book was finished. Gordon's two daughters, Susanna and Rosamond, have also kindly shared memories of their father with me. The Welchman family has generously donated a considerable amount of material, including personal items and documents, to the Bletchley Park Trust. At the beginning of the project I sought the advice of my friend and colleague Frank Carter. I regard Frank as one of the world's foremost experts on the mathematics and technologies used at BP during the war. Frank's advice and knowledge has been invaluable to me and he has contributed technical material which can be found in Appendix 2. I am grateful to John Gallehawk who directed me to a number of relevant documents in the National Archives. I would also like to thank Michael Smith for his insightful views on a suitable structure for this book. Finally, I would like to thank my lovely daughters for their interest and encouragement.

Prologue

The weather was cool and dry with slightly above average sunshine in the British summer of 1974. It was also a turbulent political time on both sides of the Atlantic. The IRA had begun its bombing campaign on mainland Britain and had targeted the Tower of London, the Houses of Parliament, and pubs in Birmingham. In the United States, after the Watergate Scandal, Richard Nixon had become the first US president to be forced to resign. Gordon Welchman and his wife Teeny arrived in England in mid-July after visiting Teeny's relatives in Germany. Her mother was Welchman's second cousin, her father Bavarian and she had grown up in a mountain valley near the Austrian border.

The couple stayed with Teeny's godmother in England and, during the visit, her son-in-law happened to show Welchman an article in the 28 July issue of the *Sunday Telegraph*. The article was part two of a preview of a book by Frederick Winterbotham called *The Ultra Secret* due to be published on 2 October. The previous week's edition of the paper was still in the house and Welchman was able to read the entire article. After scrupulously avoiding all conversation about the Second World War and his part in it with anyone apart from one or two former wartime colleagues, for almost thirty years, one can only imagine his thoughts as he read about the revelations in Winterbotham's book. As he said in *The Hut Six Story*:

> I felt that this turn of events released me from my wartime pledge of secrecy. I could at last talk to my friends, relatives, and colleagues about the activities of one of these two organizations, Hut 6, with which I was closely associated from the outset. I could even write my own account of what actually happened. I began to think of a book.

While on holiday in the UK in May 1972, he had met his old BP colleague Joe Hooper. Sir Leonard (Joe) Hooper had stayed on at GCHQ after the war and became its Director in January 1965, a post he held until

November 1973. Welchman had explained to Hooper why several aspects of his Hut 6 experience could be extremely valuable in the types of military research and development with which he had become involved. Hooper had assured him that within a few years he would be able to disclose all aspects of his experience, including the basic reasons for Hut 6's success and German failure in the field of Enigma security.

During his visit in 1974 Welchman wrote to George Goodall, a GCHQ official, to clarify GCHQ's position on the release of wartime documents and also to what extent he could use his knowledge of German battlefield communications in his consultancy work for the US Air Force. An old Hut 6 colleague, Harold Fletcher, who had remained on at GCHQ after the war until his retirement in December 1971, had put him in contact with Goodall. Welchman and Fletcher had remained friends after the war and the Welchmans visited the Fletchers in Cheltenham during their summer trip to England. Having become an American citizen in 1962, Welchman also asked Goodall if he was still eligible for a UK passport.

After returning to the US, he received a reply on 18 September. In his letter, Goodall said that there would be some relaxation on revealing the existence of material and its use but not on the means by which it was obtained. GCHQ was not concerned as long as Welchman restricted himself to the way in which German battlefield communications were organized, equipped and operated, but he should not discuss how they were exploited by the Allies. He suggested that Welchman wait to see what new policy emerged and said that he would keep him informed of developments, an undertaking he failed to honour. At least he was able to confirm that as Welchman had not renounced his UK citizenship, he was eligible to apply for a British passport at any time.

Welchman had also attached two papers he had written as part of his consultancy work for the MITRE Corporation in the USA that he thought GCHQ might be interested in: 'Selective Access to Tactical Information' (dated August 1970) and 'An Integrated Approach to the Defence of West Germany' (dated February 1974). Goodall said that they had aroused considerable interest and were still circulating in GCHQ.

Fletcher was also very interested in Welchman's current work. Like several others who had stayed on in GCHQ after the war, he had found himself in a difficult position. He could not deny to colleagues that he had been in the same organization during the war but the easiest way to avoid awkward questions about Hut 6, to friend and foe alike, was simply to say that he had been involved in other work at BP. This had become second nature to him, so his initial reaction to Welchman's questions had been to say 'please leave me out'. However, Fletcher had decided that, as it had been ten years since he had ceased to operate at a high level and over three years since he had retired completely, the time for awkwardness or potential damage caused must surely be over. Fletcher and Welchman were also delighted to learn at that time that their old friend and BP colleague Stuart Milner-Barry had been knighted in the New Year Honours list

On returning to America, Welchman and his wife held a dinner party for some friends. One of those attending was Diana Lucy, who had actually introduced Welchman to his wife Teeny. In 1969 she had been working at the local hospital and had treated a couple, Elisabeth Wimer (known as Teeny by friends and family) and her then husband Bill, who had been in a car accident. The couple's car had been written off and they needed transport to the airport. Diana had given them the keys to her house which was not far away and told them that they could relax there. After work, her husband had driven the couple to the airport. Diana kept in touch with Elisabeth by letter and in late July 1971 she had a telephone call from her. Much to Diana's surprise, Teeny was in Newburyport, visiting a distant relative, and wondered whether Diana would like to come for tea. The distant relative was none other than Gordon Welchman and Diana and he subsequently became great friends.

At the party, the subject of Winterbotham's book came up and Welchman announced to the gathering that he could at last tell them what he had been doing during the Second World War. Diana's astonished reaction was matched by Welchman's when she revealed that she had been an intercept operator throughout the war. As Diana Stuart she had volunteered for the WAAF in August 1941 and undergone four months of training with the Post Office in Manchester and three months at a coastal RAF station. She had been sent to Chicksands Priory where she remained until 1945. After the war she had married an American, Frank Lucy, and settled in Newburyport in the spring of 1946. Later she would prove to be a valuable source of information to him about the inner workings of the intercept stations within the 'Y' Service.

In late 1981, just before his book was published, Welchman had become aware of the work of the Poles and in particular of Marian Rejewski, which had taken place years before GC&CS arrived at BP. His book, *The Hut Six Story* had been written with little knowledge of the immense contribution of the Poles and, as his book was about to go to press, he was only able to make minor corrections and include Rejewski in the dedication. Following its publication, MITRE was forced to withdraw his security clearance, which in effect prevented him from continuing to work for them as a consultant. He decided to put the record straight in 1985 by publishing a paper in the first issue of a new academic journal, *Intelligence and National Security*, titled 'From Polish Bomba to British Bombe: The Birth of Ultra'. Scarred by his previous experience, he submitted his article to the Defence, Press and Broadcasting Committee (better known as the D-Notice Committee) which subsequently cleared the article in writing on 8 July 1985. About one week later, Welchman received a letter from the then Director of GCHQ, Sir Peter Marychurch. This was only the second official letter that Welchman had received from GCHQ since the war. It included the following extraordinary statement:

> I ask you to consider not only the direct damage to security but also the knock-on effect of your actions; each time a person like yourself, of obviously deep knowledge and high repute, publishes inside information about the inner secrets of our work, there is more temptation and more excuse for others to follow suit.

The so-called inner secrets that Welchman had published were about technologies which had been obsolete in intelligence terms for many years. Despite an apparent vendetta against him by the intelligence services, Welchman, along with most of his former BP colleagues remained largely unknown to the general public. After his death his case was taken up by commentators on the intelligence services such as Nigel West and David Hooper .

As Sir Stuart Milner-Barry said in a letter to the *Guardian* after his death:

> To talk of 'direct damage to security' in the context of Welchman's article in 'Intelligence and National Security' is surely absurd. The secrets of the Enigma and how it was broken are of fascinating interest historically, and it is a sad pity that the authorities still prevent the story being properly told. But to suppose that the battles which we had to wage before the birth of the first electronic computer (which must seem to present-day cryptanalysts rather like fighting with bows and arrows) could be relevant to security now is just not credible.[1]

Chapter 1

Origins: From Algebraic Geometry to Cryptography

Fishponds, a suburb of Bristol known for its aeronautical industries in both world wars, was the birthplace of William Gordon Welchman on 15 June 1906. Gordon, as he became known, was the youngest of three children of William Welchman (1866–1954), a missionary who became a country parson and later Archdeacon of Bristol, and his wife, Elizabeth, daughter of the Reverend Edward Moule Griffith. Gordon's paternal grandfather George and great grandfather William were also clergymen.

When Welchman was about eighteen months old, his father became vicar of the medieval Temple Church in Bristol. The vicarage was in Berkeley Square, Clifton, which had a large central area of lawn, trees and flower beds on rising ground. The road outside the Welchman house fell gently to the left, and on the other side of the road was a stone ramp sloping up to railings that enclosed the lawn area. One day, Gordon was left in his pram outside the house but the brakes had not been properly adjusted. Before long the pram started to move down and across the road. When it reached the ramp on the other side, it turned over and threw him out. Miraculously, a pillow inside the pram also flew out and he landed on it unhurt. If his head had hit the pavement, one can only speculate on how history may have been changed.

Welchman was much younger than his brother and sister and felt out of place in his clerical home. While his sister Enid May pursued a career as a nurse, his brother Eric, thirteen years his senior, was one of the first officers to be killed at Mons in 1914 at the beginning of the First World War. Gordon overcame a childhood stammer through singing and this no doubt led to his lifelong passion for music and in particular, madrigals. He also decided to teach himself to dance and practised his steps with a broomstick, with which he became quite proficient. After completing his early schooling, he was sent to Marlborough College, a public school in Wiltshire, which seemed to suit him very well. Founded in the 1840s, Marlborough was much younger than Harrow, Eton or Winchester. In the early twentieth century, many believed that institutional longevity was more important than academic strength, the latter being quite evident at Marlborough. Its Officer Training Corps offered marches, drills and lessons in map reading and target practice. In later life, Welchman shared with his son Nick,[1] who would also go to Marlborough, happy memories of elaborate wargames and manoeuvres. A career as an artillery officer might have beckoned but he had developed a close bond with a mathematics teacher called Alan Robson, an alumnus of Sidney Sussex College, Cambridge, which would set him on a different course.

While at Marlborough, Welchman would frequently cycle to a farm where his cousin Sara lived with her husband George Hussey and their two daughters, Myrtle and Gladys. Welchman became quite close to both girls and little did he know that Myrtle in due course would marry a Bavarian gentleman and have a daughter whose path he would cross many years later.

After attending Marlborough College from 1920 to 1925, he became a Mathematical Scholar at Trinity College, Cambridge, in 1925 and distinguished himself in the Tripos, gaining a first class in Part I in 1926 and was a 'wrangler' in Part II in 1928. 'Wrangler' was the quaint Cambridge word for a student who gained first-class honours in the third year. After teaching at Cheltenham Boys' School for one year, he returned to Cambridge in 1929 and was elected a fellow of Sidney Sussex College. The college needed another supervisor in mathematics and he was considered to be an admirable choice. Apart from having the highest professional qualifications, he also had considerable artistic and athletic interests that allowed him to find common ground with an unusually large number of undergraduates. His students remembered him as having a genial approachability and a capacity to understand and respond to their points of view. The College soon elected him to the office of Dean.[2] He was a musician and in great demand by the madrigal groups.[3] Music would continue to be a prime leisure interest throughout his life.[4] Unfortunately, a motorcycle accident would hamper his expertise as a budding trombonist.

Welchman was a university-standard hockey player and while at Sidney Sussex he would sometimes turn out for Cambridge University Wanderers. He was well known among Cambridge University's leading climbers and explorers and in 1932 led a University expedition to Spitzbergen, the largest and only permanently populated island of the Svalbard archipelago. This was a much more daunting journey in 1932 than today and he wrote a long account of the expedition in the College's magazine, *The Pheon*. Years later he told friends that during the expedition he had gone to relieve himself and saw, much to his horror, that his urine was a bright red colour. He was in a state of panic until his colleagues reminded him that they had eaten beetroot for breakfast.[5]

Former students always seemed to remember two things about him; an impeccable dress sense and continual, unsuccessful efforts to light his pipe throughout lectures. He was in great demand at University dinners and parties because of his good looks and ability to talk on a range of subjects. One can well imagine him fitting in well at Cambridge in the 1920s and 1930s. Academically, he had specialized in the field of algebraic geometry and in 1934 had been commissioned by Cambridge University Press to write a book titled *Introduction to Algebraic Geometry*. The subject was notable for its conspicuous lack of practical application, being a branch of pure mathematics. Welchman was quite proud of the fact that he had painstakingly produced all of the diagrams that were to appear in the book.[6]

Apart from music and motorcycles, his other great interest as a young man was women. His dashing good looks no doubt were helpful in this regard but, as a gentleman, he never shared with friends or family the details of his youthful dalliances. He did, however, tell his son that he had once attached a sidecar to his motorcycle so that he could convey a young woman on a long journey. On arrival, he discovered that a missing bolt could have separated him from his *amour* at any stage en route.

Attitudes to women and motor transport at Cambridge between the wars were, to say the least, traditional. In the spring of 1919 there had been insistent calls for the reopening of the whole question of the position of women in the University. The *Cambridge Review* in June 1920 addressed the issue in an editorial as follows: 'so long as the sun and moon endureth, Cambridge should remain a society for men, and any sister institution should by its own arrangements produce a charter, and, as a separate institution, confer its own degrees'. It also went on to deplore the prevalence of young married fellows in Colleges and recommended a period of 'at least ten years' celibacy on election'. The problem for the anti-feminists was that the view of the country as a whole was against them and in 1918 the Representation of the People Act had been passed, enfranchising women over the age of thirty who met minimum property qualifications. Before the end of 1920 Oxford University had approved the admission of women to full membership. By 1926, women had become eligible for teaching posts and just before the war Dorothy Garrod became the first woman professor in either Oxford or Cambridge. In 1928, women were granted equal voting rights to men in the UK.

Arcane attitudes were not just restricted to the role of women at Cambridge in the 1920s. In 1925, two Indian tennis stars, D. R. Rutman and S. M. Hadi, were turned down for the captaincy of the University team, even though on the basis of ability and seniority, the role should have gone to one of them. Yet, the prevailing view at the time supported an unwritten law that 'gentlemen of colour' should not be elected. Concerns were raised about the morality of young Cambridge men who were often noisy, obstreperous and ingenious. The arrival of the motor car created even more of a stir with the Senate being told in 1925 that 'the motor habit, when it becomes an obsession, induces a state of mind out of harmony with the best traditions of Cambridge'. There was also a concern about under-graduate immorality being stimulated and facilitated by the use of the motor car after dark. The majority of these young men had been educated at public schools. Sidney Sussex was not a college overly concerned about its social image, yet in 1929, only 25 per cent of its freshmen were from state schools.[7]

In 1931, at the age of twenty-five, Welchman became friends with Betty Huntley-Wright, a beautiful young actress and vocalist.[8] While family and friends believed that the relationship was purely platonic, Welchman may well have had other ideas as this poem written by him and sent to Betty suggests:

> Dear Betty, I am greeting you
>   The day that you are twenty.
> Of birthdays you have had a few
>   And may you still have plenty.
> I wasn't there when you were 'naught'
>   (Oh Betty, were you naughty?)
> But hope to drink your health in port
>   The day that you are forty.
> When sixty years have rolled away
>   I hope you'll still be merry,
> And on the happy natal day
>   I'll drink your health in sherry.
> And if we both should be alive
>   I hope we'll still be 'matey'

When I'll have got to eighty-five
And you'll have got to eighty.[9]

It was almost certainly music which brought Welchman together with his first wife, Katharine Hodgson, as they met at a summer music camp around 1936. Welchman was a member of the Cambridge University Madrigal Society and regularly performed with it. Katharine was a professional musician and came from a very strong military family. Her father, Francis Faith Hodgson, was a captain in the 84th Punjabis, Indian Army. Her mother's sister, Do, was married to Colonel Arthur Crookenden, a powerful figure in the family who went on to write a history of the Cheshire Regiment in the First World War. His three sons were also gallant soldiers who all ended the war with physical damage.

Gordon Welchman and Katharine Hodgson were married on 20 March 1937 at the parish church in the village of Pangbourne in Berkshire. They eventually settled in a house called Brandon Hill on the outskirts of Cambridge. Their first child, Jeremy Nicholas (Nick) was born on 11 January 1938 and family life was initially idyllic. Following the signing of the Munich agreement on 30 September 1938, the *Cambridge Review* was able to report that while a few meetings had been abandoned and a few lectures shortened, the course of University life seemed to be running as smoothly as ever.

Against this back-drop of life in 1930s Cambridge, in the latter part of 1938 Welchman received a letter which would change the course of his. Unknown to him, two former Cambridge dons, who had worked in the British Admiralty's cryptographic section, NID 25, (euphemistically known as Room 40 after the room that originally housed it in the Old Admiralty building) during the First World War, had been trawling through the staff and student lists at both Oxford and Cambridge. They were looking for men of 'the professor type' who were deemed suitable for secret work within the Foreign Office. In 1919, the remnants of NID 25 and the War Office's cryptographic branch, MI 1(b), had been amalgamated into a unified signals intelligence agency, the Government Code and Cipher School (GC&CS).[10] When Rear Admiral Hugh Sinclair succeeded Sir Mansfield Cumming (the first 'C') as Chief of the Secret Intelligence Service (SIS) in late 1922 or early 1923, he was also made non-operational director of GC&CS. SIS was a section of the Foreign Office and referred to within government circles as both 'C's organization' and MI 1(c). Early in the Second World War, a new cover name, MI 6 was adopted. In January 1924,

Sinclair met with the operational head of GC&CS, Alastair Denniston, and informed him that his section's work would be integrated with that of SIS. GC&CS would be responsible for cryptography and SIS for the distribution of intelligence derived from this source. Furthermore, GC&CS would have full access to SIS records. In June, GC&CS was instructed to distribute decrypted material directly to its customer departments, with copies going to Sinclair. In the spring of 1926 SIS and GC&CS moved into combined headquarters in offices within Broadway Buildings opposite St James's Park Underground station.[11]

The two dons were both from King's College. Frank Birch was a fellow during 1915–34 and a lecturer in history from 1915 until 1928. In the 1930s he had left Cambridge to work in the theatre. Frank Adcock had become a fellow in 1911 and held the chair of ancient history from 1925 until 1951. While the First World War cryptanalysts did not have much time for mathematicians, GC&CS was already putting one Cambridge mathematician through preliminary training in London and a second was recruited from Oxford in February 1939. Welchman had been noticed by one of Denniston's recruiters, hence the letter to him asking if, in the event of war, he would be prepared to defend King and Country by undertaking some secret government work. Welchman's answer was an emphatic yes and he duly attended preliminary indoctrination sessions on 20–23 and 27–30 March 1939 at the Broadway Buildings in London.[12] He had been recruited for the General Diplomatic Section and among his fellow trainees were the Cambridge mathematician who had been recruited the year before, Alan Turing, and two others who would become close working colleagues at BP, Dennis Babbage and John Jeffreys.

Following introductions by Denniston on the mornings of the 20th and 27th other instructors took over, two of whom would significantly influence Welchman and play a major role in the success of BP. Oliver Strachey[13] followed Denniston on the afternoon of the 20th and 27th with sessions on 'Transposition'. He also did sessions on the morning of the 22nd and 29th on 'Substitution'.

As Welchman wrote about Strachey in *The Hut Six Story*:

> I remember very little else about the preliminary indoctrination in London, except that I was very impressed by Oliver Strachey, a senior member of the GCCS staff, who during the coming war would head an organization known as Intelligence Services Oliver Strachey (ISOS). He seemed to be giving us an overview of the whole problem

of deriving intelligence from enemy communications, and this may well have been a strong guiding influence on my wartime work.

On the morning and afternoon of the 21st and 28th, the recruits were given an introduction to 'Book-Building' by John Tiltman.[14] Tiltman would go on to be promoted to the rank of brigadier and head the Army Section at BP.

When he wrote *The Hut Six Story*, Welchman had no memory of meeting either Dilly Knox (who would be his first boss at BP) or Knox's assistant Peter Twinn during the course in London. Twinn had been the mathematician recruited from Oxford in February 1939 and he would remain in Knox's team in the period before the war and the move to BP. Following their indoctrination, the new recruits were placed on an emergency staff list and, in the event of war, they were told to report as soon as possible to Bletchley Park in Buckinghamshire. These men of the 'professor type' would be employed by the Foreign Office as temporary civil servants and paid the then handsome sum of £600 per year.

Back at Cambridge, the political temperature was rising. The balance of opinion seemed to favour the National Government until 1935 but by 1938, the national situation was confused and Cambridge Union debates degenerated into complete irrationality. Opinion could be swung to the right one day by fascists such as Oswald Mosley and to the left by pacifists such as Bertrand Russell. In November 1938 the Cambridge Union voted 233 to 107 that the defence of Britain was not safe in the hands of Mr Chamberlain. By the end of term, the post-Munich euphoria was wearing thin as more and more details emerged about the Nazi persecution of the Jews. Churchill addressed a meeting on 19 May 1939, specifically to counter the Union vote against conscription. The meeting was lively and at the end, the chairman declared that a show of hands indicated a 10 to 1 majority in favour of conscription.

The last word on the debate in Cambridge perhaps came from John Maynard Keynes. Writing from King's College on 14 October 1939 he said:

> The intelligentsia of the Left were the loudest in demanding that the Nazi aggression should be resisted at all costs; when it comes to a showdown, scarce four weeks have passed before they remember that they are pacifists and write defeatist letters to your columns, leaving the defence of freedom to Colonel Blimp and the Old School Tie, for whom three cheers.[15]

On 1 September 1939 German forces invaded Poland and the next day, Britain and France issued an ultimatum demanding that Germany withdraw from Poland within twelve hours. On 3 September Britain and France declared war on Germany and in Cambridge, as he listened to the news as it came over the wireless, Welchman began packing his essential belongings. The next day, after saying goodbye to Katharine and Nick, he climbed into his open-topped Morgan three-wheeler and began the forty-seven-mile journey to Bletchley Park. He would be followed there in the months and years to come by a formidable team of Cambridge intellectuals recruited by Adcock and Birch such as F. L. Lucas, D. W. Lucas, L. P. Wilkinson, J. Saltmarsh, G. C. Morris, A. J. H. Knight, G. Barraclough, Max Newman, F. H. Hinsley, J. H. Plumb, H. O. Evennett, T. D. Jones, R. J. Getty, D. R. Taunt, L. W. Forster, D. W. Babbage, R. F. Bennett, E. R. P. Vincent, D. Parmée and F. J. Norton. Welchman would personally go on to recruit, among others: C. H. O'D. Alexander, P. S. Milner-Barry, J. W. J. Herivel and D. Rees.

Chapter 2

Bletchley Park:
The First Four Months

On 3 September 1939, the operational head of GC&CS, Alastair Denniston, informed T. J. Wilson of the Foreign Office that they had been obliged to recruit men from the emergency list at a rate of pay agreed by the Treasury. Welchman's name was on that list[1] as one of the men of 'the professor type' and he duly reported for duty on 4 September. He was greeted by Denniston in his office on the ground floor of the mansion at BP which had been the morning room of BP's pre-war owners, the Leon family.

BP had been bought by Sir Herbert Leon, a wealthy London stockbroker and his second wife Fanny around 1882 along with 581 acres of land. They had added servants' and domestic quarters and further extensions. The mansion, which one former GC&CS employee described as 'ghastly' and another as 'indescribably ugly', had a number of different architectural styles integrated into its façade. Apparently, the Leons travelled abroad extensively, would see some architectural feature which they liked and would return home with a sketch of it for their builders to implement. Sir Herbert died in 1926 and his wife carried on running the estate until her death in January 1937. Sir Herbert's heir, his son George, duly sold off the bulk of the estate at auction by splitting it into lots. Lot 1, which initially didn't sell and consisted of 55 acres including the mansion, stable yard and lake, was bought by a consortium of local builders and developers headed by Captain Herbert Faulkner, a keen horseman whom Welchman would later remember riding around BP in his hunting attire. Faulkner was planning to divide the land into smaller parcels for residential development and knock down the mansion and most of the other buildings on the site, He also planned to keep the lake, which stood to the south of the mansion, and build himself a house on the Leons' croquet lawn alongside it. He had already taken down some stables and removed some of the wood panelling in the mansion when he was approached by agents representing a branch of the Foreign Office, GC&CS.

The Chief of SIS and non-operational director of GC&CS, Hugh Sinclair, had become concerned that most of the British intelligence services were based in the middle of London and he had started looking for a site outside the capital to serve as a war station for intelligence activities. Bletchley Park was an ideal location as it was close to Bletchley station which was on the main north–south West Coast rail line, and near the A5, a major arterial route along which ran trunk telephone cabling connecting the north and south of the country. There were also direct rail links from Bletchley station to both Oxford and Cambridge which would prove useful as many of the people on the emergency staff list of the 'professor type' would come from the universities there. A deal was struck for the site to be leased for a period of three months and it was subsequently purchased by Sinclair on 9 June 1938 for £6,000.[2] Faulkner didn't get his house by the lake but he subsequently got the contract to build the wartime huts and brick buildings at BP, many of which still stand today.

During the Munich crisis, partly as a precautionary measure and partly as a mobilization exercise, Sinclair sent GC&CS and other Foreign Office staff to BP. Telecommunications engineers had already been working on the site since its purchase. At the end of September 1938 the Munich agreement was signed and most of the GC&CS staff returned to London. The following year it was clear that war was imminent and, around 15 August 1939, GC&CS returned to BP along with other intelligence units to begin their wartime activities.

Denniston sent Welchman to join the team led by a veteran First World War cryptanalyst, Dilly Knox. They were based in the end cottage of three within the BP stable yard which became known as 'The Cottage'. The team already included the brilliant mathematician Alan Turing from King's College, Cambridge. which was also Knox's *alma mater*. Turing had also arrived on 4 September but had been working part-time for GC&CS before it moved to BP. Other notable people working in The Cottage were John Jeffreys from Downing College, Cambridge, whom Welchman knew well, Peter Twinn, the Oxford mathematician who had been recruited earlier in the year, and Tony Kendrick, who had been Knox's only assistant in 1938. When he arrived, the team were already hard at work at unravelling the mysteries of an encryption machine with the brand name Enigma. They had begun this work well before they arrived at BP. Welchman was provided with very little information when he arrived as Knox's management style seemed to be to tell a new recruit to find something to do and get on with it. In any event, he soon realized that he could learn everything he needed to about the Enigma machine in an hour or so.

Arthur Scherbius, was an electrical engineer born in Frankfurt-am-Main, Germany, on 20 October 1878. He had invented a new system of machine cryptography at the same time as several others were making similar inventions. Their purpose was to mechanize the process of encryption so that when any letter of the alphabet was entered into a machine, it produced as randomly as possible another letter of the same alphabet. At the heart of the machine was one or more rotors or encryption wheels. Each wheel had a set of electrical contacts on each side, one for each letter of the alphabet. Inside the body of the wheel, each contact on one side was connected to a contact on the other side by a strand of wire. The other significant advance on previous machines of this type was that the wheels could rotate inside the machine. After having an earlier version of his machine rejected by the German Navy in 1918, Scherbius, with a patent secured,[3] began to offer it for sale commercially. His hope was that organizations wanting to encrypt information, such as banks, might be interested in it. The machine was not a huge success until the German Navy renewed its interest in it and decided to begin using it around 1926. It is believed by some authors that Dilly Knox bought a commercial version of the machine in Vienna around 1925.[4] In 1928, the Enigma machine went into German Army service and eventually it would also be put into service by the German Air Force. In 1926 a single Enigma cost 6,000 Reichsmarks or $144. Once the German military decided to adopt the Enigma machine, it gradually disappeared from public sale as production of the commercial version was discontinued.

The German military were interested in the Enigma machine because of its portability. They expected that their forces would be in constant motion in wartime which meant that good communication between German commanders and their troops could only be maintained by wireless communications. The machine came in a wooden box, weighed around twenty-five pounds, and could run off an internal battery which held its charge for some time. The machine was an 'offline' device in that it was only used to encrypt and decrypt messages; their transmission was a separate process. Encrypted messages would be sent by radio in Morse code.

Before an operator encrypted or decrypted a message he would have to set up a number of components on the machine. The security of the system was based on the instructions provided to the operators to do this. Each month, operators were issued with explicit instructions for setting up each component of the system for each day of the month. The daily setting was known as the key. The number of possible keys was very large and the number usually quoted is 158.9 million, million, million. Compared to the odds of winning the jackpot on the National Lottery in the UK of 14 million to 1, this is a number far too large even to contemplate. The problem facing the cryptanalysts at BP was not only the huge number of ways the machine could be set up by the operator, but also that the German Air Force and Army had a number of different communication networks, each with its own daily setting of the Enigma machine.

Some information (known as the preamble) would be put at the beginning of each message in plain German. This included call signs which identified the sending and receiving German radio station, a discriminant identifying which networks would be able to read the message, the time of origin, the number of letters in the message and whether it was a single or multi-part message. Finally it would include letters, referred to as the indicator, which defined the indicator setting and message setting (*see* Appendix 1). These settings added a final layer of security before encrypting a message.

The Germans' operating procedures exploited the reciprocal nature of the machine. When machines on a communication network were set up in the same way using the daily key and the same message setting, then the sending operator would type the message in so-called plain-text and his machine would encrypt each letter. Other operators on the same network would receive the message, then type the encrypted letters on the keyboard, and the machine would output the original plain text.

After a very short and fairly unmemorable stay, in Welchman's words, 'I was turned out of the Cottage and sent to Elmers School, where I was to study call signs and discriminants.' Due to a shortage of office space at BP, Elmers School, a private grammar school for boys located nearby, had been acquired for the Commercial and Diplomatic Sections. When Welchman arrived there, the place was empty but Knox sent Tony Kendrick[5] along to work with him. Kendrick normally gave fundamental explanations to newcomers about Enigma, something that the very busy and secretive Knox would no doubt have been loath to do.

As Welchman said in *The Hut Six Story*:

Alex [Welchman got his name wrong] Kendrick, a civilian member of Dilly's prewar staff, was sent along to get me started. He was fair-haired, walked with a stick as a result of a paralyzed leg, and was noted for the holes burnt in his trousers by a cigarette, or possibly by ash from a pipe. We occupied a fairly large room with bare walls and no view from the windows; its only furniture was a long table and a few wooden chairs. Nobody else was working in the School, so Kendrick and I felt a bit lonely.

When he arrived at BP, Welchman had known nothing about the operation of the radio networks of that time, never mind call signs, indicators and discriminants. He and Kendrick were given several collections of Enigma traffic to analyse and, ironically, his separation from the main message-breaking activity going on in The Cottage, may have been the start of the Hut 6 organization that was to follow. Colonel John Tiltman, who was in charge of Army operations at BP, had instructed his sergeant to assist the work going on in Elmers School and all bundles of messages intercepted at the Chatham intercept station, along with a report on the day's traffic, were made available to them. Again, in Welchman's words:

Kendrick started to work on the large collection of material from Chatham, and set me a good example by beginning to analyse its characteristics in a methodical manner. His approach was reminiscent of the period some five to ten years earlier when I had been doing research in algebraic geometry and had often been faced with the problem of thinking of something to think about. In those earlier days I had found the best approach to this problem was to force myself to start writing, and here was Kendrick dealing with the same problem in the same way.

As no one else at BP had studied any of this material thoroughly, it was inevitable that they would soon start to break new ground. Unfortunately, Kendrick was moved on to other work and Welchman was left on his own. GC&CS's inactivity in this area was, to a large extent, a result of the ongoing controversy about the function of signals intercept ('Y' material) and the directly related task of cryptanalysis. The Air Ministry stated at the time that:

> Cryptographers are not Intelligence Officers, but only exist to
> provide the material from which Intelligence is produced; and it is
> as well to keep the intelligence side as far divorced from the crypto-
> graphic side as possible.[6]

Edward Travis, GC&CS's Deputy Director, had disagreed and expressed
the view that: 'It is quite obvious that cryptographers will always know
more of interception than the interceptors can possibly know of
cryptography.'[7]

John Tiltman was not the only senior BP person interested in
Welchman's work. The head of BP's Air Section, Josh Cooper, also understood its potential value to BP. He had suggested that the Air Ministry
should itself be involved in the interception of high-grade traffic. In the
early stages of the war the Army 'Y' Service was intercepting a considerable
amount of German Air Force Enigma traffic. He was promptly rebuked by
Group Captain Blandy, then Deputy Director of Signals (Y): 'My Y-services
exist to produce Intelligence, not to provide stuff for people at Bletchley to
fool around with.'[8]

Cooper gave Welchman BP's sole collection of decrypted German
Enigma messages, which helped him understand the task at hand. Cooper,
according to former colleagues, was even more eccentric than Turing and
Knox. Like them he was a King's College man and had joined GC&CS as a
Junior Assistant in October 1925 to specialize in Russian codes and ciphers.
Stories abounded about his eccentric behaviour (many untrue) which
apparently included taking his evening cup of tea by the lake at BP and
then throwing his cup and saucer in.[9]

Three key figures in the history of BP, John Tiltman, Josh Cooper and
Oliver Strachey (in his initial briefing in 1938), thus helped inform
Welchman's first breakthrough of major significance for the future of the
organization he had only joined several months earlier. What he was
starting to understand was that call signs, indicators and discriminants
(part of the message preamble) could, along with the message itself, help
to build up a picture of the German order of battle. What he didn't know
at this stage was where the intercepted messages were coming from.[10]

Through Tiltman's good auspices, Welchman was able to make his first
visit to the Army's radio intercept station at Chatham in Kent at the end
of September 1939. He quite quickly befriended Commander Ellingworth
who was to prove to be 'a tower of strength throughout the war'. It was
Ellingworth who taught him how German radio nets operated and they

were able to establish a system of co-operation between BP and the intercept stations. Ellingworth ensured that the preambles of messages were sent to BP by teleprinter to give codebreakers advance material to work on.

Commander M. J. N. Ellingworth was an ex-naval man and First World War veteran, known behind his back as 'Truncy', and apparently well-liked by all his staff. Heavy bombing raids on Chatham during 1940 and the fact that German forces were just across the Channel, prompted a move to Beaumanor Hall in Leceistershire. It had been requisitioned from a William Curzon-Herrick and was about sixty-seven miles from BP. The move was interrupted by a short stay at the RAF signals station at Chicksands Priory in Bedfordshire, just twenty miles from BP. The Chatham interceptor operators worked alongside their RAF and WAAF counterparts until Beaumanor was ready. Beaumanor then became the main Army listening station and supplier of raw intelligence to BP.

Chatham, Beaumanor and Chicksands were part of Britain's 'Y' Service. In 1924 GC&CS had established an interdepartmental 'Y' committee dealing with wireless interception, though each service retained control of the personnel and installations for their own interception stations. In the years leading up to the Munich agreement, British intelligence organiz-ations were keen to gain information about the German government's intentions. This was achieved both by conventional intelligence-gathering methods and by monitoring German diplomatic and military wireless traffic. At the start of the Second World War there were three 'Y' stations in the UK, at Scarborough for the Admiralty, at Chatham for the Army and at Cheadle for the RAF. As the war progressed, the main UK intercept stations were based at Scarborough and Flowerdown (Winchester) for the Navy; Chatham and then at Beaumanor Priory and Forest Hill for the Army; and Cheadle and Chicksands for the RAF. There were also 'Y' stations in the Middle East, the Far East and behind the battle lines in North Africa, Sicily, Italy and mainland Europe as Allied forces advanced after D-Day. BP trained most of the decryption staff for the overseas centres and the intercepted encrypted signals from the 'Y' stations were all sent to BP. The allocation of frequencies to be monitored for German Army and Air Force signals was determined at BP by an intercept control team in Hut 6 and for German Naval signals in Hut 4.

Operators at intercept stations would tune in on a specific com-munications network ('net') and write the signals down character by character, at the rate of at least twenty words per minute, as they were being transmitted on short-wave frequencies in Morse code by German operators. They would then be sent by pneumatic tube to a control hut for logging and collating and then on to BP by despatch rider and later in the war by teleprinter, on a daily basis. The teleprinters operated at only 10 characters per second and were prone to errors so despatch riders augmented the teleprinter links, hurtling down dark roads to BP on their BSA M20 side-valve machines. No attempt was made to decrypt the signals at the intercept stations but considerable information could be gleaned from the frequencies, call signs and times of transmission. This work was handled by log-readers who were part of MI 8 (Military Intelligence, Section 8), the cover designation for the Radio Security Service (RSS), a department of the Army's Directorate of Military Intelligence and part of the War Office.[11]

Beaumanor was the one of the largest intercept stations with 196 radio sets in use at the end of the war and some 1,300 operators. Beaumanor was known as War Office Y Group or WOYG – the staff referred to it as 'Woygland' and to themselves as 'Woygites'. Other terms used were 'Beaumaniacs', with the more dashing males as 'Manor Beaus'. By all accounts, the tone of Beaumanor was set by its likeable commander whose personality is best exemplified by his foreword to the first Beaumanor staff magazine in October 1941 and the cartoon of him which accompanied it.[12]

Without the Y Service and the selfless dedication of around 10,000 people who staffed it, the work of BP would not have been possible.

For the first six months of the war, the German Army and Air Force continued to use the Enigma indicator system that had been introduced towards the end of 1938. Before the war the Polish Cipher Bureau had developed an elegant method for recovering part of each Enigma key by exploiting a weakness in that indicator system. Although the Poles had disclosed the details of their methods to the British late in July 1939, no information about the Polish achievements was passed on to Welchman when he joined Knox's team in September 1939. However, he was told about the operation of the Enigma machine and of the indicator system then still being used by the Germans. After a few weeks, Welchman undertook a private investigation on this indicator system. Remarkably, he re-invented one of the key Polish ideas for reducing the possibilities for part of the daily key.[13]

Welchman described in *The Hut Six Story*, the less than favourable reaction from Knox when he told him of his 'discovery'.[14] While Knox did not give him any details about the state of that development, he did say that it was being led by John Jeffreys. As they had known each other before the war, Welchman was confident that the work was in good hands. More importantly, it left him free to start thinking about the wider implications of decrypting Enigma traffic on a large scale. Knox's approach was typical of the First World War cryptanalysts, that is that each decryption of a message was in itself a cryptological success. Welchman recognized that real success would lie in its exploitation leading to military gains.

The following description of Knox that Welchman gave in his book has often been quoted by other authors:

> Dilly was neither an organization man nor a technical man. He was, essentially, an idea-struck man. He was not interested, as I was, in the administration and automatic routine needed to handle the enormous volume of Enigma traffic generated by the German army and air force.

Interestingly, Welchman saw very little of Knox at BP, even when he was part of his team. He certainly knew nothing of his pre-BP life. A book by Knox's niece, Penelope Fitzgerald, *The Knox Brothers*, published in 1977, helped to fill in the gaps.

The story of the early battle against the Enigma machine and the Polish contribution is a fascinating one and Welchman would spend much of the last few years of his life trying to unravel it and put the record straight.[15] At the end of the First World War, the newly reborn Polish state had taken control of former German territory in parts of Silesia, Pomerania and around Poznań (Posen in German). This had been part of Poland before the eighteenth-century partitions of the country by its powerful neighbours. The return of this territory to Polish control was a cause of considerable anger in Germany and an atmosphere of enmity and continual tension persisted, fuelled by the long history of numerous and bloody wars between Poland and Germany. The reborn Polish state felt seriously threatened by its neighbour to the west.

Some Polish historians claim that in December 1927 Polish military intelligence dismantled and photographed a commercial version of the Enigma machine which was discovered accidentally by customs officers at Warsaw's Okecie Airport in a misaddressed German package.[16] On 15 July 1928 Polish radio-monitoring stations at Starogard in Pomerania, Gdańsk, Poznań and Kraków-Krzeslawice intercepted the first German messages which were in a machine-generated cipher. While Polish intelligence in Germany was trying to find out about German cipher changes, a course in cryptology was started at the University of Poznań for twenty of its most advanced mathematics students who could also speak German. The course was set up at the initiative of the radio intelligence department and some of its specialist officers would lecture to the students, the most gifted of whom would be asked to volunteer to continue their studies within military intelligence. During 1931 a cipher bureau was created which was an amalgamation of the radio intelligence and cryptography sections. The new bureau was headed by Major (later Lieutenant Colonel) Guido Langer. As the new department was being organized, the course at Poznań was coming to an end and included three students who had frequently managed to solve the German ciphers that had been set for them. It was decided to set up a small section of the department for them in Poznań. Their names were Marian Rejewski, Henryk Zygalski and Jerzy Różycki.

The German military had introduced a new version of an Enigma machine with a plugboard at the beginning of June 1930 and the following year the Poles purchased a commercial model on the open market in Germany. At the same time, Captain Gustave Bertrand, who worked for French intelligence, initiated Polish–French co-operation in cryptographic matters. At the beginning of September 1931 Rejewski, Zygalski and Różycki were assigned to Section BS 4 (German intelligence) of the Cipher Office of Department II of the General Staff in Warsaw. This section was under the command of Captain (later Major) Maksymilian Ciężki.

In June 1931 a 43-year-old employee of the German Defence Ministry Cipher Office, walked into the French Embassy in Berlin and into history. Hans Thilo Schmidt had access to, and was prepared to sell, manuals and other information relating to the Enigma machine being used by the German Army. Bertrand and a colleague, who went by the fictitious name of Rodolphe Lemoine, met with Schmidt on 1 November 1931 at the Grand Hotel in Verviers, a small Belgian town on the German border, Schmidt produced some of the material that he had promised. Bertrand was delighted, and while Lemoine arranged for Schmidt's payment, he photographed the material. He then rushed back to Paris and offered the material to French cryptanalysts who promptly said that it was of no use to them. An approach to the British experts for a second opinion yielded the same answer. The material only dealt with the encryption of a message, not how to decrypt one. However, when Bertrand got permission to approach his Polish counterpart, he boarded a train to Warsaw. The Polish

Cipher Bureau, perhaps not surprisingly, received Bertrand and the material from Schmidt, with open arms.[17]

Rejewski was the most academically advanced of the three young students who had been recruited into BS 4. He had already been awarded his degree in mathematics and had spent a further year studying the subject in depth at the University of Göttingen in Germany. In October 1932 he was given a separate small room to renew the studies of Enigma abandoned by his predecessors. He was also given the commercial machine which had been purchased earlier as well as several dozen messages daily, encrypted on the military version of Enigma. In early December he received a photograph of a military version of Enigma, user instructions and a schedule of daily keys for September and October 1932. By the end of the month he had achieved one of the greatest feats in the history of cryptography. Marian Rejewski had reconstructed the internal connections within the Enigma machine and identified the indicator system currently being used by the German Army. He had done it entirely using a mathematical technique called permutation theory. Meanwhile, Zygalski had devised a technique which in essence involved cutting square holes in sheets of paper with the positions of the holes determined by some of the data in the indicator at the beginning of an intercepted message. By stacking the sheets produced from a number of messages on a light box, the holes that were aligned would be revealed by the light shining through them. This could be used to work out the ring settings that had been used as part of the daily key.

Early the following year, Rejewski, Zygalski and Różycki were brought together again to work together as a team. They fairly quickly began to read encrypted German Army messages and had considerable success for a number of years. The German Air Force introduced Enigma in August 1935 and the number of different networks to monitor grew rapidly. By 1 February 1936 the Germans had introduced significant changes and complicated safeguards to Enigma. The following year the Polish General Staff transferred BS 4 to a camouflaged high-security new headquarters in the Kabacki Woods near Pyry outside Warsaw. As the Germans changed procedures or tightened their security, the Poles would invent technologies such as the Zygalski sheets and new machines like the cyclometer and the bomba (*see Chapter 3*) to counter them. When the German Air Force and Army issued their Enigma operators with two additional wheels, on 15 December 1938, the Poles began to struggle even more. With three wheels available to the operator, he could choose from only six possible configurations. Now he could chose three from five which increased the number of possible wheel configurations to sixty. To make matters worse, the Germans had also increased the number of plugboard connections to ten.

The Poles proposed a meeting with the British and the French in the hope that they would have something to contribute as the situation was getting worse. The first tri-lateral meeting between representatives of the cryptographic services of France, Britain and Poland was held in Paris on 9 and 10 January 1939. In attendance on the Polish side were Langer and Ciężki; on the French side Bertrand and a cryptanalyst called Henri Braquenie; on the British side, Denniston, Knox, Tiltman and Hugh Foss, a cryptanalyst who had joined GC&CS in 1924. The Poles had been instructed not to reveal anything unless they got something in return. As the British and the French had nothing to offer, the meeting, while cordial, was a waste of time.

By May, tensions between Poland and Germany were close to breaking point and, on 30 June, Langer contacted London and Paris with the news that something new had come up since January. He proposed a second tri-lateral meeting in Warsaw on 24–27 July. As Knox had been included in the invitation, Sinclair instructed Denniston to include him in the British delegation. Also included was Commander Humphrey Sandwith, head of the Admiralty's interception service.[18] Knox and Denniston arrived on the morning of the 24th and stayed at the Hotel Bristol. The French stayed at the Hotel Polonia. The Poles entertained their visitors at lunch at the Hotel Bristol and ironically the fairly banal conversation was conducted in German as it was the only common language of all in attendance.

The key meeting took place the next day at the Pyry Centre. Much to the astonishment of the British and the French, the Poles demonstrated several machines and techniques which they had developed to help break Enigma keys. The news that the Poles were breaking German Enigma keys quite regularly was not received well by Knox, who maintained a stony silence throughout the meeting. Knox, who arguably knew more about the Enigma machine than anyone in Britain, had been unable to break the new military version with the plugboard. His problem had been the connections between the keyboard and the entry drum inside the machine. On the models of Enigma machines that he had successfully broken, the connection pattern followed the order of the keys left to right, row by row and alphabetically around the entry drum. So the Q, W, E, R, T keys were connected respectively to A, B, C, D, E, and so on. On the model of Enigma in mass use by the German Army and Air Force, the connection pattern had been changed and Knox's team (which included Turing) could not work out the new pattern.

This problem had also stumped Rejewski initially and he described his solution in a paper written in 1980:

> What, then, were the connections in the entry drum? It turned out later that they can be found by deduction, but in December 1932, or perhaps in the first days of 1933, I obtained those connections by guessing. I assumed that since the keyboard keys were not connected with the successive contacts in the entry drum in the order of the letters on the keyboard, then maybe they were connected up in alphabetical order; that is, that the permutation caused by the entry drum was an identity and need not be taken into account at all. This time luck smiled upon me. The hypothesis proved correct, and the very first trial yielded a positive result.[19]

So when they had all gathered at the Pyry Centre, Knox's first question to Rejewski had been; 'What are the connections to the entry drum?' Knox was furious when he heard the answer: 'A, B, C, —'. In other words, the Germans had wired it up in the simplest possible way, the Q key to Q, the W key to W, the E key to E, the R key to R, and so on.

Denniston later wrote a report on the Pyry conference on 11 May 1948 from memory and using his pocket diary to check dates:

> It was only when we got back in the car to drive away that he [Knox] suddenly let himself go and assuming that no one understood any English raged and raged that they were lying to us now as in Paris. The whole thing was a pinch he kept on repeating – they never worked it out – they pinched it years ago and have followed developments as anyone could but they must have bought it or pinched it.[20]

Knox remained aloof and withdrawn over dinner that night, almost as if he had a grudge against the Poles. The next day, Knox met Langer, Ciężki, Rejewski, Zygalski and Różycki and was apparently 'his old self'. However, that still didn't stop him from writing to Denniston a few days later saying that the Poles had 'got the machine to Sept 15th 38 out by luck. As I have said only Mrs B. B. had seriously contemplated the equation $A = 1$, $B = 2$. Had she worked on the crib we should be teaching them.' Despite his grumpiness, he ended his letter with kind words for Rejewski, Zygalski and Różycki: 'The young men seem very capable and honest.'[21] Unfortunately, Mrs B. B. has never been identified.

In the end, Denniston attributed Knox's fit of pique to the formality of the meetings held on the first day of the conference and pompous declarations by senior officers. Knox and Denniston had been friends and colleagues since coming together in Room 40. Yet in a letter to Bertrand, dated 3 August 1939 and written on Hotel Bristol note paper, Denniston is remarkably candid about Knox:

My dear Bertrand,

I have finally had a day off and I take this opportunity to write to you a very personal letter, 'from the heart', which seems necessary to me.

I have seen D [Dilly Knox]; in his opinion I may have said something bad about you and that is why I wish to emphasise that we owe everything solely to you and I look forward to the co-operation of our trio and that to reach our goal you must remain in the leading position. In Warsaw it was you who advised me to return and think about it – and you were right.

Maybe you understand my problem in the shape of Knox. He is a man of exceptional intelligence, but he does not know the word co-operation. You surely must have noticed that off duty, he is a pleasant chap loved by all. But in the office his behaviour is different.

In Warsaw I had some deplorable experiences with him. He wants to do everything himself. He does not know how to explain anything. He can't stand it when someone knows more than him. Unfortunately, I cannot do without him, he knows more about the machine than anyone else in the country. He built a machine of the type used by the Spanish, and frequently by the Italians in Spain, which is not to be sneered at, even if not so much has been done as has been done by our friends in Z [the Polish Cypher Bureau].

You must forgive me for being so keen to keep him, but I will tell you in all sincerity, that I will never take him to a conference again if I can only avoid it. From now on, we must establish the rules of our co-operation in order to avoid unnecessary effort.[22]

On 10 September 1939 the Poles closed the Pyry Centre, destroyed all trace of their machines and evacuated their workers. The Second World War had begun. Ten days later, Bertrand delivered a replica Enigma to Colonel Stewart Menzies in London as a gift from the Poles.

One cannot overstate the Polish contribution to the ultimate success of BP. They had recognized in the early 1930s that the age of machine cryptography had begun and that mathematicians would be needed to deal with it. While it is likely that Knox came away from the Pyry conference with the missing link in his attempt to re-construct the Enigma machine itself, Denniston clearly saw the bigger picture and it is to his credit that he too had already started to recruit mathematicians for GC&CS. More importantly, the Poles had demonstrated to the British that encryption machines like Enigma could be broken, if the right mathematical minds were allowed to concentrate on the problem.

In early drafts of *The Hut Six Story*, Welchman had carefully avoided saying anything critical about Knox, though after reading Penelope Fitzgerald's account of Knox and his brothers, he felt he could say something about his treatment at Knox's hands. He used carefully chosen words such as being 'turned out of the Cottage' and more tellingly:

> Certainly during my first week or two at Bletchley, I got the impression that he didn't like me. I don't remember what I learned in the Cottage, but after a week or so he gave me some sort of test and appeared to be, if anything, annoyed that I passed.

In her excellent and loving biography of Knox, Mavis Batey argues that, quite to the contrary,

> The records show that Welchman was not 'banished' to the School because, as he thought, Dilly did not like him. Where Dilly was concerned, lack of communication was not a sign of dislike but merely of total absorption in a project to the exclusion of all else.

She goes on to quote from a confidential note from Knox in November 1939 in which he says that Welchman 'was doing well and is keen. I hope to get him back here to learn about the machines'.

Unknown to Mavis Batey, who was one of Knox's team in The Cottage and a brilliant cryptanalyst, Welchman had other reasons for thinking that Knox disliked him. Welchman told Winterbotham in January 1975 that Knox had not been happy with his proposed reorganization of BP's code-breaking activities.[23] He had gone to Travis with the proposal and Travis had then got him the full support of Tiltman and Cooper, so he was allowed to go ahead. He went on to say:

> Incidentally, this early initiative on my part was never forgiven by Dilly Knox, but please do not mention this to anyone. Dilly was much loved by all of us, and he made a tremendous contribution. On the other hand Denniston soon became enthusiastic about what I was doing.

Denniston's support had obviously been important and as Welchman said to Denniston's son Robin in February 1979:

> I had the impression that Dilly Knox disliked me from the start, and may well have complained to your father about my assignment to the Cottage.
>
> Another matter of great personal interest to me is that your father gave strong support to my plans for the creation of Hut 6, and must have followed our progress closely. Before his illness he called me to his office, congratulated me on my achievements, and assured me that I would be rewarded after the war.[24]

Welchman had also corresponded with another Cottage veteran, Peter Twinn, after *The Hut Six Story* had been published.[25] In answer to Twinn's question about what Welchman thought of Dilly he said:

> Over Dilly, I intend to quote Rejewski's feeling that he was very quick to grasp what the Poles told him, which suggested that he had got a long way himself. But I would like to say more than that. David Rees, who was one of the Sidney Sussex mathematicians that I recruited in the very early days, left Hut 6 to join Dilly. He felt bad about Dilly's insistence that he must not tell me about a success. He did tell me about it in confidence, and, though I remember no details, I was very impressed by the brilliance of what Dilly had done. I gathered that Dilly was afraid that I would jump in and take the exploitation of his success away from him. It is sad that he should have felt this way, but he was a very sick man.

So what is one to make of Alfred Dillwyn Knox: an amiable but absent-minded professor, or an ill-tempered and secretive loner? His eccentric behaviour has been well documented as has his secretive nature and his apparent dislike of men. Even one of his closest colleagues, Peter Twinn, has said that Knox told him very little. The National Archives hold a number of letters from Knox to Denniston with threats of resignation over one issue or another.[26] There was also, of course, his health, as Knox was ill during his time at BP. Set against this was his sheer brilliance as a cryptanalyst. He had broken the basic military Enigma without plugboard on 24 April 1937 and, as Twinn said proudly of the work of Knox's team: 'Three different species of Enigmas were solved by us without any help from anyone except the incompetence of the German cypher authorities and their operators.'

It would seem that differences between Welchman and Knox were not personal as both men said complimentary things about the other. Knox was one of the people to whom Welchman dedicated *The Hut Six Story*. It is clear however, that they had a different vision of the future of cryptography and how best to deal with the threat posed by Nazi Germany. Quite simply, Knox's approach would not have worked when thousands of intercepted messages came flooding into BP on a daily basis. What remains a mystery is why Knox was unable to make the same guess as Marian Rejewski about the connection pattern of the Enigma keyboard to the entry drum. At the end of 1984 Welchman received a letter from an American academic, author and expert on machine cryptography, Cipher Deavours. In it, Deavours provided an interesting slant on the connection pattern, or as he called it, the entrance permutation:

> This business about Knox and the entrance permutation has always puzzled me to no end. Had the British been about their proper intelligence gathering business, this snag need never have happened.
>
> The Enigma company had four models of the machine. The machines were publicly exhibited at both the 1923 Congress of the International Postal Union in Berne, and at the 1924 congress held in Stockholm.
>
> Enigma 'A' and 'B' were Scherbius Enigmas each employing a common cryptographic method. These machines each had four rotors which were driven by four 'gaptoothed' gearwheels of sizes 11, 15, 17, and 19. Each wheel had 6 gaps. The rotor movement was, thus, very irregular with more than one rotor usually moving at once and other rotors pausing. Had this rotor movement afforded more variation, the machine would have been indeed very strong cryptographically. This model of the Enigma was used by the Abwehr during the war.
>
> Enigma 'C' and 'D' were the glow lamp models with which we are all familiar. Enigma 'D' was the widely sold commercial model and it was this version which was used by the Italian Navy (rewired of course) and solved by the British. Enigma 'C' seems to have been the model from which the Wehrmacht modification came. This 'C' model has the same reflecting rotor construction as the German military version with the slight difference that the reflecting rotor could be set in one of two possible positions internally. (Model 'D' had a completely settable reflecting rotor.) The point here is that both

the keyboard and the glowlamps in Model 'C' were in the standard A–Z sequence. Had Knox seen pictures of the machine, he would immediately have seen the possibility that the entrance permutation was not based on the typewriter sequence as in Model 'D'. Why he did not have this information is beyond comprehension. First, the machine photos were publicly available and second, in 1927, Dr Siegfried Türkel published the work 'Enciphering with Apparatus and Machines' (English Translation) which contained numerous photos of all Enigma models from 'A' to 'D'. It would seem impossible for the British to have completely missed the Türkel work.

As you know, the British solved Enigma 'D' messages of the Swiss government during and after the war. The method used probable text beginnings in German and French and was equivalent to the 'Baton' method. The British obtained the wirings of the Swiss machine through bribery. Knox must have been involved in this and so it seems likely that this was his method. The Baton method sometimes works even when the plugboard is present in the machine, particularly if only a few steckers are in use. I would imagine that Knox tried to refine this approach for better results. Given his background in manual cryptography, this would be quite natural.

Given Knox's temperament it is likely that he occupied himself with two problems at once; determining the machine's wiring connections, and analysis of the message keys. This might have been the real cause that he did not progress satisfactorily on either problem. His secretive nature certainly did not help any.

Chapter 3

The Ultra Architect

As students drifted back to Cambridge for the start of the 1939/40 academic year, a certain lecturer in algebraic geometry was conspicuous by his absence. The rumour making the rounds of the common room at Sidney Sussex College was that he was doing important war work of a secret nature. A number of students he had been supervising before the war began would be seeing him again soon enough. While secrecy was paramount at BP, it would seem that not everyone was in total ignorance of the activities taking place there.

Diana Neil, who worked in Hut 4 from March 1944 to December 1946, was from Bristol and Welchman's father had married her parents during the First World War. When he and his wife had moved to Bristol and he became an archdeacon, Diana and her family attended his church. As she later recalled:

> Mrs Welchman had died in 1938, the church was burned down by incendiary bombs in 1940 and the Archdeacon went to live with his brother in Bradford on Avon. One day I thought I would go and visit the dear old gentleman when I was on leave. I duly did in my Wren uniform, and was invited to stay for tea. During tea he asked, 'Now my dear, where are you billeted in the WRENs?' I replied how fortunate I was to be living at Woburn Abby. 'Really my dear,' he said. 'And where do you work?' I hesitated but then thought this dear old man would never know in any case, so told him I worked at a small place nearby called Bletchley. 'Do you mean Bletchley Park my dear?' Oh, my goodness what have I said, so had to admit it was. So he said: 'My son Gordon, who had a First Class Honours Degree in Mathematics at Cambridge, he's working at Bletchley Park, on very secret and important government business.'[1]

*

Just before the beginning of the Second World War, the Polish crypt-analysts had shown the British and French how the Enigma traffic of the German Army and Air Force could be broken by a manual method involving large numbers of perforated sheets. In September 1939, a great deal of this Enigma traffic was being intercepted, but it was not being properly analysed by GC&CS, now based at BP. After being assigned to the neglected task of traffic analysis by Dilly Knox, Welchman soon realized that BP was almost certainly going to be able to break a great deal of this traffic. To exploit such a great opportunity, they were going to need the co-ordinated efforts of several specialized organizations, including the radio intercept stations and he had already established close contact with one of these stations. BP was faced with an unprecedented situation, quite different from the one that cryptanalysts had encountered in the First World War, when messages were broken one by one. If they could discover the key which told German Enigma operators how to set up their machines on a particular communications network, they would be able to decrypt all messages using the same key. The Germans were already using several keys which were valid for twenty-four hours and even in the summer of 1939, before Germany invaded Poland on 1 September, the British intercept stations were intercepting hundreds of messages each day. As Welchman remembered in *The Hut Six Story*:

> Previously I suppose I had absorbed the common view that Crypt-analysis was a matter of dealing with individual messages, of solving intricate puzzles and of working in a secluded back room, with little contact with the outside world. As I studied the first collection of decodes, however, I began to see, somewhat dimly, that I was involved in something very different. We were dealing with an entire communications system that would serve the needs of the German ground and air forces. The call signs came alive as representing elements of those forces, whose commanders at various echelons would have to send messages to each other. The use of different keys for different purposes, which was known to be the reason for the dis-criminants, suggested different command structures for the various aspects of military operations.
>
> Even more important perhaps, was the impression I got from the messages themselves. Although my knowledge of German was very limited, I could see that the people involved were talking to each other in a highly disciplined manner. They were very polite to each

other, in that the originator of the message would be careful to give the full title of the officer or organization to which the message was to be sent. Furthermore, in the signature that came at the end of the message, the originator would be careful to give his own title in full. These early impressions proved to be of immense importance later on, and it was fortunate that I had this period of secluded work.

As no one at BP seemed to have recognized that intercepted German messages represented a potential intelligence gold mine if the traffic as a whole were analysed, Welchman drew up a comprehensive plan. He called for the close co-ordination of radio interception, analysis of the intercepted traffic, breaking Enigma keys, decrypting messages on the broken keys, and extracting intelligence from the decrypts. He presented the plan to Deputy Director Edward Travis, who immediately saw the urgent need to act on it.

Having convinced Travis that a large scaling-up of the effort would be needed when these methods of breaking Enigma produced results, he sketched out what a room containing codebreaking machinery and British-built Enigma machines might look like. He also foresaw that processes akin to mass production would be required. The codebreaking procedures that he had been introduced to in March were ones in which the various tasks of decryption, translation, and writing the resulting out-going message were all performed, essentially, by one cryptanalyst. He had realized that this approach would simply not scale to handle the volumes of intercepted traffic envisaged. It would have to be replaced by a clear division of labour amongst a team of experts. Remarkably, Travis persuaded Whitehall to back this gamble, even though at that stage not one German Enigma message had ever been broken in the UK either before or since the war began.

It is not surprising that Welchman decided not to discuss his ideas with Knox, given that he had felt excluded from Knox's team in The Cottage. However, it is surprising that he chose to approach Travis rather than Alastair Denniston, the Director of GC&CS and that Travis in turn by-passed Denniston and went straight to Stewart Menzies, head of MI6. There is some evidence that Denniston was away from BP at the time due to ill health. Travis may also have been concerned that Denniston and Knox had been together in Room 40 in the Admiralty during the First World War, and had become close friends. Travis had joined the Royal Navy in 1906 and worked on the security of Royal Navy ciphers, and on liaison on such matters with the Navy's allies in France and Italy beginning in 1916.

It is likely that he had little contact with the codebreakers in Room 40. They had come together in 1919 in the newly formed GC&CS, with Denniston taking responsibility for cipher-breaking, and Travis for cipher security under him. This separation of roles had continued in the early days at BP, even though the cipher 'Construction Section' was now based in Oxford. Travis had been made responsible for the service sections of GC&CS in 1938. Denniston's management style did not include spending much time out of his office and in effect 'visiting the troops'. In any event, he was very busy coping with the administrative problems arising from the move to Bletchley and the subsequent expansion. But Travis did make it a habit to get out, seeing the work on the ground and talking to the staff. So it seems that Travis was made responsible for the 'Enigma Section', though Dilly often continued to write straight to Denniston. Travis would have had a direct interest in the security of Enigma as at this time he was concerned with the deployment in the British services of the Typex machine, which was designed on very similar lines. On 18 November 1939 Denniston received an unsigned memo, proposing that, once they were in a position to decrypt traffic:

> I should like to see Research divorced from Production and the work organized on the following lines:-
>
> Research Section who should investigate the still unknown problems such as the Naval and T.C.D. [Gestapo Enigma?] This should be done by Knox, Kendrick, Turing, Miss Nugent, and such of the clerks as Knox requires.
>
> The production section requires dividing into several subsections as follows:-
>
> i) Receiving, sorting and W/T Liaison. This section would prepare data for Netz and Bombes. Staff: Welchman, Twinn and 4 clerks.
> ii) 'Netz' party. The work of finding machine settings etc., from sheets punched from cyclometer results, Jeffries [*sic*] + X assistants.
> iii) 'Bombes' machines run by Dawson + 1 assistant.
> iv) Decyphering Section. This should include staff to test 'Netz' and 'Bombes' results. They will decipher all available traffic with minimum loss of time and pass to Service Sections for translation. It will require someone (or ones) with good German to scrutinise traffic before passing on for translation. Two female typists must be trained by R.A.F. to work their machines.
>
> A special hut will be required for the Production section.[2]

While no copy of Welchman's original proposal to Travis seems to have survived, from his account in *The Hut Six Story*, this memo was clearly based on it. Welchman would say later in life that his proposal to Travis was probably his greatest contribution to the war effort and many historians would agree with him. The memo itself was certainly not written by Welchman as he would never have proposed himself for any specific role. At the top right of the front page of the memo are the words 'Paper? By EWT.' It seems highly unlikely that Travis would have used the words 'I should like to see' to his superior. However, he may well have gone above Denniston's head to his superior, Menzies, and felt empowered to write this memo.

The Welchman proposal was for an organization which would remain basically unchanged throughout the war, with the hut numbers becoming, in effect, the cover name for their activities. Army/Air Force codebreaking and intelligence would be based in Huts 6 and 3 respectively. Their Navy counterparts would be in Huts 8 and 4.

Denniston and Travis were quite different in personality and management style. While Denniston allowed creativity and innovation to flourish in the early days at BP, Travis proved to be the ideal person to fight the battle in Whitehall to get authority for the resources that would be needed for the expansion. It is unlikely that Denniston, for all of his qualities and huge personal contribution to the ultimate success of BP, would have been as successful in Whitehall. Subsequently, Travis continued to take direct responsibility for the Enigma huts as they came on stream, their staff, and the mechanization programme. Denniston remained 'in charge' as Operational Director of GC&CS.

Recruitment of the high-quality staff that would be needed started almost immediately and the future Hut 6 was Welchman's priority. The emergency list of 'men of the professor type' that had been drawn up the year before had been quickly exhausted and a new intake was needed as soon as possible. The men who would form the first management team of Hut 6 came from a number of places but not surprisingly, much as Birch and Adcock had done before him, Welchman returned to the fertile recruiting grounds of the Cambridge colleges.

The first two recruits to Hut 6 were in Argentina at the outbreak of war representing the British chess team in the Olympiad. Stuart Milner-Barry had come up to Trinity College, Cambridge, in the same term (October 1925) as Welchman and they had been friends ever since. Milner-Barry had studied classics. He had entered the world of stockbroking when he had the call from Welchman to join him at BP.[3] He duly recruited his friend and fellow chess player C. H. O'D. (Hugh) Alexander, a scholar of King's College and a mathematician. He was working as Director of Research at the John Lewis Partnership and while that was not an ideal role for him, his management experience there would prove to be valuable in the years ahead. Following a year in Hut 6, he joined the newly opened Hut 8, where he would remain until March 1945. Following their arrival at BP in January 1940, Milner-Barry and Alexander were billeted at the Shoulder of Mutton inn about one mile from BP. Writing years later, Milner-Barry had fond memories of the hospitality of the inn-keeper, Mrs Bowden, and he and Alexander would remain there until they left BP at the end of the war. Welchman lived with them for a while but soon moved out to live with his wife in a nearby town.

Welchman admitted after the war that he shamelessly recruited former friends and students, and before long he was back in Cambridge. He appeared one evening at the door of one such student. John Herivel and his friend Malcolm Chamberlain had been supervised by Welchman for six terms. Now here he was in Herivel's rooms, asking him for help with secret war work that he was doing at a place called Bletchley. Bored with the ghostly atmosphere of Cambridge at that time, Herivel agreed and duly arrived at BP on 29 January 1940. Chamberlain joined them around the same time. They found that another of Welchman's students, David Rees, was already there, having arrived in December 1939. Rees was a brilliant mathematician and would become one of Welchman's 'wizards' in Hut 6. Non-mathematicians were also recruited from Sidney Sussex, including Howard Smith and Asa Briggs who arrived in 1939 and 1942 respectively. Welchman was helped in his recruiting drive by John Jeffreys, a former Research Fellow at Downing College, fellow maths supervisor and close friend. Jeffreys had arrived at BP about the same time as Welchman and had been on Denniston's emergency list of 'men of the professor type'.

Another former colleague on the same list eventually arrived at BP at the end of 1939, but not without some difficulty. Dennis Babbage was a fellow geometer and friend from Magdalene College, Cambridge. He had attended the same pre-war sessions between Cambridge's Lent and Easter terms in 1939 as Welchman and, like him, was told that he would be summoned in the event of war, which they felt was inevitable. He had heard nothing after the declaration of war on 3 September and in frustration made contact himself. He had heard rumours that there were limits on numbers at BP, but eventually Tiltman 'smuggled' him into BP as a soldier of sorts. He spent some time in The Cottage with Knox's team in January 1940 but learned very little from him before he moved to Hut 6 to become another of Welchman's 'wizards'.

Two other friends from Cambridge would also arrive in Hut 6 in due course, Harold Fletcher in August 1941 and Houston Wallace in March 1942. Fletcher was working in a reserved occupation when he was recruited by Welchman. After overcoming the difficulties of being released so that he could be placed on the special reserve and employed for wartime duties by the Foreign Office, he duly arrived at BP.

Welchman even went back to his old school, Marlborough College, looking for recruits and asked his old mathematics teacher there, A. Robson, to send him his best young mathematicians. This produced another group of excellent people, including John Manisty, who arrived in 1941. The old boy network would yield other recruits to Welchman's team including Alex Aitken, the Scottish chess champion, and David Gaunt, a classics scholar from Cheltenham College. Even Travis got into the recruiting game, producing two scientists in early 1940, John Colman and George Crawford, who had been a former schoolmate of Welchman's at Marlborough. Travis also persuaded some of the London banks to send him bright young men to handle the continuous interchange of information that he envisaged would take place between Hut 6 and the intercept stations. Through this route and other personal contacts came Reg Parker, Frederick Braithwaite, Edward Smith and later John Monroe.

Then there were the young women who would prove to be vital cogs in the Hut 6 organization. The first recruit was Dorothy Chads, followed in early 1940 by Mary Wilson, Sheila Dunlop and Jean d'E. Mylne. While Welchman was not involved directly in recruiting most of the female contingent in Hut 6, he did recruit two important women. The first was Joan Clarke, whom he had supervised in geometry for Part II of the Cambridge Tripos. She duly arrived at BP on 17 June 1940, but instead of working in Hut 6 was collected by Alan Turing and taken to work in Hut 8. She remained there for the rest of the war and in 1944 became its deputy head. As Welchman's wife Katharine and son Nick were still living in Cambridge, he returned home as often as he could and on one such trip in early 1940, recruited June Canney and, in due course, drove her to BP. She would soon become his secretary and play a key role in the administration of Hut 6. As Welchman said jokingly to his agent many years later: 'Sad that I was far too busy to take advantage of the society of so many attractive and intelligent young ladies.'[4]

By 1941 the government had curtailed Welchman's personal recruiting programme and introduced regulation. In reality, this simply meant getting access to scientists and mathematicians through C. P. Snow of Christ's College, Cambridge. As Welchman had known him before the war, the flow of recruits to Hut 6 continued unabated. In any event, enough staff were already in place to begin populating the newly opened Hut 6 in late January 1940. While they had not yet broken any Enigma traffic, an organization was being put into place because Welchman was confident that it was only a matter of time before they were breaking large numbers of Enigma encrypted messages on a daily basis.

Hut 6 formed the Production section and its subdivisions followed Welchman's plan for a production-line approach.[5] All intercepted traffic came into Hut 6's Registration section headed by Welchman himself and as his deputy, Milner-Barry. By March, their team included Colman as statistician; a part time typist, Mrs P. H. Edwards; four team leaders including Howard Smith and Michael Banister; and seven female team members. The section's job was to acquire a grasp of the whole German wireless traffic (W/T) organization, so that the available intercepting stations could be used to the best possible advantage. For this purpose they had to keep in close touch with the Intelligence Section in Hut 3, with the Air Section, with the Military Section, and with the intercepting stations. They watched for peculiarities in the traffic and for signs of any change in German procedures. Once Enigma results were produced they looked for ways that they could help other sections. They also investigated other lines of attack and, as far as possible, prepared themselves for emergencies. At the same time they had to keep abreast of all developments in Enigma theory and be ready to modify their methods of registration when necessary.

Once documented, traffic was passed to the Netz section (or Party as it was quaintly called). Their task was to find the daily key on particular German communication networks using the various tools developed by John Jeffreys and his team. Research and development of new tools was an ongoing activity and a bombe machine group was set up to test the early prototype of that device. It consisted of Miss E. E. Dawson and one assistant. An order for the first bombe had gone to the British Tabulating Machine Company (BTM) in November 1939, The Bombe Section was officially established and strengthened upon the arrival of the first prototype (called Victory) in Hut 1 on 18 March 1940.

Once the key was 'out' the Deciphering section staff tested results from the Netz and Bombe sections and decrypted all the available traffic as quickly as possible. It was then passed to the service sections in Hut 3 for translation and analysis. In early 1940, Hut 3 had only three staff, Malcolm Saunders, S. C. Edgar and F. L. (Peter) Lucas.

The Poles had exploited a weakness in the Germans' procedures for Enigma in the 1930s. Henryk Zygalski had devised a method that used this weakness to help work out some of the settings used in the key for any given day. It was based upon a catalogue of perforated sheets and it had the huge advantage that it was not compromised by the plug connections on the Enigma machine. As there were only six wheel orders in operational use at this time (the operator could mix up his three wheels in six ways), a complete catalogue contained 26 perforated sheets each roughly 20 inches square, one for each of the possible ring settings on the right-hand wheel. Thus $6 \times 26 = 156$ sheets had to be manufactured. In December 1938 the Germans introduced two additional wheels so that each day, the Enigma operators chose three from a total of five available. This increased the number of wheel orders from 6 to 60 and, at that point, the Poles had managed to produce by hand, only two of the original six sets that they were working on.

One of the positive outcomes of the conference in the Pyry Forest in July 1939 had been that the British, with greater resources at their disposal, agreed to produce the Zygalski sheets. The task was assigned to a team led by John Jeffreys and a machine was built to punch out the holes. It was a monumental task and apparently a small party was held to celebrate the punching of the two millionth hole. The Poles were doing the same work by hand with razor blades! The Zygalski sheet method was called the Netz method (or just Netz) at BP and because Jeffreys led the work, some authors have subsequently confused the Netz with another perforated sheet method which he developed. The Jeffreys sheet method was actually a catalogue of the effect of two wheels and the reflector. The Netz method was the one that Welchman reinvented in his early days at BP.

The Poles had developed two machines to help with their work and they demonstrated both of them at the Pyry conference. The cyclometer helped with the task of constructing a card-index system containing information about all possible Enigma start positions that could have been used. The bomba had three pairs of Enigma wheel systems driven by an electric motor and exploited the same weakness as the Zygalski sheets. The Poles built six machines, one for each possible wheel order. When the number of possible wheel orders increased to sixty, the Poles would have needed sixty bomba machines and they did not have the resources to manufacture them.

A key part of Welchman's plan was to install Jeffreys and his team along with the Netz in Hut 6 as soon as they were operational. This would form the basis of Hut 6's attack on the encrypted Enigma messages. However, when Jeffreys had produced two sets of the sheets, BP could not get them to work, so Turing was dispatched to meet the Poles, who had now fled Poland and were working at the headquarters of the French Cipher Bureau, code-named Bruno and located outside Paris at the Château de Vignolles. The Poles demonstrated to Turing how the British-made sheets could be used along with their other methods to find the settings in a wartime Enigma key. At the end of his trip, a farewell dinner was held and Zygalski asked Turing why each side of the square perforations on the British sheets was such an odd measurement, eight and a half millimetres. Turing explained that the British worked in inches and in fact that each perforation was one third of an inch square, much to the amusement of all present.[6] Turing returned to BP and on or around 23 January 1940, a second set of the sheets was successfully used for the first time at BP. Shortly after this, the principal Luftwaffe key was broken. This, according to Milner-Barry, was a great event because:

> The first bombe was not yet in action, nor had cribs as yet been thought of. (Except probably in the fertile imagination of Welchman, ranging as usual a long way ahead of the event.)

With the rest of his team in place, Welchman arranged for Jeffreys and his group to move into Hut 6. During the transition period, other breaks were occurring but not on an operational basis. Much of this traffic was days or weeks old and of little use for intelligence purposes. It did, however, prove useful for training. In his early work on call signs and discriminants, Welchman had adopted the technique of colour-coding different German communication networks by using coloured pencils. Thus the principal Luftwaffe key came to be known at BP as 'Red'.

Milner-Barry would later say that:

> I can still remember Welchman talking about dealing with the traffic on an operational basis at a time when the phoney war was still in progress and when the terms carried no significant meaning to me.

By summer 1940 Welchman had put the hut on a twenty-four-hour rota to avoid the Registration Room having an accumulation of some fifteen hours of traffic. The first members of the night shift were David Gaunt, Michael Banister, Sheila Dunlop and June Canney. There were three shifts: 0000–0800, 0800–1600, 1600–2400 with three or four staff per shift. With keys changing every day at midnight, the main task was to break the current day's Red key. On one very successful day, it was broken at 5.00 a.m. and a thousand messages which subsequently came in on it were read. Plans were also put in place for a mobile Hut 6 after Dunkirk. At this stage, the whole Hut 6 operation was still fairly informal with none of the rigid differentiation of function between various members of a shift that later proved necessary. The Machine Room had been set up and the staff there would start by examining traffic on the registers, which were a continuous list of messages by each station with essential preamble detail. These lists were known as blists, a shortening of Banister Lists after their originator, Michael Banister. Machine Room staff would arrange the data in a suitable form for the Netz Room to try to complete the key by using the Netz method and other techniques. The registrar would underline Red discriminants with a red pencil to distinguish them from traffic on another network.

Many of the secrets of the Enigma were unlocked by Knox and his team, which on occasion included visitors from Hut 6 such as Rees and Babbage. Knox had pioneered the technique of looking for wheel order tips by using Enigma operator mistakes, which were called cillies. It was an esoteric mystery presided over by Knox in The Cottage, assisted by Hut 6 visitors. One example of a cilli occurred when a German Enigma operator, after encrypting a message, proceeded to encrypt the next message without moving his wheels.

Another extraordinary mistake made by the German cryptographic departments was the procedure imposed on those producing the monthly key sheets for each communication network. BP called these the Rules of Keys[7] and discovered them for Red in June 1940, and confirmed them during the following months. Many of the rules were discovered by members of Hut 6 whose names would be attached to them for the amusement of all involved as well as posterity. Nigel Forward, for example, arrived in Hut 6 in February 1941 and made the remarkable discovery that all German Air Force keys selected their wheel orders, not from the sixty possible, but from a list of only thirty. This dramatically reduced the amount of bombe time needed, particularly towards the end of each month. The discovery became known as the Nigelian Wheelorder Rule. Lionel Clarke arrived in July 1940 and about a year later discovered that in the columns on the monthly sheets which gave the wheel orders for each day, no wheel was followed by a consecutive wheel. In other words, if the wheel order on day one was 123, then on day two, the left-hand wheel would not be 2, the middle wheel 3 nor the right wheel 4; this rule was named the Clarkian Wheelorder Rule. John Monroe joined this illustrious band of rule discoverers when he realized that, on some keys, all five wheels would always be used on consecutive days. While this was not as absolute as the other rules, the Monrovian Wheelorder Rule was born. Some other rules were discovered including:

- On any two consecutive days in the same month, the same wheel could not be used in the same place. Within a month the same wheel order could not be used twice.
- In the first 26 days of the month, each ring setting was a unique letter, then arbitrary for days 27 to 31.
- Consecutive plugs were never used on the plugboard apart from A and Z. There were only 300 possible pairings but repeats in a month were avoided if possible.

Many of the Rules of Keys provide compelling evidence that the Germans believed throughout the war that their Enigma systems could not be broken. The rules must have been introduced on the basis that the enemy would never know any of the settings from a previous day of the month!

Hut 6 was now ready to take the lead in the attack on Enigma. Despite his outbursts and peculiar behaviour, Knox had been the Enigma pioneer in Britain and his energy and enthusiasm had inspired all in the early years. But now that enough of the Enigma secrets were exposed and Hut 6 was up and running under Welchman, Knox had to accept his new 'Research' role and turned his attention to other things such as the Enigma machine being used by the German military intelligence organization, the Abwehr. This device did not have a plugboard but was extremely complex with three moving wheels with multiple turnover positions and a reflector which moved during operation (in contrast to the standard service Enigma which had a fixed reflector). Yet Knox's team achieved great success against it. Knox worked on until, tragically, he succumbed to the cancer which had plagued him throughout the war, on 27 February 1943.

Throughout the whole history of Hut 6, there appear to have been extraordinarily few examples of innovations in German technique of which BP did not have adequate warning. Someone always seemed to be willing to take on the next problem and come up with a solution. By the beginning of May 1940, Hut 6 had broken four Army and five Air Force keys. Red, which was used by the Luftwaffe's general operational network and first seen by Hut 6 in September 1939, was being broken on a daily basis. Then, around 10 May, Hut 6 traffic registers showed up a change in German operator procedures.

The existing procedure had been for the sending operator to choose a three-letter message setting, say KAR, which would be the starting position of the Enigma wheels after the machine had been set up using the daily key settings for both encryption and decryption of the message. He would then choose another three letters, say GQX, and turn the wheels until these letters appeared in the window for each wheel. He would then type in KAR twice which might yield TLFQEP. The letters GQX would be sent in the preamble and TLFQEP would be the first six letters of the encrypted message. The receiving operator, having set his machine up with the daily key settings, would turn his wheels to GQX, type in TLFQEP to recover KARKAR. He would then set his wheels to KAR and begin decrypting the message by simply typing the encrypted message text on his machine. As the lamps lit up, they would reveal the plain text of the message. When staff in the Hut 6 Machine Room saw that there was an extra three-letter group in the preamble of the message, they quickly guessed that the Germans had stopped the double encryption of the message setting. For the example above, the preamble now contained the two three-letter groups, GQX TLF.

The news must have been shattering to the staff in Hut 6 because it meant that the Netz method was useless to them and consigned to history. It had been based entirely on the double encryption of the message settings and patterns which resulted from this. However, it could not have been entirely surprising, particularly to Welchman, Turing and other colleagues who had recognized that the Netz method was fragile, based as it was on a German mistake which could be rectified at any time. In fact, a machine-aided method which was not dependant on the German indicator system had been under discussion at BP for some while. According to Peter Twinn, in 1984 correspondence with Welchman, the idea of Enigmas linked together and going through all possible positions was certainly in many people's minds before Turing started thinking about their use after the change to the German indicator system. Thinking about a machine-based solution had yielded the bombe but the prototype was not fit for general use.

Before the German procedure change, with his usual foresight, Welchman had asked Milner-Barry to make a study of decrypted messages. He hoped that this would yield an intimate knowledge of the Enigma operators and mistakes that they might introduce due to 'human factors'. What it yielded was a catalogue of operator errors which helped Hut 6 break back into Red on 22 May. During the campaign in France, this resulted in over 1,000 decrypted messages a day and Welchman decided to concentrate most of his then limited resources on it.

The possibility of using operator errors had been pointed out by Dilly Knox as early as January 1940 and the name for them – cillies – could well have been originated by him or one of his team in The Cottage. In any event, it led to what Welchman referred to as a comedy of errors and a more detailed explanation about how they were exploited can be found in *Appendix 3*. The classic example of a cilli was an operator's choice of the six letters for his indicator settings. As only the first three letters would appear as plain text in the preamble, operators were choosing memorable six-letter words like HITLER or BERLIN. A particularly amusing example was recalled by Art Levinson, one of the American contingent at BP.[8] The first three letters sent by the operator in plain text were TOM, followed by the encryption of his second three letters, say XGH. Levinson and his colleagues immediately tried to think of six-letter words beginning with TOM such as TOMTOM or TOMMEY. Much to their surprise, it turned out that the six-letter word chosen by the operator was TOMMIX. Tom Mix was a Hollywood cowboy who, much to the astonishment of the Americans at BP, appeared to have a large fan club in Nazi Germany!

John Herivel was a man on a mission and once he understood the working of the Enigma machine, he spent much of his time thinking about how it could be broken. His eureka moment occurred when he imagined himself as an Enigma operator setting up his machine for the day. He realized that when the operator set the position of the ring around each wheel, the physical arrangement of the machine meant that he might well end up with the ring setting at the top of the wheel. All three ring settings would then be viewable through the windows adjacent to them. A lazy operator might then use these as his indicator setting for his next message or perhaps just turn one or two wheels by a position or two. If this happened, Herivel came up with a method which, if successful, would produce the ring setting for the day. Welchman encouraged him to carry on with it, even though it did not yield useful results at first. Then, when he arrived at Hut 6 on 10 May

1940 to take up the evening shift, Welchman was waiting for him. In the corner of the Hut surrounded by a group of his colleagues, David Rees was in the process of completing the breaking of Red with the aid of Herivel's method. Welchman took him to one side and said 'Herivel, this will not be forgotten.'[9] The Herivel Tip (or Herivelismus) as it became known, would prove to be a key tool for Hut 6 until the arrival of the bombes.

Welchman was true to his word the following year when Prime Minister Churchill visited BP in early September. Travis accompanied Churchill on his tour around the site and, on arriving in Hut 6, informed Welchman, who had been asked to give a short presentation, that he had five minutes. Welchman said that he had three points and after completing the first two, Travis said 'That will do Welchman.' The Prime Minister winked at him and said 'I believe there was a third point, Welchman?' He then took Churchill over to where Herivel was standing and said 'Sir, I would like to present John Herivel who was responsible for breaking the German Enigma last year.' Herivel was moved to end his own memoir published sixty-seven years later with the words 'So Floreat Welchmani memoriam!'

As his workload increased, Welchman was finding it more and more difficult to get back to Cambridge. After Katharine had given birth to their second child, Susanna, on 1 January 1941, the family decided to move closer to BP. After living in the villages of Fenny Stratford and Loughton, they eventually settled in the town of Stony Stratford. Their Queen Anne-style fronted house was on Watling Street, a Roman road which ran though the centre of the town. The town had been an important stopping-off point for mail and passenger coaches travelling between London and the North of England. This coaching history is the source of the supposed origin of the phrase 'cock and bull story'. In the height of the coaching era – the eighteenth and early nineteenth centuries – the Cock and the Bull were two of the main coaching inns in the town and the banter and rivalry between groups of travellers is said to have resulted in exaggerated and fanciful stories, which became known as 'cock and bull stories'. The Welchman house lay along the main road, a short walk from the two inns which were still thriving businesses. However, rather than horse-drawn coaches, the road in front of the house was now choked with military convoys. On one occasion, Welchman was involved in an accident on the main road when his car was sandwiched between two military vehicles. His black car and the heavily blinkered headlamps in use in wartime no doubt contributed to it. The Welchmans would often entertain friends at home and, in particular, musicians would arrive for impromptu musical evenings with Welchman providing beer from one of the nearby pubs. The household also included a nanny, Miss Ring, and occasionally a maid, which became essential when Katharine joined the ATS in 1942.

By the end of 1940, Welchman's plan for the subdivision into huts was gathering pace and a staff list produced on 2 December 1940 shows staff numbers as: Hut 6 – 93, Hut 3 – 60, Hut 8 – 37, Hut 4 – 40. The number of staff listed in Knox's Research Section in The Cottage was 8![10] By July 1941 Welchman needed more staff and he wrote to Travis on the 4th, stating his requirements:

> As you know, the work of Hut 6 is getting more and more difficult. We need more staff and more space. The male staff will probably not need many additions, but I should like permission to engage up to 6 seniors and 6 juniors in addition to our present staff. The girls are divided into 4 sections which are likely to require an average staff of 25 each. In fact we shall need at least 4 Temporary Junior Assistant Principals and 100 Temporary Assistants or Grade II clerks. At present we have 3 girls capable of being Temporary Junior Assistant Principals, and 64 others of whom 12 are probably not up to the work. I should like permission to engage up to 48 more girls either as Temporary Assistants or as grade II clerks and up to three more Temporary Junior Assistant Principals.
>
> Of course more space will be needed. We are very overcrowded already. I should think that an addition equivalent to about one quarter, or possibly one third of our present space would be sufficient.[11]

Failure by senior BP management to deal quickly with urgent requests such as this led Welchman to take more dramatic action. In late October 1941, Welchman, Turing, Alexander and Milner-Barry all signed a letter to the Prime Minister, Winston Churchill. Milner-Barry then proceeded to London where he took a taxi to No. 10 Downing Street and handed in the letter to one of Churchill's staff. The consequence was a marked improvement in the situation because on receipt of the letter Churchill had put an 'Action This Day' stamp on it with a handwritten note to his chief military assistant, General Ismay, saying: 'Make sure they have all they want on extreme priority and report to me that this has been done.' The letter may well have led indirectly to Denniston's replacement as Operational Director of GC&CS by his deputy, Edward Travis in February 1942. This followed a review of the administration of signals intelligence by Sir Stewart Menzies, Chief of SIS.[12]

Turing's work at the start of the war on a machine solution had quickly reached the build stage and the British Tabulating Machine Company at Letchworth had been contracted to carry out the work. Their Research Director, Harold 'Doc' Keen, needed to be briefed on BP's requirements and Peter Twinn was given the task, as he explained in a letter to Welchman in 1984:

> Keen's first introduction to the problem was from me and took place in the White Hart at Buckingham. Travis asked me to put the matter to Keen first because he thought, erroneously in my opinion, that Alan Turing's manner and occasional incoherence might put Keen off and create the wrong impression.

By early 1940, the manufacture of the prototype bombe, a complex electro-mechanical machine, was well under way. The first prototype, named Victory, was installed in Hut 1 on 18 March 1940 but did not prove particularly effective. It was only when a second and improved machine was installed in Hut 11 in August that real results were achieved. This machine, named Agnes, incorporated a brilliant design modification invented by Welchman and called the diagonal board (*see Chapter 4*). Victory was then moved to Wavendon as a training machine as it was unreliable and six more machines were on order by November. The first of an even more sophisticated model, the Jumbo bombe, arrived in Hut 11 in March 1941.

With the arrival of the machines, the whole Hut 6 operation changed and fundamental to its success was the concept of the crib. The idea was to guess a plain text phrase that was embedded somewhere in an intercepted encrypted message. If the plain text phrase could be matched to a run of encrypted characters within the message, it provided a crib which could be used with a bombe to help deduce some of the key settings such as the wheel configuration. A crib was not a new concept and Knox and his team had used it quite effectively several years earlier. However, they were using hand methods and it was now proposed to use a machine to speed up the process. A new structure to do so was gradually put into place during 1941.

Up to the end of 1940, Welchman had personally directed all of the Hut 6 activity. But a more complex infrastructure was now required to deal with the growing Enigma traffic. In early 1941 the Governing Body was formed and included the heads of Control (Colman) the Crib Room (Milner-Barry) and Machine Room (Babbage) with Welchman in the chair. Fletcher, as Head of the Registration Room, Decoding Room and Netz Room was added to the group in early 1942. He handled most of the administration of Hut 6 throughout the war and had the crucial responsibility of liaising with BTM at Letchworth, which had been contracted to manufacture the bombes.

The group had weekly meetings and considered weekly reports from section heads (compiled into a Hut 6 weekly report), but had little operational decision-making authority. They concentrated on laying down policy and had grown to nine members by 1944. The Governing Body continued to meet until March 1945, when it was dissolved.

Hut 6 Administration was created to enable individual members to carry out their jobs with the minimum amount of distraction from the administration of GC&CS. The office had five staff, including three secretaries, and their duties consisted of the supply of furniture and office equipment, accommodation, statistics and staffing.

The position of duty officer was introduced in 1941 and in theory he was Hut 6's chief executive officer. It was filled by a senior member of the hut who carried out other duties until August 1942 when a permanent assistant duty officer was appointed on the day shift. The roles of the day duty officer and the head of the Decoding Room were combined in April 1944 and eventually it was almost solely responsible for liaison with Hut 3 on matters of decoding priorities.

Welchman had recognized by early 1940 that the problem of interception required a special section and the Control Room had been created under John Colman. The section had a wide-ranging role which included recognizing radio set requirements; pressing for suitable interception and communications facilities; organizing and maintaining relations between Hut 6 and intercept stations; maintaining a continuous service to direct cover and assist interception. It consisted of a body of watch officers, each with an assistant, who maintained a round-the-clock rota keeping control by direct line of the main home intercept stations. Policy on cover was set by the Governing Body of Hut 6. Priorities between different requests were determined by the control officer (order of priority usually cryptography, intelligence, traffic analysis), with Colman, as head of Control, the final arbitrator.

The scope of minute-to-minute management of interception from the Hut 6 Control Room developed considerably and staff numbers grew to around twenty-five. By late 1941, Hut 6 maintained liaison officers at two main intercept sites. In the summer of 1943, a small special section, the Overseas Party, was created to tackle problems associated with overseas interception. Control had a special telephone exchange set up with direct lines to the main intercept station. In late 1943, a larger switchboard was installed and was in use twenty-four hours a day, seven days a week. A priority teleprinter system was put into place with a performance target of twenty minutes from time of intercept to time of teleprinting. While despatch riders were rarely necessary to send important traffic, Chicksands, only thirty minutes away, sent riders to BP hourly. Hut 6 Control communicated with intercept stations at Beaumanor, Bishop's Waltham, Chicksands, Forest Moor, Harpenden, Denmark Hill, Whitchurch (Shropshire), 'Santa Fe' (Bexley, Kent, US Army), Wick and Montrose.

In his memoir, John Herivel observed that:

> Nobody was recruited to the Machine Room in Hut 6 who was not a mathematician; mathematicians, moreover, who were of two sorts only: those who had been students of Welchman's at Sidney Sussex College, and those who had been friends of his at Cambridge; in other words, he had packed the house!

With the arrival of effective bombes, the Machine Room was set up to produce instructions for the women (usually members of the Women's Royal Naval Service or WRNS) who set up the bombes, operated them and then tested the results that were produced. The instructions were in a diagrammatic format and called menus, apparently because they were the diet that was fed to the bombes! A separate Testing Room was set up and as a direct descendant of the old Netz Room, carried on with the name until 1943.

The Crib Room was formed on 1 October 1940 under Milner-Barry. The art of cribbery, that is finding usable cribs, was steadily developed and the members of the section, the cribsters, became gradually surer in their touch. They gained experience which would prove to be the foundation stone of the later success of Hut 6. Sometimes the cribsters would be helped by German Air Force and Army Enigma operators' use of stereotyped language. An Army unit stationed in North Africa but seeing little action used the same phrase in its encrypted daily report to headquarters every day for a month 'KEINE BESONDEREN EREIGNISSE' (this loosely translates as 'No special occurrences'). In 1940, when the German Air Force was operating in France, each day its airfields would receive instructions for their targets. Each message would begin with the phrase 'BESONDERE ANORDNUNGEN FUER DIE . . .' ('Special Orders for the . . .') followed by each airfield's designation.

The Research Machine Room began informally in autumn 1940 as a separate body of people entrusted with the specific task of trying to break 'odd keys' while Red and another Luftwaffe key known as Brown, used to send information about navigational beams, were broken daily by routine shifts of the Machine Room and Crib Room. The Research Machine Room had variable membership of at most two or three people at a time who were seconded from the routine shifts for a week or fortnight. They worked permanent days rather than shifts. Once progress was made with a key, and if its contents were sufficiently important, it would be quickly transferred to the routine shifts. An example was Light Blue, used by the Luftwaffe in Africa. It was broken using cillies in March 1941 and at once became a current key for the Machine Room. Another example was Orange, which was used by the SS and broken initially by the Research Machine Room on 10 December 1940.

A Research Crib Room was created in April 1942 and became permanent in September 1942 when Derek Taunt was assigned to it.

The Decoding Room decrypted all of the traffic using British Typex encryption machines, which had been converted to emulate Enigma machines. Once a key was broken, Typex machines could be set up using that key and all traffic that had been intercepted on it could then be decrypted. The section operated much like a typing pool with women typing in thousands of encrypted 200–250 character messages. The machine would produce the German text on thin strips of paper tape which were then stuck on to sheets of paper and passed to Hut 3 for translation and analysis. They also decrypted broken naval traffic for Hut 8 until it established its own Decoding Room.

The Typex machine was the British equivalent of Enigma.[13] In 1926, the British Government had set up an Inter-Departmental Cipher Committee to investigate the possibility of replacing the book systems then used by the armed forces, the Foreign Office, the Colonial Office and the India Office by cipher machines. O. G. W. Lywood, a signals officer with the RAF, believed that it would be possible to develop an improved version of the commercial Enigma machine. He proposed to incorporate parts from Creed teleprinters, in order to produce printed text. The committee refused to proceed so the RAF went it alone with Lywood's ideas in 1934. Unlike the military Enigma, which was a standard machine with virtually no variations between machines apart from the additional three wheels used by the German Navy and two settable reflectors, Typex had a minimum of 120 different wheels or inserts in service. As five wheel inserts could in effect be selected from a set of 28, the Mk. VI version operators could arrange their wheels inside the machine 7,687,680 different ways, compared to 60 or 336 with Enigma. Typex had 20 or more completely different sets with no common wiring between them. The Germans would have had to find the wirings for between 120 and 250 wheels – a huge task. Ironically, the Typex infringed several patents on Enigma held by the German company Chiffriermaschinen Aktiengesellschaft. Of course no royalties were ever paid!

The old Registration section became the Registration Room, recording all Air and Army traffic in a form suitable for the Crib and Decoding Rooms. The registration of traffic remained its main function until September 1942. From summer 1941 until autumn 1943, it also documented operational keys. A separate group of staff within the section formed the Research Registration Room and dealt with research keys, that is those that were problematic. All messages were registered on blist forms and numbered. Details of incoming discriminants were recorded on a chart called the 'Hanky-Panky' or just 'Hankey', which also directed messages bearing identified discriminants to the correct blist. The 'Hankey' was named after its designer John 'Hank' Hancock.

Before autumn 1942, the training of staff in Hut 6 came from doing the work itself. The Decoding Room was the first to find a more specific requirement and a school was set up on 14 September. A Registration Room school followed in late September, which laid the foundations for systematic training for all new staff. The need for training was driven by the large influx of staff and the scope of the work becoming more difficult. Therefore, a formal training syllabus for Hut 6 staff was put in place.[14]

About 200 distinct Enigma keys were identified, named and broken in the history of Hut 6 and details can be found in Appendix 4. With a very large number of live keys at any one time a system was needed to manage it effectively. A parentage system was created to make best use of the available cryptographic resources and the special talents of each person. It also ensured that each key got its fair share of attention, and incidentally proved useful in countering boredom and staleness. One or sometimes two people (the parent) took responsibility for a key or set of keys and had specialized knowledge of related cribs and cillies on a key. Changes in allocations of keys to a parent were made at intervals.

Space was an ongoing problem until Hut 6 moved to the spacious Block D in February 1943. The research branches of the Machine, Crib and Registration Rooms had to be housed in the Mansion until Block D was completed. All organizations, no matter how harmonious, have their problems and Hut 6 was no exception. According to the authors of the 'Official History of Hut 6',[15] there were artificial and arbitrary divisions of responsibility. Every day questions arose which neither party could settle on its own. As cribs became more important, the balance of power shifted from the Machine Room to the Crib Room and members of the former 'felt degraded from their former proud position to little more than menu-makers and testers of stories'. Meetings were held in the autumn of 1941 but the situation persisted into 1942. A solution was deferred until the move to Block D but a fusion process ensued in which Machine Room members spent time in the Crib Room and vice-versa. In February 1943, the Machine and Crib Rooms merged as the Watch and the Netz Room became the Machine Room. A similar merger took place between their Research Section counterparts with a similar information exchange. Milner-Barry took over the Watch, and Babbage the Research activities. The 'Official History of Hut 6' summarized the merger as follows:

> The final moral of the Machine Room/Crib Room story may be stated thus: While in a complex cryptographic organization like Hut 6, a considerable degree of specialization is unavoidable as between interception, traffic analysis and cryptography, it is undesirable that there should be any watertight divisions in the initial processes of breaking. Any specialization that is necessary here should arise from divisions of the material to be broken – e.g. Watch/Research and later Air/Army – not from different lines of approach to the same material.

Over a few years, Welchman had managed to put in place a remarkably efficient organization. It would provide a model for its sister organization, Hut 8. Hut 6 was run in a very loose and informal style with only an indispensable minimum of formal routine meetings. Heads of departments had a free hand with their advice and it was almost always accepted without question. By the end of the war, Hut 6 had around 550 staff.

As the architect of the hut-based process at BP, Welchman knew that some problems would eventually emerge. While he had established an excellent working environment in Hut 6, the same could not be said for Hut 3, led by Malcolm Saunders. This was of concern to him as he had envisaged Hut 6 and Hut 3 working as an inter-service organization under Foreign Office administration.

R. V. Jones was a frequent visitor to BP in his capacity as Assistant Director of Intelligence (Science) in the Air Ministry. Travis had given him the impression that he regarded Hut 3 as 'a lot of exploiters of Hut 6's efforts' and asked that he come to BP in November 1940 to give Hut 6 a talk on his work. This was to be exclusively for Hut 6 because on a previous visit during the summer he had given a talk to Hut 3 and they had not invited Hut 6. After his morning talk to Hut 6, Jones encountered Saunders and others from Hut 3 at lunch. They were furious that they hadn't been invited. As Jones recalled in a letter to Welchman:

> The only way I could placate them was to stay and repeat the talk to Hut 3 during the afternoon, which I knew would involve driving back into London after the nightly attack had started. As I described in my book, I crashed into an unlit lorry abandoned outside St. Albans Hospital, and Charles Frank and I went through the windscreen. I feel that the rivalry between the huts still owes me for the car, for this was the first year in which I had not insured it comprehensively and it was a write-off. I am sure that you with your point about reading German, did not feel that Hut 6 were unnecessary middlemen, but my impression may have been unduly biased by Travis, and relations between him and Saunders may not have been too good.[16]

During the autumn of 1941 the Whitehall intelligence departments had become increasingly concerned about BP's control over intelligence. In particular, they were annoyed by BP's right to communicate directly with fighting commands, even though it speeded up the process of getting vital information to commanders in the field. Inter-service rivalries had also surfaced in Hut 3 between the senior liaison officer with the Air Ministry, Robert Humphreys, backed by C. R. Curtis, head of the Army section and the nominal head of Hut 3, Malcolm Saunders. Humphreys had lobbied effectively for BP in Whitehall but was a poor team player and had caused great dissent in both Hut 3 and Whitehall. Nigel de Grey described the situation as 'an imbroglio of conflicting jealousies, intrigue and differing opinions'. Eventually, an RAF officer, Eric Jones, was brought in to assess the situation. His report, dated 2 February 1942 and classified Most Secret provides a fascinating and objective commentary on the work of Huts 6 and 3 in early 1942.[17]

Jones's conclusions and recommendations were very clear. He recommended the removal of Curtis whom he described as 'a charmingly naive plagiarist who puts to the War Office as his own, interpretations borrowed from others'. He also recommended the removal of Humphreys, as he was 'inclined to make personal capital out of the work'.

The outcome of Jones's report was the removal of Saunders from Hut 3 along with Humphreys and Curtis. They were initially replaced by a management triumvirate of the three senior officers in the Hut, but Jones himself was confirmed as overall head in July 1942. Jones would go on to replace Travis as Director of GCHQ in 1952.

Welchman had been one of the first to recognize the indivisibility of the whole Enigma effort, from interception right through to intelligence. All sections – interception, cryptographic, traffic analysis and intelligence – operated as parts of a whole. Hut 6 also defined some basic principles of cryptography which would prove invaluable to Britain's own intelligence security. An assessment of how the Germans measured up against these principles was included in Hut 6's end of war report:

1. The cipher must be theoretically secure – i.e. unbreakable if no errors are made in the construction of keys and encoding of messages. This was easily achieved by the Germans. While the first two indicating systems used by them were inadequate, the system introduced in May 1940 made Enigma theoretically unbreakable

2. The construction of keys must be wholly random i.e. there must be no rules of keys or key repeats (other than such repeats as can occur by chance). The Germans never properly realized the importance of this and failed, particularly on Air Force keys.

3. The effect of possible errors by the cipher clerks must be obviated. This was the hardest to achieve and the Germans failed despite great efforts and a wealth of ingenuity. The main reason why the theoretical security of Enigma did not give practical security was that the Germans failed to control their cipher clerks. They introduced new devices in a piecemeal fashion such as the plugable reflector D and the use of dummy words and repeated characters. The supervision of their cipher clerks was not thorough enough or sufficiently co-ordinated. German cryptographers were never allowed to inspect genuine traffic or keys.[18]

By October 1943, Welchman's main work for Hut 6 was complete. He had put in place an effective infrastructure, efficient processes, the provision of the tools to do the job and a high calibre of staff. Although improvements were still possible, he was needed for another role at BP. According to Milner-Barry:

> Welchman's originality of mind, strong mechanical bias, and imaginative vision were invaluable assets for one presiding at the birth of an infant organization and planning its future growth.

Chapter 4

Turing, the Bombe and the Diagonal Board

Three men, Alan Turing, Gordon Welchman and Harold Keen, were ultimately responsible for the machine which enabled BP to read millions of encrypted messages during the Second World War. Only Welchman would live long enough to see some information about their magnificent achievement reach the public domain. The first accounts were laughable and, in some cases, wildly inaccurate. Winterbotham was the first to attempt to describe a machine that he knew little about in his book *The Ultra Secret* in 1974:

> I am not of the computer age nor do I attempt to understand them, but early in 1940 I was ushered with great solemnity into the shrine where stood a bronze-coloured column surmounted by a larger circular bronze-coloured face, like some Eastern Goddess who was destined to become the oracle of Bletchley, at least when she felt like it. She was an awesome piece of magic.

This was followed by Cave Brown in his book *Bodyguard of Lies* in 1975:

> The machine was installed at Hut 3, a large Nissen hut under the trees in Bletchley's parkland, and the time soon came to begin operational trials by feeding Enigma intercepts to 'The Bomb'. These intercepts were simply obtained from the string of tall-pyloned wireless interception posts which the British government had established around the world. The posts recorded all enemy, hostile and suspect wireless traffic and radioed it to Bletchley Park, where Enigma transmissions were identified, put on tape and fed into the 'Bomb'. If the 'Bomb' could find the keys in which the transmissions had been ciphered, the cryptanalysts at Bletchley could then 'unbutton' these messages.

Cave Brown had clearly been doing his research but unfortunately, had conflated three key developments at BP: a machine to help with the decryption of Enigma messages, the world's first electronic computer which used paper tape to input data and was nothing to do with Enigma, and a hand technique developed by Dilly Knox to tackle messages encrypted with early versions of the Enigma machine. The first machine was the bombe, the second Colossus and Knox's technique was called 'buttoning-up'. Ironically, Cave Brown's book was approved by the American authorities before publication.

It is unlikely that Winterbotham and Cave Brown were trying to deceive their readers but, rather, were writing in ignorance of the real facts. In a modern computer world it is all too easy to think that the bombe was indeed a computer which magically worked out the daily key settings that operators on a German communications network were using on their Enigma machines. The reality was far from that, as Welchman pointed out in a letter to Robin Denniston in February 1984:

> The technical point that must be made to cryptographers of today is that we had a manual method and later on a Bombe that enabled us to ignore the enormous number of alternative plugboard connections in the first stage of the attack on an Enigma key. This, indeed, was all that the Bombes did.

The use of machines by the Poles to assist in the attack on the Enigma machine has been described extensively in the literature and in *Chapter 3* of this book. Rejewski published his own accounts which appeared in English in the early 1980s.[1] Twinn confirmed to Welchman in their correspondence in the 1980s that Knox's team had descriptions of the Polish bomba available in the Cottage. Knox had also used the idea of a crib with his hand methods to great effect in the early part of the war. As part of his team, Turing would have had access to this information.

Alan Turing's work and life has been admirably covered by Andrew Hodges in his fine biography, *Alan Turing: The Enigma*. In 1935, Turing had gone to a Part III course on Foundations of Mathematics given by M. H. A. Newman. Something important had lodged in Turing's mind: was there a definite method, or as Newman put it a mechanical process, which could be applied to a mathematical statement, and which would come up with an answer as to whether it was provable? Max Newman would eventually be a colleague of Turing at BP and head the section named after him (the Newmanry) that would commission Colossus, the world's first electronic computer. Stimulated by Newman, Turing went on to publish in 1936 his seminal paper with the tongue-twisting title of 'On Computable Numbers, with an application to the Entscheidungsproblem'. It was a remarkable piece of work, summarised by Hodges as follows:

> Alan had proved that there was no 'miraculous machine' that could solve all mathematical problems, but in the process he had discovered something almost equally miraculous, the idea of a universal machine that could take over the work of any machine. And he had argued that anything performed by a human computer could be done by a machine. So there could be a single machine which, by reading the descriptions of other machines placed upon its 'tape', could perform the equivalent of human mental activity. A single machine, to replace the human computer! An electric brain!

Three years later, Turing found himself at BP, working in The Cottage with Dilly Knox. The eccentric ways of both gentlemen have been well documented and it is fascinating to imagine how these two characters got on, considering Knox's apparent dislike of most of his male colleagues. Given Welchman's difficulties with Knox, one wonders if Turing ever experienced anything of a similar nature. What does survive is a memo from Knox to Denniston in which the author says:

> Turing is very difficult to anchor down. He is very clever but quite irresponsible and throws up suggestions of all sorts of merit. I have just, but only just enough authority and ability to keep his ideas in some sort of order and discipline. But he is very nice about it all.[2]

With Welchman dispatched to Elmers School to work on traffic analysis, it was Turing who began to look at how cribs and mechanization could help with the decryption process. A crib was a guessed phrase that could be matched character by character, to a string of encrypted characters in the message. A crib was independent of the German indicator system. Even before the Pyry conference, the idea of mechanizing two Enigma wheels three positions apart to exploit the repeated characters (known as 'females') caused by the German Enigma operators encrypting the message setting twice, had been discussed at BP.[3] It is important to note that at this point Turing's idea for a machine solution had nothing to do with his earlier ideas about a 'universal machine'. What he envisaged was a bespoke solution, specific to the internal wiring of the Enigma wheels and constructed around the crib.

As Turing's ideas developed, Welchman had moved from Knox's team to begin building his own team in Hut 6 and putting in place his ideas for expansion. Like Turing, he was also thinking about machine solutions for the Enigma-related problems facing them. With their ideas taking shape, BP needed to turn them into reality and for this they looked to BTM and the company's brilliant engineer Harold Keen.[4]

In 1910, BTM had been awarded the contract to mechanize the 1911 British census. To meet this commitment, the company had recruited new staff and so Keen joined in 1912. In 1921, most of the company, including Keen, moved to a new factory in Letchworth, Hertfordshire. By 1923, he was head of the Experimental Department and eventually became regarded as one of the most successful British innovators in the field of punched-card machinery. He had also picked up the name 'Doc' because of his habit of carrying papers and tools in a small bag, much like the one used by doctors. In 1939, Travis visited BTM and following discussions with Keen and the Managing Director, a Mr Bailey, a contract was signed to produce the bombe machines under the codename 'Cantab'. Peter Twinn briefed Keen on the technical details.

As the machines were urgently needed Keen adapted, where possible, suitable and proven components already being manufactured on a large scale for BTM's existing products. The design, manufacture and assembly of the machine took place in his own department to ensure security. All BTM equipment was based on the requirement to record numerical and textural information by means of accurately punched holes in Hollerith cards. The holes were sensed by small metal brushes and used to activate electro-mechanisms. Timed electrical clock pulses were distributed within or between mechanisms by using commutators with circular rows of contact segments and rotating brushes. This technology, along with the company's expertise in the use of electromagnetic relays as switches, lay at the heart of the machine that BTM would produce for BP.

Keen decided to use circular wheels (known as drums) to replicate the wheels of an Enigma machine. Each so-called scrambler in the bombes (also called Letchworth Enigmas) consisted of three drums which were internally wired to replicate the Enigma wheels that they represented. Rather than sitting side by side like the wheels in an Enigma machine, the bombe's drums were attached to the machine in vertical columns. Operators had to have clear access to individual drums so that they could easily change them during use. Each drum had a different colour to help the operators to identify them and the colours used for wheels I–VIII were red, purple, green, yellow, brown, blue, black and grey respectively. Only the German Navy used wheels VI, VII and VIII.

In early versions the sensing rate of the commutator segments was 20 to 25 per second. Based on the lower rate it took 22 minutes to test all positions of three wheels and therefore to test the possible wheel configurations available to the German Army and Air Force operators took 22 hours. This was eventually reduced to around 15 hours. Standard BTM units and components were employed to provide the various functions.

Twinn had told Keen that up to 40 scramblers (each with three drums) might be needed to satisfy Turing's design requirements. A compromise was agreed that limited the number in the first two prototypes to 10. The next two prototypes incorporated a significant modification invented by Welchman (the Diagonal Board) and had 12 scramblers. By the end of 1941, the bombes had 3 banks of 12 scramblers, close to Twinn's original prediction. To provide the flexibility to interconnect the various components of the machine, the machine had 230×26-way jacks and batches of 26-way plug-in cable connectors.

By the summer of 1941, there were four to six bombes at BP in Hut 11 and a similar number in some converted stables at Adstock Manor in the village of Adstock, where coincidentally, Travis lived throughout the war. The machines were delivered in ordinary unobtrusive covered lorries like the ones used for BTM's own machines and therefore attracted no undue attention. Eventually some machines were installed in the villages of Wavendon and Gayhurst, 70 in all. Then a purpose-built facility was opened in Stanmore in August 1942 and in 1943 at Eastcote. By the end of the war, BTM had produced around 211 machines.

The Enigma machine had a weakness in its design and in its use. Its weakness in design was that it could not encrypt a letter as itself. Its weakness in use was that the operators, particularly those in the German Air Force, became lazy and over-confident and their continual habit of re-using the same phrases in messages day after day, provided Hut 6 with an ample supply of cribs. The standard procedure was to write the letters of the guessed phrase and the intercepted message in its encrypted form on slips of paper. By placing them on a table, one above the other, one slip could be moved left or right. What the cryptanalyst was looking for was a position where each letter in the phrase had been encrypted as one of the other 25 letters in the alphabet. The relationship between the guessed phrase (called a crib) and corresponding encrypted characters in the message could then be tested on a bombe. If the test was successful, part of the setting of the Enigma machine that had produced it would be revealed and further hand testing might reveal the rest of the setting. A detailed description of cribs and how they were used at BP can be found in *Appendix 2*.

A bombe did not magically tell BP's cryptanalysts how Enigma operators on a German communication network were setting up their machines before they encrypted a message. It simply eliminated enough of the 158.9 million, million, million possible ways they could have done it to allow the actual settings to be worked out using hand methods. John Herivel, who worked in Hut 6, wrote the following elegant description of the bombe many years later, using the German word 'stecker' for plug:

> The whole basis of Turing's approach was the idea of running a crib through all 17,576 different positions of the drums for a given wheel order and accepting or rejecting a given position by testing to see if possible stecker pairs could or could not be found for it. This was a very remarkable idea as although in theory the steckers made the identification vastly more difficult, in practice they provided a method for spotting possible positions. Thus the steckers were used to work for a solution and their 'difficulty' was thus neatly compensated for by their 'utility'.

There were problems with Turing's original design as only certain cribs worked effectively. The solution came to Welchman in flash of inspiration and involved interconnecting the scramblers in the bombe in a way that meant that almost any crib could be effective. As he wrote in *The Hut Six Story*:

> When this new method of interconnecting the scramblers came to me, I couldn't believe it. But I sat down with a few coloured pencils, drew a simple wiring diagram, and convinced myself that the idea would indeed work. Armed with this diagram I hurried once again to the Cottage, this time to talk to Turing. On this occasion I had a better reception than I had received from Dilly. Turing was incredulous at first, as I had been, but when he had studied my diagram he agreed that the idea would work, and became as excited about it as I was. He agreed that the improvement over the type of the Bombe that he had been considering was spectacular.

Welchman took the idea to Travis and with Turing's backing he was dispatched to brief Keen at BTM. His idea proved to be reasonably straight-forward to implement and Keen grasped the principle behind it quite quickly. It became known as the diagonal board and speeded up the solution of Enigma keys by orders of magnitude. Welchman and Keen worked closely together for the next few years and also become close friends. Bombes with a diagonal board became the default configuration for the machine for the rest of the war. Welchman had wanted to call it the modified device the 'spider' to distinguish it from the early prototype but, in the end, the name bombe was used for the rest of the war. However, Travis tended to use the term spider when referring to a bombe.

The machines themselves were spectacularly successful and the performance records recorded in the Official History of Hut 6 show availability figures across all machines throughout the war at just under 98 per cent. Given that there was regularly scheduled down time for main-tenance and that they ran twenty-four hours a day, seven days a week, their performance was extraordinary and a testament to the skills of Doc Keen and his team at BTM. Other variants of the bombe would follow including the Jumbo which did more automatic testing than the 'spider'. It also printed out results which eliminated much of the hand-based work which had previously been necessary. As not many of these machines were made, they were reserved for important messages which caused difficulties for the spider. A 'Giant' bombe was built in June 1944 just after D-Day and consisted of four bombes linked together. However, it never left BTM's Letchworth factory as it proved to be unreliable. Once the Americans became involved in BP's work, they began producing their own version of the bombe.

Joan Clarke had been recruited by Welchman in 1940, but rather than working in Hut 6 she had joined Turing in Hut 8 on 17 June of that year to help with work on the German Naval Enigma problem. The German Navy was much more security-conscious than its Army and Air Force counter-parts and in the early years of the war, its Enigma-encrypted messages had proved to be unbreakable by BP. An excellent cryptanalyst in her own right, Clarke had been present when Turing had fully realized that Welchman's invention of the diagonal board would significantly improve the performance of the bombe. She had also been engaged to Turing for a time and while it had not worked out (Turing had warned her that this might happen because of his 'homosexual tendencies'), they did remain colleagues and good friends even after the war. Sometime in the late 1970s, as Joan Murray, she produced a document for the NSA about her personal memories of the bombe development.[5] The following extract provides some insight into Welchman and Turing's working relationship:

> The heads of both Hut 6 and Hut 8 were involved in the vital developments in the logical design of bombes, which took place near the time of my arrival. The first was Welchman's idea of the diagonal board, which made use of the reciprocal property of the stecker. I understood later from Turing that Welchman's objective in specifying this was simply to provide entry to a secondary chain of constatations [one pair of matching plain/cipher text]. With the original form of test on the bombe, this secondary chain would need to include a closure in order to be of any value in reducing the number of bombe answers. Meanwhile, both Welchman and Turing were looking for a general method of achieving simultaneous scanning, i.e. testing all stecker assumptions for the input letter at the same time. I remember Turing jumping up with the remark that 'the diagonal board will give us simultaneous scanning,' and rushing across to Hut 6 to tell Welchman. Turing's contribution was the realization that a wrong stecker assumption for the input letter would imply all wrong steckers, if one allowed an unlimited number of re-entries into the chain. In the electrical implementation which provided simultaneous scanning, 25 relays represented the other steckers for the input letter, and the new test was whether any of these relays was not activated. When I mentioned the subject to Turing after the war, when he was visiting GCHQ at Eastcote as a consultant, he minimized his own contribution compared with Welchman's idea of the diagonal board, saying that Welchman or someone else was bound to have realized it before long – but I doubt whether anyone else would rate Turing's contribution to bombe theory so lightly.

On 15 July 1941, Welchman, Turing and Alexander were invited to the Foreign Office in London by Lord Cadogan.[6] Cadogan was Permanent Under-Secretary for Foreign Affairs, 1938–46. In an unpublished extract from his diaries he had mentioned a visit to Bletchley on 11 January 1941: 'Very interesting – I should like to spend a week there so as to try to understand it. A charming young Cambridge Professor of Geometry – Welchman – did his best. A good show, I think.' According to Cadogan the three of them were referred to simply as Menzies's 'Brains Trust' and all presented by Menzies and given £200 each.'[7] It was Welchman's impression, supported by Joan Clarke, that they were recommended for a decoration but had to be given money instead.

Chapter 5

Expansion and Consolidation

By the end of May 1942 Welchman had already presided over three key periods in the development of Hut 6 and, through its efforts, the success of BP. The first period had begun with Dilly Knox's pioneering pre-war work in breaking the early version of the Enigma machine without a plugboard. Knox had devised a number of ingenious tools and methods to help with this work with arcane names such as rodding, buttoning-up, lobsters, crabs and boils. He had also been the recipient (although not initially a grateful one) of the results of the ground-breaking work by the Polish cryptanalysts in the 1930s. This had led to the construction of the Zygalski sheets and the successful adoption of the Polish methods at BP in late January 1940. A further development called the Jeffreys sheets was also put to good use. As this initial period ended, Welchman had assembled the nucleus of the original members of Hut 6.

The second period of activity from January to July 1940 had seen the Germans occupy Norway and France as well as the disaster of Dunkirk. Hut 6 was a limited operation initially with the Netz Room engaged in moving the sheets around to allow the holes punched in them magically to reveal part of the daily key; the Machine Room arranging the data for them and completing the key; the Registration Room logging all incoming traffic and finally the Decoding Room turning the incoming messages from gibberish to German and, it was hoped, vital intelligence. By March they had managed to break fifty daily keys across three German communication networks (called Red, Blue and Green). However, the Norwegian campaign saw the real start of Hut 6's continuous operational breaking of German keys.

Disaster had struck on 29 and 30 April when the new indicator system appeared in some of the traffic coming into Hut 6. As was often the case, the Germans had provided Hut 6 with ample warning of this change. Remarkably, they used the very system that Hut 6 was breaking on a daily basis to inform Enigma operators about new security measures being introduced to the system. In fact, throughout the whole history of Hut 6, there appear to be very few examples of any innovations in the German cryptographic system of which Hut 6 did not have adequate warning. However, the new indicator system rendered the Polish method, including the Netz, obsolete.

The 10th of May 1940 was a turning point, not only for Hut 6, but for Britain and Europe as a whole. As Hitler launched the invasion of Belgium, the Netherlands, Luxembourg and northern France, the volume of wireless traffic coming into Hut 6 rose to levels previously unimagined by most at BP, except perhaps Welchman. On the same day, the man who would become BP's biggest supporter stepped onto the world stage. Winston Churchill became Prime Minister at the head of a coalition government. With limited resources at his disposal, Welchman had a difficult decision to make. It was obvious from the volume of traffic on the main Air Force network (using the Red key) that it was of paramount importance. While there was a considerable amount of Army traffic coming in which could have contained high-grade intelligence, resources were not yet available to break it. Therefore, Welchman took the decision, in consultation with other senior figures at BP, to concentrate Hut 6's attack on Red.

With the Netz Room out of action and the machines which would ultimately lead the attack not yet available, Hut 6 turned to hand methods. Breaks at this stage were based on cillies, which helped to reduce significantly the number of possible key settings used by the operator. A method based around cillies had originated in The Cottage under Knox and new classes of cillies were regularly exploited by Hut 6. The German Army and Air Force operators were allowed to choose 'at random' the three letters which would make up the message setting. This was in effect a final scrambling of the wheels before encrypting the message. It proved to be a serious mistake as human beings are not random and their choice of letters often proved to be anything but (*see Appendix 3*). The Herivel Tip was another example of how analysing the behaviour of Enigma operators could reveal errors in procedure which could be exploited by the skilful cryptanalyst.

The third period ran from August 1940 to May 1941, when Britain stood alone against the threat posed by Nazi Germany. It also saw the arrival of the bombes and the evolution of the crib into an art form in its own right, known at BP as cribbery. With the first bombes incorporating the diagonal board now operational, Welchman turned his attention to integrating cribbery into Hut 6's production-line approach. Likely looking messages were usually identifiable by a combination of length, frequency, time of origin, time of intercept, call sign, and similar standard features. Different sections of the message would be written down on strips of paper. Based on their experience, the cribsters would make an educated guess as to a phrase which was likely to be hidden somewhere in the encrypted message. They would also use their experience to determine which section of the message was likely to contain the phrase. The guessed phrase would be written down on a separate slip of paper and placed on a surface above or below the appropriate section of the encrypted message. By moving the guessed phrase left and right, the cribsters hoped to identify the encrypted version of the phrase. The technique was based on the fact that the Enigma machine could not encrypt a letter as itself. If they were successful the cribs were handed on to the Machine Room where they were turned into their graphical representations known as menus. The Crib Room became the 'chief breaking agency' and under Welchman's direction, took charge of general bombe policy and relations with both Hut 3 and the naval sections.

The whole course of the Second World War changed when Adolf Hitler, realizing that Britain would not be bombed into submission, instead looked east and on 22 June 1941, attacked the Soviet Union. At the same time, BP entered its fourth period of development, one of expansion and consolidation. The peak of its success in terms of the quantity and quality of intelligence was probably achieved in the months following D-Day. However, from June 1941 to the end of 1943, BP, and particularly Hut 6, got almost completely on top of the Enigma system. As access to resources such as bombes, radio sets and staff increased, the Luftwaffe's communication system was at the mercy of Hut 6. By the end of December 1942 the Hut 6 team was breaking almost every key that was generating a large amount of traffic with a reasonable frequency. Even more impressive was the fact that a satisfactory solution had been found for every technical problem presented to them.

As Germany initiated new campaigns, prepared to meet expected attacks by the Allies or split up existing keys because of alterations in their system of key distribution and allocation, the number of keys increased dramatically.

By June 1941 cillies had become very rare and the opportunities for the mathematicians to show their prowess in hand-breaking were scarce. The Machine Room spent its time in testing endless bombe 'stops'[1] and morale began to suffer. In the end the testing of the bombe stops was put out to the bombe outstations. Hut 6 would only be sent the output from tested stops which offered possible key settings.

As long as there were enough different coloured pencils, the Army and Air Force keys were just given corresponding colour names. With the invasion of Russia, Hut 6 began to run out of coloured pencils and keys named after birds, such as Kestrel and Vulture, sprang up. In 1942 the German Air Force started to use a large number of subsidiary keys and John Colman set about giving them names on some kind of logical basis and from then onwards, he was responsible for key name allocation. The Army keys were birds, Air Force keys fell into a number of groups including insects, vegetables, flowers and mammals.

It became necessary to have more than a single person on each shift as there were so many keys to tackle. In June 1941 there was often only one person in the Watch room. In later years the number increased, often to five. In preparation for D-Day, two separate watches were put in place, one for Army and one for Air Force keys. There were three main tasks on the watches. The first of these, essentially supervised by the head of the Air Force shift, was to know what the bombes were doing and to have a ready supply of jobs waiting as bombes became free if a key 'came out' or 'went down'. The head of shift had to be in a position to brief his successor as head of shift. New jobs were passed through a hatch to the Machine Room where its head of shift was in direct telephone contact with the bombe outstations and could advise them on job priorities. The head of the Army Watch usually left instructions with the head of the Air Force Watch shift about their priorities.

The second task under the head of shift was known as e.p. (after the chess term *en passant*, meaning 'in passing') and involved receiving decrypted messages from the Decoding Room (through another hatch) and noting anything of cryptographic interest before putting them on a conveyor belt to Hut 3. Each key had someone responsible for it (at least one parent) taken from members of the Watch, whose job included keeping records about the key, The final check by the head of Watch had to be done fairly quickly to avoid unnecessary delays.

The third main task was to deal with incidents of re-encrypted messages. With the proliferation of keys many messages were encrypted on at least two different keys. This was manna from heaven for the cryptanalysts in Hut 6 and it was essential to record them carefully. The Registration Room made out a slip of paper with brief particulars of a re-encrypted message and added a cross in the corner in the colour associated with the key on which it had been sent. These slips were consequently called kisses. The person responsible for this in the Registration Room sorted the kisses and checked for other re-encrypted messages on a key, regardless of whether it was 'out' or not. If a promising re-encrypted message was discovered and neither the original or new key was 'out', he would wait until one key was 'out' and then ensure that the message on the other key was promptly decrypted and record it. If one key was already 'out', this person had to obtain a copy of the decrypt either by having a duplicate done in the Decoding Room or by finding it in Hut 3.

Other things needed attending to on shifts, including assisting the Machine Room with difficult settings and preparing menus, which were in effect, instructions for the bombe operators. In the latter stages of the war two female operators were employed to prepare the menus on the instructions of one member of the Watch. These then had to be checked by another member of the Watch. There were also 'jobs' which, when they became available, the US-based bombes were better suited to deal with. While the American bombes gave priority to naval jobs, they had a great deal of spare time, which was used by Hut 6 for research projects under the direction of John Manisty.

By 6 August 1941, the various inter-relationships in Hut 6 had settled down pretty well, but Welchman was still finding that, perhaps because he was the originator of the various information-handling procedures, he still had a more complete overview than anyone else. This was partly why he started regular management meetings and insisted on weekly reports from all sections being posted on all bulletin boards. The big expansion of Hut 6 and Hut 3 and their supporting activities had started in early 1941. The people who arrived after that were fitted into an existing organization. While their jobs were well defined, they were under pressure as soon as they started working in the huts.

As the workload increased, Welchman started to look at streamlining the organization to make it even more efficient. While he prided himself on having created a very friendly and collegial working environment, problems did occur. Space was becoming increasingly limited and when the Machine, Crib and Registration Rooms established research sections, they had to be housed in the Mansion. This problem was relieved in February 1943 when they were able to move into the spacious accommodation of the newly opened Block D. This building had state-of-the-art pneumatic tubing and pulley systems installed to allow documents to be moved from section to section. Block D was also large enough to house Huts 3 and 8 as well as several other related BP sections.

Setting up of the Watch in February 1943 was Welchman's last major reform in Hut 6 and produced an immediate and permanent improvement in the atmosphere. The changes allowed one man to have complete responsibility for a key and also raised the status of research in the Hut 6 operation. Up to the spring of 1943, research had always been something of a poor relation, but not in Welchman's eyes. Harold Fletcher remembered Welchman as someone 'who always saw the long term importance of things more clearly than anyone else'. For a time, at least two bombes were even allocated to research but this proved hard to maintain.

As the number of keys started to multiply during 1942, many of them proved to be a mixture of other keys. This was detected because Reg Parker had been keeping meticulous records of broken German keys. Parker had joined the Hut 6 Control team in May 1940 and had taken it upon himself to keep logs of all broken keys. His reasoning followed the classic approach to cryptography, that is to get inside the head of your enemy. Parker reckoned that someone in Germany had to produce a multitude of setting sheets every month and this must be a very boring job. To produce a monthly setting sheet, he would have to create for each day of the month a wheel order (three numbers from one to five), the ring settings for each wheel (a three-letter group) and ten pairs of letters to be plugged together on the plugboard. There were also the discriminants and call signs which had to be included with each day's key settings. The chap was bound to be tempted to re-use some of the settings that he had previously worked out, following the various rules that had been imposed upon him for this task.

After faithfully doing this for several months, Parker finally discovered that this was exactly what was happening. The normal practice was to make up a key out of the wheel order and ring settings of an existing key and the discriminants and plug connections from another. John Monroe remembered one month during which Red had the plug connections of the previous month's Mustard. As this latter key had been broken two days out of three, it could be used to help break Red quickly. It became even more interesting when it was discovered that the wheel order and ring settings for Mustard had also been used the next month by a fairly unimportant key named Cockroach. It was thus possible to break Red by first breaking Cockroach, then using the resultant wheel order and ring settings on the previous month's Mustard to work out its plug connections which had then been used in Red. This method became known as Parkerismus in Hut 6.

The whole catalogue of German mistakes seems to have been founded on their belief that the Enigma machine and their procedures for its use could not be broken. The 'Official History of Hut 6' concluded that:

> It must be emphasised that, theoretically, if the enemy is not breaking your keys then you can use repeats, partial or otherwise, as much as you like, although there is a chance that a capture might give you away. If, however, you feel you must use repeats then use them in a completely patternless manner so that even if the enemy does establish that one key is constructed from another he can only ascertain which day is used for which day by breaking both without the aid of the repeat.
>
> From all this it seems that one of the most desirable attributes of a key compiler is full confidence in the ability of the opposing crypto-graphers.[2]

It could well be advice such as this that persuaded GCHQ to wait until June 2006 to declassify the three volumes of the 'Official History of Hut 6'.

In June 1942, 1,170 messages per day were being decrypted and by August, 500 breaks had been made and at least 50 separate German communication networks recognized. Increasingly, a definite attempt was also made to use known and forthcoming Allied intentions to guide Hut 6's activities. As the amount of decrypted material flowing to Hut 3 increased, Welchman wanted a broad overview both of the cryptographic situation and of the present and future work of Hut 3. In the hope of achieving a much closer and more effective interrelationship between the two huts, he persuaded the new head of Hut 3, Eric Jones, to appoint a spokesperson for Hut 3. This individual would acquire an overview of the ever-changing needs of both huts and establish an effective intelligence liaison between them.

Jones appointed Oscar Oeser to the role as head of a new group called 3L. Throughout his professional career, before, during and after the war, Welchman demonstrated the admirable quality of being able to separate personal issues from professional ones. His relationship with Dilly Knox was a good example of this and another was his relationship with Oeser. They became good friends and Oeser occasionally visited the Welchman family at their home during the war. While he even enjoyed working with him, he told colleagues that Oeser was a bad choice to head 3L. According to Welchman, Oeser never understood the co-ordination of many activities that was essential to the success of Hut 6, so he could not explain what really mattered either to his own 3L staff or to the key people in Hut 3.

More systematic consultations were arranged with Hut 8, Hut 6's sister section for naval decryption and Hut 4, the sister section for Hut 3 which had moved into Block A adjacent to Hut 8. Access to the bombes was also hotly contested so a rota of bombe directors from Huts 6 and 8 was set up and given the power, during their turn of duty, to decide on the distribution of the bombes. This group was eventually disbanded and replaced by weekly meetings at which intelligence and cryptography staff from both huts were represented.

Hut 6's final period of activity would run from the beginning of 1944 until the end of the war in Europe in May 1945. The work would be led by Milner-Barry as Welchman would be promoted and moved to a new role. For almost three years he had been the driving force behind Hut 6's many successes. He also carried the burden of being one of the few people at BP who understood the reality of their position. In a note to Travis dated 15 December 1941, he warned that:

> The enigma code as now used by the German Air Force and German Army is, as far as is known at present, theoretically unbreakable. Our methods of breaking now are purely opportunist and are based on taking advantage of the enemy's mistakes. We have been extra-ordinarily fortunate in that he has continued to make mistakes in just sufficient number to enable us to break some of his codes fairly regularly.
>
> Our success has always hung by a thread, and must continue to do so, unless indeed we can devise some new methods or invent some new and powerful machinery; and nobody has yet any idea how this could be done. What is required and is essential in order to break, is a certain minimum of positive data, and if the Germans were to use their machine properly it is admirably adapted to withholding such data from us altogether.
>
> Now there is conclusive evidence that the German security officers are very much alive to the dangers of this practice even though they may not be aware of the exact means by which we take advantage of it. We often decode messages in which operators are hauled over the coals for doing just this kind of thing. This source of success is, therefore, now of relatively less importance.

Cribs are now our main line of attack against the major keys. Provided we can guess at the exact (letter for letter) German text of any single message or part of a message up to a length of say, 20–40 letters, this will give us sufficient data (if everything else goes right) to enable the bombe to give us the answer.

In sum, it would, I think, be much easier for the German security officers to prevent their operators from giving us the benefit of cribs than stop them from using favourite indicators when they are in a hurry. But, secondly – and this is the main point of these notes – even on the hypothesis that the Germans never guess, we can never be confident of continued success. The good luck which has so far attended us in the matter of cribs is little short of miraculous.[3]

*

1943 was something of an anti-climax after the rapid pace of the previous two years. It was also a transitional period as key repeats like those exploited by Parkerismus ceased and thus the pace slackened. It also saw the move to Block D in the spring as well as setting up of the Watch and the larger Research Section under Babbage. With a lull as the Germans were forced back into fortress Europe, the main attack switched to the research keys, especially the Army ones. Derek Taunt and Bob Roseveare led on the Air Force research while David Gaunt and Doug Nicoll led on Army research. Babbage and Aitken were known as the 'senior partners' and oversaw their work.

In September 1943, the Germans dropped discriminants from Army traffic and in Milner-Barry's opinion this was the most dangerous period BP ever went through. The Air Force duly followed suit by dropping them at the beginning of November. Hut 6 had been forewarned of this from a decrypted message in March. The Germans had been using discriminants for years which had made sorting and identification comparatively straightforward. Hut 6 was desperately afraid that sorting might become next to impossible. A scheme was devised and duly put into action on 1 April 1944. Welchman regarded it as overly complicated, but it did produce a solution. A new section was set up called the Duddery and run by David Gaunt and subsequently saved the day by successfully identifying the keys as they came into the Watch.

Hut 6 managed to defeat most of the technical innovations thrown at it by the German cryptographic sections. In the last year of the war, new modifications to the German Enigma machine presented Hut 6 with fresh challenges. Each machine had a component called the reflector (*Umkehr-walze* in German) which acted like a stationary wheel with letters wired in pairs. The current running through the Enigma machine passed out of the left-hand wheel and back into it through the reflector before making its way to the lampboard. The first modification was the introduction of a pluggable reflector, Umkehrwalze D. Up to that point, the Air Force and Army had used Umkehrwalze B and the Navy, Umkehrwalze B followed by C. The wirings of both of these reflectors were known, so there was quite a stir when a decrypted message revealed the existence of an unknown reflector. Preparations were made to deal with it and when the Red key was 'out' on 1 January 1944, it was found that some signals on certain networks could not be read (known as duds at BP). It was fairly quickly established that this new reflector was pluggable and could be changed daily along with the rest of the key settings. While the D reflector proved to be a major problem when it was used exclusively on a network, again German mistakes provided the solution. On most keys, the B reflector was used as well as the D reflector, so once the key was broken with the B reflector, the connections on the D reflector could be found,

Just after D-Day, Hut 6 started finding a number of messages that started, when decrypted, with a number spelt out in German and then ended with meaningless characters. Once again, another decrypted message revealed the existence of the Enigma *Uhr*. This turned out to be an attachment to the Enigma machine which made it possible to change the plug connections in a number of additional ways. Remarkably, this new problem was solved on a regular basis by Hut 6. The recovery of the connections on the D reflector and the *Uhr* settings in connection with any broken key was normally an additional function of the Watch, with the task being assigned by the head of the shift to a member competent enough to take it on.

Annually, in the spring, the Germans rearranged all the frequencies of their networks, so they all had to be rediscovered. Intercept operators were, however, able to identify the idiosyncrasies of the wireless operators. In February 1945 the Germans started to change the frequencies daily and encrypt the call signs, which proved to be unbreakable. John Monroe remembered working two twelve-hour shifts with Nigel Forward in an attempt to identify frequencies. Fortunately, the Germans reverted to their normal frequency-setting regime fairly quickly.

*

In the summer of 1941 BP had its first warning that German submarines were being issued with new four-wheel Enigma machines and new code books. The German Navy as a whole was much more security conscious than its Air Force and Army counterparts. It did not use the stereotyped language which had provided many of the cribs being used by Hut 6. It also did not leave the choice of message setting to the operators but instead issued them with elaborate code books for this purpose. The message setting gave the starting position of the wheels in the Enigma machine and had to be worked out along with the daily key before the decryption of messages could begin.

The Navy Enigma was generally considered to be unbreakable in 1939 and when Alan Turing arrived at BP in early September little work was being done on it. He became interested in it 'because no one else was doing anything about it and I could have it to myself'. Through a brilliant piece of analysis, he fairly quickly worked out how this code book system worked. However, even Turing could not reproduce the tables in the code books and it was felt at BP that only 'a capture' would allow them to make further progress. The situation got so desperate that an extraordinary scheme to capture the secret code books was considered. Lieutenant Commander Ian Fleming was personal assistant to Rear Admiral John Godfrey, Director of Naval Intelligence. He visited BP twice a month and was well aware of the problem. He wrote to Godfrey on 12 September 1940 with the following plan:

> I suggest we obtain the loot by the following means:
>   Obtain from Air Ministry an air-worthy German bomber.
>   Pick a tough crew of five, including a pilot, W/T operator and word-perfect German speaker.
>   Dress them in German Air Force uniform, add blood and bandages to suit.
>   Crash plane in the Channel after making S.O.S. to rescue service in P/L [plain language].
>   Once aboard rescue boat, shoot German crew, dump overboard, bring rescue boat back to English port.
>   In order to increase the chances of capturing an R. or M. with its richer booty, the crash might be staged in mid-Channel. The Germans would presumably employ one of this type for the longer and more hazardous journey.

While similar scenarios by Fleming would eventually yield him fame and fortune through his James Bond books, in this case common sense prevailed. The cancellation of Operation Ruthless, the name given to Fleming's plan, was a major disappointment to Turing and Twinn. As Frank Birch, the head of the Navy Section at BP, wrote in a letter on 20 October 1940:

> Turing and Twinn came to me like undertakers cheated of a nice corpse two days ago, all in a stew about the cancellation of Operation Ruthless. The burden of their song was the importance of a pinch.

Eventually captures (or pinches as they were called at BP) were made and Hut 8 began to decrypt German Navy Enigma messages.

In February 1942 the warnings about a four-wheel Enigma become a reality and Hut 8 could not read the Enigma traffic coming from the U-boats. They were attacking Allied convoys crossing the North Atlantic and almost 700,000 tons of vital Allied ships and cargoes were sunk around the world that month. Only eleven U-boats were sunk in the first six months of 1942. Salvation came in October and the story behind it was worthy of a Hollywood film. Regrettably, one was made years later in which the heroes of the hour were American rather than British.

On 30 October 1942, the submarine *U-559* under Lieutenant Hans Heidtmann was operating in the eastern Mediterranean. It was detected by British radar and four destroyers were sent to search for it. One of these was HMS *Petard*, a P-class (for Pakenham) fleet destroyer. Its captain, Lieutenant Commander Mark Thornton, and his first lieutenant, Antony Fasson, had discussed in detail how they would board a captured U-boat and had drilled a boarding team. The British ships attacked *U-559* that night and badly damaged it. Once it was clear that it was stopped and being abandoned, Fasson rang the cease-fire bells. Rather than wait for a whaler to be launched, he stripped off and swam over to the submarine. He was joined by a young seaman, Colin Grazier, and a fifteen-year-old civilian canteen assistant, Tommy Brown, who had lied about his age to get aboard ship.

Once on board the badly listing submarine, Fasson and Grazier managed to pass documents up to Brown who in turned handed them to shipmates who had pulled up alongside in the whaler. After three bundles of documents were passed up to him Brown shouted at his colleagues to come up. They had just started on their way when the submarine sank with Fasson and Grazier on board. Brown managed to jump off and was picked up by the whaler. Three weeks later, the documents rescued by Fasson and Grazier reached BP, including the current edition of the Short Signal Book and the second edition of the Short Weather Cipher. Their heroic efforts had helped to turn the tide in the Battle of the Atlantic in favour of the Allies.

Hugh Alexander had originally joined Hut 6 but was then moved to the newly formed Hut 8 to act as Turing's deputy. He eventually became head of Hut 8 when Turing moved on to other projects and remained in the position for most of the war. Huts 8 and 4 copied much of the Hut 6/3 model, which was not surprising given that Alexander had started off in Hut 6 and was a close friend of Milner-Barry. With the vital code books in their hands, a start could be made on the messages emanating from the U-boats. In his post-war report on Hut 8 Alexander said that in November they finally started to read the U-boat traffic using weather reports and the captured Short Signal Book (from *U-559*).[4] The German Navy's obsession with weather forecasts would provide Hut 8 with cribs for the rest of the war.

The U-boats had the four-wheel machine, but for a time they used only three of the wheels for some of their messages and this enabled Hut 8 to work out the wiring of the new wheel and decrypt a small number of signals. However, four-wheel bombes were needed to read the U-boat messages on any significant scale.

Travis asked Welchman to oversee the development of a four-wheel bombe. Travis had been told, presumably by the head of MI 6, Stewart Menzies, not to give the job to BTM and Keen's production team. The reasoning seems to have been that if they gave the job to Keen, they would be 'putting all of their eggs in one basket'. Travis was put in touch with Professor Patrick Blackett, a government advisor on military strategy and developing operational research, who suggested that they approach the Post Office's research establishment at Dollis Hill in north-west London. In the late summer of 1942, one of Dollis Hill's leading engineers, Tommy Flowers, was briefed on the problem and Charles Wynn-Williams, a brilliant physicist who was doing research at the Telecommunications Research Establishment (TRE) at Malvern was called in to help on the project.

The Dollis Hill team developed an attachment to the standard three-wheel bombe being manufactured by BTM. The device was called the Cobra because of the snake-like form of its multi-wire connections leading to the bombe (approximately 2,000 wires). It provided the extra-fast readout required for the four-wheel bombe, and used electronics for the first time to provide the twenty-six-fold increase in tests needed because of the fourth wheel. It used gas-filled thyratron valves as electrical switches as well as radio-type vacuum valves and had no moving mechanical parts. Its valves performed the same functions as relays but much faster. Harry Fensom, one of Flowers's key assistants, helped install the first Cobra at Stanmore in the spring of 1943. Its cable apparatus was built by an engineering firm at Dursley near Stroud in Gloucestershire and the valve attachment at Dollis Hill. The Cobra proved to be noisy and unreliable and was not a success.

As the pressure grew on Hut 8, Welchman had a series of meetings with Frank Birch, starting on 7 December 1942 and continuing until 5 April 1943. Birch wanted assurances that everything possible was being done. As late as 29 March 1943 Welchman was at Dollis Hill talking to Flowers and the Director of the Dollis Hill Research Station, W. G. Radley, about the 'four-wheel problem'. All concerned had been instructed not to tell Keen about this further development of his bombe. When he found out, he refused to have anything more to do with bombe-related developments. Faced with what he described as 'the monstrosity designed by Flowers', Welchman needed Keen back on board. He and Fletcher went to see him and eventually Welchman managed to talk him around.[5] Keen added a row of super-slow drums, using available parts and then drove the whole assembly a lot faster using valves instead of relays for the sensing. This was an extremely simple use of valves compared with Flowers's design. Neither Flowers nor Wynn-Williams would have known, as Keen did, that the fast drums of the three-wheelers could be driven a lot faster and still provide good electrical contacts. Keen's relays operated in one millisecond and were copied from a Siemens design. BTM's development of its four-wheel bombe did not have a significant effect on their existing three-wheel bombe production as the basic three-wheel design was retained. Four-wheel machines were installed at Stanmore and Eastcote from early 1943 and a total of fifty-nine were built. Fletcher estimated that the delay caused by Keen not being briefed initially had been from four to six months.

All of this did not go down well with Radley and Flowers. Welchman had met them around 22 May 1943 and they had attacked Keen, questioning his competence as an engineer and the actual relay system he had designed. They also threatened to take the matter higher unless their point of view was accepted. Welchman investigated their charges but the people he interviewed were more than satisfied with the work of BTM. Not surprisingly, Keen and his Letchworth colleagues were not happy with this turn of events. Denniston was forced to take the matter up with Radley who pulled back from making a formal charge against Keen or BTM. He did, however, insist that Dollis Hill employed the best relay engineers in the country and that Keen's relay apparatus would not stand up to continuous use. When Denniston pointed out that Keen's apparatus was already being used successfully, Radley insisted that Dollis Hill's valve-sensing equipment (the Cobra attachment) should also undergo the same tests as Keen's solution. This was a small concession to make to keep the Post Office on board for future developments. Welchman had wanted to launch a formal enquiry but as Radley agreed to withdraw his charges against Keen, Denniston persuaded him to not to proceed with it. Denniston went on to summarize the outcome of his discussions with Radley:

> At this point the interview terminated with expressions of goodwill. I am however quite certain that this whole matter will recur at a later date and although I have formed a good impression of Radley I am not convinced that there is not some motive behind some of his statements and actions. He was very ready to deny that he or Flowers had said this or that to Welchman, although Welchman had produced to me written notes of his conversation, written immediately after the interview that I was definitely inclined to doubt Radley's veracity, in other words, when I made a direct frontal attack he seemed only too ready to pipe down.[6]

*

In his dealings with those who could provide technical solutions to BP such as Keen's BTM engineers and Ellingworth's intercept operators, Welchman had learned that it was a mistake to tell them how to do their jobs. Unfortunately, some cryptographical staff at BP simply approached technologists with demands for solutions without first discussing with them the problem at hand. The large installation of standard IBM and BTM tabulating equipment at BTM under F. V. Freeborn, was a case in point.[7] Freeborn was supporting a number of cryptographical activities at BP yet members of these departments tended to try to tell him how to use his machines in support of each problem instead of presenting their problems to him and discussing possible solutions.

BTM had been doing some work in Freeborn's section for Freddie Jacob of the Military Section at BP and for Wilfred Bodsworth from the Naval Section. In May 1940 an initial installation of Hollerith punch-card equipment was established at BP and when further processing was required, it was decided that this should also be done at BP. The original staff from BTM consisted of Freeborn and two brothers, Ronald and Norman

Whelan. They started off in a small hut outside the perimeter fence but then moved into Hut 7 within the grounds of BP and staff numbers quickly increased. They originally had a six-week job but demand was so great that they remained for the rest of the war. Many jobs undertaken were on a once-off basis as their 'customers' were not very good at explaining the problem and what was required. To manage the increasing workload, the operation was split into five teams working eight-hour shifts, seven days per week. The operation grew to over 500 staff by the end of the war and was consuming some two million Hollerith punch cards each week.

The daily Hollerith processing carried out in Hut 7 and then in the larger Block C in dealing with Navy Enigma messages was given the highest priority. Messages were split into groups and punched onto Hollerith cards. Naval messages were transmitted in four-letter groups and the Hollerith equipment was used to find a pair of such groups in more than one message, with the separation between them being the same in each message. This could involve searching through around 80,000 cipher text characters in a day. In other words, the Hollerith equipment was being used as an early 'search engine' to find cribs which could be used on the bombes.[8] Given the difficulty of finding cribs in German naval messages, Welchman had encouraged Alexander to use Freeborn's facility by carefully explaining the problem to his team. Ronald Whelan recalled one visit that Alexander made to Freeborn years later:

> He was a frequent visitor to our building in BP and on one of his calls to discuss processing requirements Freeborn handed him a newspaper cutting which he thought would be of considerable interest. Alexander glanced at the paper for a second or so, apparently with scant attention, before handing it back with the comment that he found it interesting. Freeborn indignantly accused him of not reading the paper, whereupon he solemnly delivered the whole text, word for word, to Freeborn's astonishment and near collapse.[9]

In addition to Block C, Freeborn's team also had equipment located in the village of Drayton Parslow about four miles from BP. The original BTM group had taken up residence in a large house in the village and purpose-built buildings were quickly erected to establish a new machine room. The facility was mainly used for compiling cryptographic material. Whelan recalled that Freeborn drove the BTM group hard and they worked seven days a week from 8.15 a.m. to 6.00 pm. and once the Drayton Parslow facility was in place, they worked most evenings as well. After their first three months at BP, Whelan had one day of leave and after that, his leave amounted to a couple of days every six to eight weeks. They did have some respite on each Christmas Day when they would leave work around 4.30 in the afternoon!

Welchman had established a close working relationship with the Army's intercept station at Chatham and its commander officer, Ellingworth, in 1939. By 1940, Hut 6 had a twenty-four-hour intercept control section working under John Colman which kept in continual telephone contact with Ellingworth's duty officers. When the main RAF station at Chicksands became operational, its head, Wing Commander Shepherd, was willing to learn from Ellingworth and Colman and before long Colman's team was also working well with the duty officers at Chicksands. Welchman's belief that traffic analysis could be used effectively alongside the work of the cryptanalysts in Hut 6 was beginning to bear fruit. Colleagues had not been convinced, as Milner-Barry recalled:

> I had been entirely sceptical of the possibility of ever finding or recognizing standard routine messages of the requisite length, and only the persistence and optimism of Welchman, independent as it seemed to me of any evidence, induced me to make the attempt.

However, Colman's team were not the only people trying to analyse the German Enigma traffic. In Hut 3, Major D. L. B. Lithgow, who had been in charge of a 'Y' station in France and then moved to BP after Dunkirk, had established a group called the Special Liaison Party (SLP). Independent of the BP work, MI 8 (the cover designation for the Radio Security Service) had set up a small section in London in May 1940 called No. 6 Intelligence School (later called the Central Party). Hamish Blair-Cunynghame, Neil Webster and Chris Wills had been brought together to break the call-sign system being used by the Luftwaffe. Another group in the same building, including Edward Crankshaw and Bill Tozer, were studying the German armed forces radio network using decrypted German messages. This would ultimately reveal order of battle information.

The German radio communication system was based around 'stars' with a control station at the centre through which went all communications for that 'star network'. Intercept operators kept a log which was a listing of enemy Morse signals as they arrived along with other information at the beginning of each message. Apart from the radio frequency being used by the sender and sometimes preliminary unencrypted chat, there was other information which was of particular interest. The preamble of a message was the opening sequence of characters consisting of time of origin, urgency prefix if any, indicator (three-letter starting position for decryption), number of letters in the message and the first five letter group including the discriminant. Discriminants were three-letter labels which indicated which Enigma key had been used. Each key could be recognized by the use of any one of four different combinations of three letters allocated to it (e.g. SFY, SZY, ZKQ, BQI). Call signs were labels consisting of three alphanumeric characters which identified separate units of the German Army and Air Force (e.g. P7J, SF9, 5KQ). They were changed daily using a fixed programme laid out in a call-sign book, one of which would eventually be captured. The log readers summarized from the logs the pattern of communications of a star by means of a diagram with arrows giving the directions of the messages, a list of message preambles and notes of significant chat. These summaries made it possible to recognize stars and some of the stations on them from day to day even without knowing the call sign. This was the same data that Welchman had been studying when he first arrived at BP.

The London group moved to Harpenden in the spring of 1941 and log reading became increasingly important. The initial team consisted of Philip Lewis, Hamish Blair-Cunynghame, Edward Crankshaw and Bill Tozer. When the intercept station at Chicksands became operational in addition to Harpenden and Chatham, problems occurred because different logs were being compiled in different formats. A process of 'reconciliation' was attempted in order to compare and combine logs from different intercept stations. This inevitably led to a rivalry developing between the team in Hut 6 and the Harpenden group. As reports of their findings came to Welchman's attention, he was made aware of the re-encryptions which were being detected in increasing number. These were messages which were encrypted more than once on different keys. The log readers would spot them in their summaries of all communications on each star. However, he was having problems with some of the key people involved in the log-reading process. Lithgow had been promoted in Hut 3, much to Welchman's displeasure, and he wrote a memo to Travis on 9 May 1941 lobbying for 'a combination of the four mutually interdependent parties, working in a civilian basis under leaders who are themselves experienced in the actual work of their sections and under your leadership'.[10]

In another memo to Travis Welchman was particularly critical of Majors Lithgow and Tozer:

Both Major Tozer and Major Lithgow are apt to dress up source information as W/T I [wireless intelligence] and to display it in their own shop window. Major Tozer is even less reliable than Major Lithgow. There is a danger that he may destroy the value of accurate intelligence by the addition of wild ideas of their own . . . in spite of [Tozer's] enthusiasm he is a nuisance.[11]

Welchman was keen to move the Harpenden group to BP but instead they were moved to Beaumanor in the summer of 1941. Blair-Cunynghame was put in command with Lewis as second in command. A weekly wireless intelligence summary called 'The Beaumanor Weekly' began to be published and it reported on log-reading findings network by network.

Around June 1942, the Beaumanor group was moved to BP as a result of Welchman's persistence and the valuable contribution of Blair-Cunynghame. It eventually absorbed Lithgow's group and became part of Hut 6, using the name of the original London group, the Central Party. One of the Central Party's main functions was what they informally called 'fusion'. The 'Fusion Room' compared decrypts from Hut 6 with corresponding data extracted by the log readers from the daily radio traffic between enemy stations. This enabled a complete picture of the enemy order of battle to be constructed.

One pleasant by-product of the Central Party's move to BP was that Welchman could now tell his wife that he was engaged in intelligence work. Welchman had felt that he was the subject of a certain amount of disapproval from the military branch of her family. It seemed to him that his wife's Aunt Do was the main instigator of hostility towards him. He must have been an easy target as a person who worked in some mysterious office, wore no uniform, and showed no evidence of doing anything useful for the war. Welchman's experience was matched by many of his BP colleagues. Katharine had volunteered for service with the ATS in 1942 and been posted initially to Aldermaston and then London. She was then sent to the log-reading group at Beaumanor and moved with them to BP.

The log readers of the Central Party had a huge task as enemy wireless traffic increased. They also made use of a growing number of decrypted messages and captured documents. By the beginning of 1943 they were examining some 12,000 pages of logs each day. The material had to be condensed and sorted before use and diagrams continued to be used to show the flow and peculiarities of the traffic. By going through this process day after day, log readers gained an intimate knowledge of groups of wireless stations which were working together as a unit. Even when call signs or frequencies were changed, the log readers could usually recognize the individual stations in a group by monitoring their traffic over a period of time. This huge amount of information was distilled into a weekly report which in 1943 was running to some 100 pages. This drew attention to any unusual wireless activity which in turn might point to interesting enemy movements or the need to increase the coverage of a particular group.

Lewis recalled the work of his team years later in correspondence with Welchman:

> If 'fusion' meant anything it covered our attempts to identify units and signals procedures on the basis of evidence submitted by the log readers. By then we were fully aware of the patterns of signal procedures, frequencies, participants in nets, etc. that might provide evidence to you of continuity. Though it was not until we moved to BP that, from every source of information, we built up our own large Order of Battle primarily to encourage the log readers to understand the overall picture and the importance of the work they were doing. In essence the Fusion Room was a Common Room where the initiates could meet in seclusion. The term was not used at Harpenden and was of only nominal significance at BP where we had ample space for private discussions. Thus the term 'Fusion Room Officer' has no esoteric meaning whatsoever. In my time we never called ourselves thus; such a term would have been risible![12]

Another important part of the work of the Central Party was suggesting probable re-encryptions. Re-encryptions of a message from a key already broken were likely to provide an excellent crib. These took various forms including, from one day's setting into the next day's setting, from one Enigma key to another or from one Enigma key to a hand cipher.

A steady flow of information was sent to Hut 6 and Hut 3 both as a result of the routine log reading and as the result of investigation suggested by a study of decrypts. For example, a message sent on a certain key might be refused by a station which did not possess that key. The same message might then be sent to the same station on another key. This type of re-encryption was spotted immediately by the log readers. They also detected cillies which were often of use to the cryptanalysts in Hut 6. The Central Party provided a similar service to other sections at BP including those working on the Fish[13] and German Police systems.

Lewis believed that the work of the Central Party was ancillary and subordinate to that of Hut 6. Its members did not regard themselves as prime producers of intelligence but it was essential that they be fed with as much information as possible as the Enigma keys were broken to enable them to chase up idiosyncrasies of the individual radio networks. They were provided with the whole logs delivered by despatch riders. Lewis remembered that they had an 'excellent man' (Sergeant Carteret) who was responsible for collecting all the despatches and making sure the log readers received them as soon as possible. He did not recall receiving any tele-printed material, only the log pads. They were concerned with the radio frequencies, the amount of traffic and the participants in the networks, as well as the preambles with the call signs. Many German operators had their own peculiarities, both in relation to the preamble and the signing-off procedures. Some seemed rather proud of their signing-off flourish and the Central Party was always delighted when they could follow idio-syncratic behaviour.

In addition, Lewis had problems with Lithgow's team in Hut 3.

> Early on we ourselves realised the dangers of what you aptly term 'tunnel vision'. I mean early on at BP. That was why we had the weekly briefing session I have already mentioned when the whole organization assembled to hear the latest developments in our researches, with call signs becoming real units and their movements linked to the Order of Battle map. So many people were concerned with their own task that they had no idea of the interlinking nature of the whole intelligence exercise. Again various people tried to run their own little empires or elderly regular officers felt they had to have some say, so that overall coordination and control was lacking, which could have been (and maybe was) disastrous or at least time-wasting with regard to priorities. These priorities were of the utmost importance and we needed firm direction from a small control unit in that respect. I assumed that I took my priorities from you. You may have assumed that we were capable of providing more infor-mation on our own than in fact we were.

Eventually, Sixta (short for Hut 6 Traffic Analysis) was created in November 1943 and incorporated the Central Party and SLP. It was inde-pendent of Hut 6 and Hut 3 and had overall responsibility for traffic analysis of German Army and Air Force networks. The development of W/T I and subsequently Sixta, according to Milner-Barry, 'was down to

Welchman–Colman, Welchman–Blair-Conyngham [*sic*], Welchman–Lewis.' Many of Welchman's colleagues had thought that traffic analysis was a fad but Milner-Barry, effusive as ever in his admiration for Welchman's contribution in this area, went on to say:

> Again it was Welchman with his strange and uncanny knack of grasping the ultimate significance of things who fought throughout for the recognition of the importance of W.T.I.
>
> Welchman's prescience was to be brilliantly justified after his departure, when the knocking down of the various props which had made identification almost a rule of thumb matter – first discriminants, then changing frequencies and finally encoding of call signs – made the cryptographer largely dependent on the complete and accurate knowledge of the German W/T organization which Sixta had steadily been building up. Then what had been from the cryptographer's standpoint a luxury became a basic necessity of life and, if Welchman had not fought for its development in the early years, we should have no hope of weathering the storms which nearly overwhelmed us in the last eighteen months.
>
> Battles were successfully fought to provide us with enough tools to do the job at the breaking as well as at the intercepting end. That again under the Director, was almost Welchman's achievement, not only when he was Head of Hut 6 but when he was translated to a higher sphere.

Chapter 6

The Americans

In late April 1943 a car drove through the gates of BP with three American visitors inside. One of the three, a dapper man with a tiny moustache, was William Friedman, the doyen of American cryptography. Friedman's visit to BP was intended to cement further the relationship between his SIS operation and BP.[1] Its Operational Director, Alastair Denniston had visited Friedman in 1941 and they had become good friends.[2]

The US Army had created a cryptographic service during the First World War, designated MI-8. At the end of the war, it was felt to be un-American to snoop on other countries in peacetime so a successor organization to MI-8 was set up in New York and known by those involved as the American Black Chamber. It attacked the codes of many countries throughout the 1920s under the leadership of Herbert Yardley.[3] The US Navy also had established a Communications Intelligence Organization in 1924. The American cryptographic groups were under threat from the American Secretary of State, Henry L. Stimson who, after being appointed in 1929, famously said 'Gentlemen do not read each other's mail.' Nonetheless, on 19 July 1929, three Army officers and one civilian met to plan a new cryptographic service, the Signals Intelligence Service (SIS). The civilian present was William Friedman whose official role had been to create codes and ciphers for the US Army.[4] Once the Army agreed that he should take up the position of Director of the SIS, he had set about recruiting young men who combined mathematical expertise with linguistic skills. What followed was remarkably similar to GC&CS's recruitment drive for 'men of the professor type'. Friedman trawled the listings of American Civil Service examination results looking for mathematicians who had top scores and a good knowledge of a foreign language. By 1939 the SIS had received a considerable increase in funding and by early December 1941 its numbers had swelled to 181 officers, enlisted men and civilians in Washington, and 150 in the field.

In early February 1941, four passengers landed from HMS *King George V* after it had anchored in Scapa Flow, the Home Fleet's remote base in the Orkneys. The ship was returning from its maiden voyage to the USA. The four passengers were greeted by John Tiltman, who was to be their host during their stay in Britain. The four had with them a package containing gifts and were on their way to Bletchley Park, the first Americans to enter BP. The American party were Abraham Sinkov and Leo Rosen from the US Army's Signals Intelligence Service and two young US Navy communications officers, Robert W. Weeks and Prescott H. Currier.[5] The gifts they had brought with them were replicas of the Japanese encryption machine that the Americans had named Purple. Japan had developed the machine to encrypt diplomatic traffic and, like the Enigma equipment used by the Germans, the Purple machine was also used to decrypt messages. The development of the American Purple replica was arguably an equivalent feat to the early Polish work in reconstructing the Enigma machine. It could even be compared to the work of the brilliant mathematician Bill Tutte in his later reconstruction of the Lorenz SZ 42 machine at BP (*see Chapter 7*).

The breaking of the Japanese diplomatic traffic had been the crowning achievement of Friedman's SIS and in particular the brainchild of one of his first recruits, Frank Rowlett. In the mid-1930s, the SIS team had been ordered to make decryption of Japanese diplomatic messages its top priority. The messages were being encrypted on a machine based on code wheels which the Japanese called Cipher Machine Type A. Again, paralleling Welchman's use of colours to identify German communication network keys, the Type A became the Red machine. This was broken by Rowlett and his colleague Solomon Kullback, paralleling Rejewski's early work on Enigma. It was a hugely significant development because the system would eventually be used to send diplomatic traffic between Japan and Germany. Hundreds of diplomatic messages were decrypted. In this case the US Army and Navy co-operated and pooled resources to deal with the huge volume of traffic. In late 1938, much like Enigma decrypts had warned BP of changes being made by the German cryptographers, a Red intercept revealed that the Red machine would be replaced in major embassies by the Type B cipher machine which was given the codename Purple. The new system was more complex than Red and the Navy cryptanalysts soon gave up trying to break it, Rowlett and Leo Rosen discovered that the new system was based on telephone switches rather than wheels. It took the SIS team about one year to design and build its own Purple replica. They decided to demonstrate it to the Director of the Navy Department's Communications Intelligence Unit, Laurence Safford. They wanted approval to share their work with their naval intelligence counterparts. Following the demonstration, Safford assumed that they had stolen the machine and was astonished to learn that they had actually built it. General Mauborgne, the Chief Signals Officer, was also impressed and took to referring to his cryptanalysts as 'magicians'. This led to the Americans referring to intelligence produced by cryptanalysis as 'Magic', much in the same way as BP's output was known as 'Ultra'.

The Americans never achieved the complete inter-service co-operation, collaboration and communication which Welchman believed made BP unique. Evidence of the American failure in this regard is provided by events leading up to the infamous attack on Pearl Harbor by the Japanese Navy on 7 December 1941.[6] Some historians have claimed that Churchill knew well in advance about the devastating air raid on Coventry on 14 November 1940 and that warnings were not issued because it might reveal the Ultra secret to the Germans. This has been categorically disproven by wartime records.[7] Some authors have made the same claim about the Americans and Pearl Harbor. However, the American situation was different and more a result of inter-service rivalry.

In the early hours of 7 December 1941, the Navy intercepted the fourteenth part of a long Japanese message to their Washington Embassy which said:

> The Japanese Government regrets to have to notify hereby the American Government that in view of the attitude of the American Government it cannot but consider that it is impossible to reach an agreement through further negotiations.

Two more messages were subsequently decrypted. The first instructed the Japanese Embassy to destroy its cipher equipment, all machine codes and all secret documents. The second was very unusual and said:

> Will the ambassador please submit to the United States Government (if possible to the Secretary of State) our reply to the United States at 1:00 p.m. on the 7th, your time.

This material was shown to General George Marshall, the US Army's Chief of Staff. It was agreed that US outposts should receive fresh warnings about a possible attack as soon as possible. Unfortunately, he was not told that due to atmospheric problems, the Army's communication facility was having trouble contacting Hawaii by radio that morning. The Navy had a more powerful transmitter but red tape and inter-service rivalry meant that the notion of the Army giving the Navy a message for transmission was out of the question. Instead, it was sent via Western Union with no greater priority attached to it than any other telegram being sent from one person to another. A messenger was attempting to deliver the telegram to Army headquarters at Fort Shafter in Hawaii as Japanese bombs and bullets were destroying much of the American naval fleet.

Following the attack on Pearl Harbor, the scale of the whole SIS operation was expanded, much as BP had moved from the days of The Cottage to a hut-based production-line approach. In June 1942, the SIS was given total responsibility for handling Japanese diplomatic traffic. The Navy's cryptographic section was now free to concentrate on Japanese naval codes and ciphers. At the same time, the Army decided to set up a signal intelligence school and the SIS was tasked with taking charge of it. Larger accommodation was needed and, again, with echoes of BP, a posh girl's school called Arlington Hall, three miles from Arlington, Virginia, was purchased and became Arlington Hall Station. The Navy was also faced with a shortage of accommodation and soon secured another girl's school in north-west Washington, DC, called Mount Vernon Academy. The facility became known as Naval Communications Annex and would house the main US Navy cryptographic section, known as OP-20-G. By December 1942 this section had grown to 1,188 staff.

Denniston had visited Washington in 1941 after the first American visit to BP and established what would become a lifetime friendship with Friedman. He also laid the groundwork for possible future technological collaboration between the two countries.[8] After he was replaced as Director of GC&CS, Denniston's new role was as head of a 200-strong operation based in London and responsible for diplomatic and commercial signals intelligence. In 1943 Friedman was able to spend some time in London with Denniston before travelling on to BP. In a future role at BP, Welchman would be responsible for the ongoing liaison between BP and the American cryptographic stations Arlington Hall and Mount Vernon. He would become friends with one of OP-20-G's top technical experts and his American counterpart, Howard Engstrom, and their paths would cross again in peacetime.

The urgent need, and doubts about the British engineering workload, had already prompted the Americans to start investigating designs for a bombe, based on the full blueprints and wiring diagrams received by US

Navy Lieutenants Robert Ely and Joseph Eachus at BP in July 1942. Throughout the summer of 1942, engineers of OP-20-G hoped for break-throughs in technology which would allow them to develop a high-speed electronic bombe. For this work to succeed, they needed the advice of the more experienced British engineers. In August, OP-20-G informed GC&CS that it intended to build its own machine. Joseph Wenger, OP-20-G's operational head, had been given all of the resources that he needed for such a project. Due to its urgency, the project was also free from the usual bureaucracy of the US Navy's procurement arm, the Bureau of Ships. The electrical-research laboratory of the National Cash Register Corporation (NCR) based in Dayton, Ohio, was taken over by OP-20-G as a research centre and a possible production site for the machine. The project would be led by the laboratory's head, Joseph (Joe) Desch.

Funding for a full $2 million Navy development effort was requested on 3 September 1942 and approved the following day. Edward Travis and Frank Birch, head of BP's Naval Section, travelled to Washington later that month. On 2 October 1942 they signed an agreement with Carl Frederick Holden, Director of US Naval Communications, one of the first deals to establish the special signals intelligence (sigint) relationship between the two countries. The agreement went some way to clarifying the respective roles of Britain and the USA in the European war and in naval code-breaking work.

At the end of 1942, Alan Turing was sent to Dayton to check on the American bombe project and duly arrived on 21 December. The advice that Turing was able to offer was limited, given Desch's apparent desire to design his own machine. However, he was able to pass on GC&CS's experience in a number of areas which would prove invaluable to the American project. For example, the British had learned that laboratory testing alone could not anticipate all of the problems with key components of the bombe. Turing wrote a short report on his visit to Dayton[9] and was impressed enough with some of Desch's design ideas to say that 'Starting from scratch on the design of a Bombe, this method is about as good as our own.'

Turing was also able to show that it was not necessary to build 336 bombes, one for each possible wheel order available to the German Navy Enigma operators (who chose three wheels from eight). In 1940, Turing had developed a technique called Banburismus which significantly reduced the number of possible wheel orders that needed to be tested so the initial order was scaled down to ninety-six machines. In the end, the US Navy bombes contained sixteen four-rotor Enigma-equivalents and were claimed to be faster than their British counterparts.

While all the American services had technical liaison people at BP, as the war developed this was proving to be inadequate. Following protracted negotiations, it was agreed that an American detachment would be integrated into BP. A strong team from the US Army arrived on 30 August 1943, led by William (Bill) Bundy[10] and consisting of nine officers and ten enlisted men with the designation 6813th Signal Service Detachment. There was also the 6812th group[11] that would work on the bombes and the 6811th which would be involved in radio interception. The cover story of the cryptanalysts among them was that they were messenger pigeon experts in the Signal Corps. This aroused the suspicions of an officer who was checking their identities. He was concerned that there was no record of any of them taking the Army General Classification Test. They agreed to take the test so that the paperwork would be in order. One of their number, Art Levinson, remembered the officer coming back after grading their test and saying: 'What scores! You guys ought to be in intelligence.'[12]

Bundy's group consisted of seven cryptanalysts and two translators and, after settling into their billets, they made their way to Block D at BP. The two translators were taken to the offices occupied by Hut 3 and indoctrinated by its head, Eric Jones. Bundy and his team of cryptanalysts reported to Welchman for an introduction to the work of Hut 6. Welchman admitted years later to being slightly nervous until one of the Americans, Bill Bijur, asked if he could smoke and proceeded to produce an enormous cigar which he lit. With the ice broken, Welchman went on to amaze them with the exploits of his team. As he recalled in *The Hut Six Story*:

> Among my most pleasant memories of the whole war is the way those Americans came to Hut 6. By then we had moved to our new brick building, so I was able to receive them in respectable though by no means luxurious surroundings. There must have been eight or ten of them. They were ushered into my office to be briefed on our activities. I felt somewhat ill at ease as I started to tell them the Hut 6 story. But their attitude was simply that they wanted to be told what to do so that they could be helpful as soon as possible. There were no fanfares. No arguments,. No difficulties. They simply melted into Hut 6 and were liked and welcomed by everyone. Very soon each of them had found their niche and was contributing. Their leader joined our management group and before long he became a major contributor to the key-breaking activities of the Hut 6 watch.

The success of the Americans in Hut 6 would owe much to the leadership of Bundy and the close working relationship that Welchman established with him. They remained friends for the rest of Welchman's life. Years later Bundy wrote a paper which concluded with a point that would prove poignant, given his long association with Welchman:

> The only gap it leaves, which at least one of my wartime colleagues wishes to fill but has so far been thwarted by British Security concerns, is a truly professional account of the breaking techniques. An extraordinary combination of mathematical theory and brilliant opportunism in catching constant German errors produced the first Enigma breaks in 1940; the machine techniques then developed were in a very real sense the foundations of modern electronic computer technology. This is a book that remains to be written.[13]

*

Frederick Winterbotham's Special Liaison Units (SLU) were tasked with briefing Allied commanders in the field as Ultra intelligence was sent to them from BP. When the USA entered the war, it was agreed that American commanders would also have to be briefed, and mobile SLU units would be assigned to them. There were concerns expressed in British intelligence circles about sharing the Ultra secret with the Americans and these fears were almost justified in 1944. At the beginning of the year, the legendary James Doolittle, who had led the carrier-borne air strike on Tokyo in April 1942, had taken command of the US Eighth Air Force. In due course, Doolittle had been briefed personally about Ultra by Winterbotham. In May, a vacancy on Doolittle's staff was filled by Arthur Vanaman, who was in turn briefed by Doolittle about Ultra. As Vanaman's job was to select targets and ask men to risk their lives to attack them from the air, he felt he should experience action for himself. He presented his case to Doolittle who gave him the green light to go on a real mission. On 27 June 1944, Brigadier General Vanaman boarded an American bomber for a raid over eastern France. German flak soon put an end to the mission and, after successfully parachuting to safety, Vanaman was picked up by German troops. He was taken to a hospital in Frankfurt for treatment to flak wounds and then on to Berlin. By August, he was in the largest German prisoner of war camp, Stalag Luft III. Conscious of the fact that he talked in his sleep, Vanaman would put tape over his mouth before falling asleep and developed techniques for self-hypnosis in an attempt to exorcise any memory of Ultra from his mind. In the end, Vanaman was released, apparently so that he could carry special radio codes to Supreme Allied Headquarters for possible negotiations over prisoners of war. Vanaman eventually returned to the US in 1945 without having given away the Ultra secret to the enemy. Nonetheless, he was demoted to colonel, evidently for embarrassing the US Air Force in the eyes of the British and other US services. Perhaps not surprisingly, his superior Doolittle, who had approved Vanaman's mission, was never reprimanded for the event.[14]

Remarkably, the Royal Air Force experienced a very similar and equally embarrassing incident. On the evening of 6 May 1944, a Lancaster bomber, was shot down over southern France and the crew bailed out.[15] Amongst them was Air Commodore Ronald Ivelaw-Chapman, who had commanded the Bomber Command base at Elshaw Wolds in Lincolnshire. Like Vanaman, he wanted first-hand experience of action even though he was 'Ultra cleared'. He was captured by the Gestapo on 8 June, the most senior Bomber Command officer to have been captured by the Germans. Fortunately, the Germans did not realize his importance and he was treated as an ordinary prisoner of war. Unlike Vanaman, Ivelaw-Chapman was promoted to air vice marshal after the war.

Chapter 7

Bletchley Park:
The Last Two Years

When Edward Travis replaced Alastair Denniston as the Operational Director of Bletchley Park in February 1942, he increasingly turned to Welchman to assist him in a range of activities not directly related to the work of Hut 6. In September 1943 Welchman was appointed head of the Machine Co-ordination and Development Section and his role in Hut 6 came to an end. At his recommendation, Milner-Barry took over as the Head of Hut 6 and Manisty took over the Watch. It was a tough act for Milner-Barry to follow.

By the end of 1943, BP had moved from an operation whose infrastructure included the movement of documents between Huts 6 and 3 in a wooden tray on wheels pulled by string, to the pneumatic tube and conveyor belt production line of Block D. Staff numbers in Hut 6 had grown to 401 and they occupied 29,230 of the 40,000 sq ft of the available office space in their new building.

Welchman was now based in Room 10 in the newly opened Block F and getting to grips with his new role. He wrote to Travis on 2 December and categorized the areas he believed he would now be working in: assistance to cryptographers, security of machine ciphers, development of cipher machines, communications, interception, after the war, policy and plans.[1]

In March 1944 Travis restructured his senior management team.[2] Three Deputy Directors would be responsible for the three main functions of the establishment, designated DD1, DD2, and DD3. Nigel de Grey (DD1) became Travis's chief deputy and took on responsibility for security, and the production and distribution of intelligence. Alan Bradshaw (DD2) took on responsibility for planning and administration matters, while Edward Hastings (DD3) took on liaison with Allies and the research sections, comprising Intelligence Service Oliver Strachey (ISOS) and Intelligence

Service Knox (ISK). The different services at BP were also under the command of a Deputy Director: Tiltman – Military, Birch – Naval, Cooper – Air and Wilson – Cipher Security. Finally, four Assistant Directors were appointed: Welchman – Machines and Mechanical Devices, Jones – Hut 3, Elsdale – Communications and Interception and Page – ISOS & ISK.

One of Welchman's functions in his new role was to keep an eye on the security aspects of new technological developments in British communications. He quickly found himself concerned about trends in military thinking on communications which were beginning to appear. He continued to work closely with Keen and BTM,[3] Flowers and the Post Office Research Station at Dollis Hill and Wynn-Williams at the Telecommunications Research Establishment in Malvern. Welchman was also responsible for ensuring that BP had a sufficient stock of replica Enigma machines for the decoding rooms in Huts 6 and 8.

In early 1944, Katharine was pregnant with their third child, Rosamond, and left the ATS. The Welchmans were at last able to buy the home that they had sought for a number of years. Rippington Manor was a fine Elizabethan house in the village of Great Gransden in Bedfordshire. The original house was a cell of the monastery at Repton, which was then called Rippington. The house the Welchmans acquired was built towards the end of the sixteenth century, during the reign of Queen Elizabeth I. They had arranged to purchase it some years before and, once they took possession, they remained there until the end of the war. Great Gransden was a remote place, not easily visited by people who lacked a motor car and the petrol to make it go. Two country buses ran from the village, one to Cambridge, the other to St Neots in Huntingdonshire, a small county that no longer exists. The village was also fairly close to the Cambridge/Bletchley rail line and Welchman had fond memories in later life of cycling to and from the village of Gamlingay, the location of the nearest station. Despite its remoteness, the Welchmans were able to entertain friends and colleagues from BP and Cambridge. On several occasions, Welchman was able to take his children to the rooms he had lived in at Sidney Sussex College and for a punt on the river.

Part of the original land belonging to their house had been requisitioned by the government and used as a camp for prisoners of war. Initially, Italian prisoners were housed there and Welchman's son Nick befriended some of them. Eventually the Italians were relocated and replaced by German prisoners, who were segregated from the locals. The Canadian Air Force had a base near Great Gransden, and the village children were invited to a splendid Christmas party in 1944. Like many families living in the countryside, the Welchmans took in a boy who had been evacuated from London.

In 1943, another major activity was rapidly growing in complexity at BP. The German high command had commissioned a new encryption system which was more suited to very long strategic-level communications. This system did not use Morse code to transmit messages but instead was based on the international teleprinter system. This had a thirty-two character alphabet and was an online system. The operator would type his message on a teleprinter attachment to the encryption machine which would add a randomly generated character to each character of the message using the properties of the teleprinter alphabet and its addition table. So, for example, if the first character of the message was 'A' and the encryption machine generated a 'B', the two would be 'added' together producing 'G'. A radio transmitter was integrated into the system to send the messages off to another operator. Using the example above, if the receiving encryption machine was set up exactly the same as that of the sender, the first random character it generated would be 'B'. It would then automatically add it to the first incoming character, 'G'. Following the rules of the teleprinter addition table, this would produce 'A', the first character of the message. Each character in the message would be processed in the same way and printed on the teleprinter attached to it. A mistake by a German operator using this system on 30 August 1941 had allowed Bill Tutte, following some crucial work by John Tiltman, to reconstruct the encryption machine producing the random characters and subsequently break the system. After developing machines called Robinson to speed up the decryption process, the world's first electronic computer, Colossus, was designed by Tommy Flowers and his colleagues at the Post Office's research laboratory at Dollis Hill in London. Colossus speeded up the decryption process to an acceptable level for intelligence purposes. While not directly involved in the day to day operation of this work, Welchman did have overall responsibility for it as the work of BP's Newmanry and Testery sections that did take on this system was part of his remit.[4]

His assistant, Houston Wallace, remembered accompanying Welchman to one of the intercept facilities to address operational problems:

> You and I went to Denmark Hill together to see what could be done
> to reduce the error rate in the tapes that reached Newman's people

at BP. In those days, we had no equipment for comparing two tapes. I believe we decided that, to get error-free operation, it was necessary to punch three separate tapes from each oscillograph trace (undulator tape), and to compare them visually by laying them on top of each other on a long table.[5]

In his new role, Welchman established a committee to discuss desirable improvements to BP's various technological capabilities. Its members were Alexander, Turing, Freeborn, Gerry Morgan, Head of Research in the Military Section, and Max Newman, head of the section responsible for the Colossus machines.

On 17 February 1944 Welchman embarked on a month-long visit to the USA in his role as Assistant Director for Mechanization. His first task was to work closely with a Canadian colonel, Benjamin Deforest (Pat) Bayly.[6] Bayly, was a communications expert who had developed a new encryption machine based on teleprinter traffic which was christened the Rockex. Travis wanted Welchman to work with Bayly on improving the security of this machine as well as the whole problem of government communications. He also wanted the two of them to carry on the British–American technological liaison on Enigma and other problems that had already been initiated.

One project which emerged from this liaison was the development of a replacement for the Typex machine. The new machine needed to be highly secure, easy to operate and deployable in forward areas. Welchman, now a cryptanalyst-turned-cryptographer, worked with Bayly, Turing and Alexander to design the RM-26. It was to house 24×26-point rotors, each containing the same scrambled wiring. The 24 rotors were to be in three banks of eight, with complicated interdependent motion. Unfortunately, it never progressed beyond the prototype stage due to the increasing necessity for a machine compatible with the new generation of American cipher devices.

Bayly was originally from Moose Jaw, Saskatchewan, and had become a professor at the University of Toronto. At the height of the war, he had been hired by William Stephenson, the senior representative of British intelligence for the entire western hemisphere. Stephenson had been sent to the United States on 21 June 1940 covertly to open and run British Security Co-ordination (BSC) in New York City. The BSC office, headquartered in room 3603 in the Rockefeller Center, became an umbrella organization that by the end of the war, represented the British intelligence agencies MI5, MI6 (SIS or Secret Intelligence Service), SOE (Special Operations Executive) and PWE (Political Warfare Executive) throughout North America, South America and the Caribbean.

Bayly had first visited BP near the end of Denniston's tenure as its operational head. Sir Stewart Menzies had instructed Richard Gambier-Parry to escort him to BP and introduce him to Denniston. Gambier-Parry had been given the task at the beginning of the war of leading MI6 Section VIII (SIS Communications), the section devoted to all forms of secret communication. He went on to orchestrate its complete overhaul and modernization. Menzies had forgotten to tell Denniston of Bayly's visit, which was unfortunate, because, according to Bayly, it was clear that Denniston 'loathed Gambier's guts'. Bayly left them to their inevitable row, retiring to the guardhouse until it was all over. Denniston met him a year later in London and was most apologetic about their previous meeting.

On arrival, Bayly's first request was to be taken to the teleprinter room where he promptly sent a message to his office to ask his wife Bun, to be there in thirty minutes or so. Shortly after, Bayly and his wife were having an asynchronous conversation via the teleprinter link. While operators on security networks frequently used 'chat' as a way of testing their communications, the ultimate purpose was always to send a secure and/or receive a secure message. Here, Welchman witnessed Mr and Mrs Bayly, years ahead of their time, using the same technology for normal family conversation!

Bayly recalled his first meeting with the legendary American cryptographer William Friedman, in a series of letters to Welchman in 1983. It gives a good insight into the subsequent work which would occupy not only much of Welchman's and Bayly's time for the remainder of the war, but also that of Alan Turing:

> My first meeting with Billy Friedman was interesting. Bill Stephenson was faced with the problem of being in New York and having to talk to Washington about rather delicate matters. This was just after Pearl Harbor. I was supposedly doing purchasing with side tones of setting up communications in the Western Hemisphere where they might become necessary, so Bill asked my opinion on phone scramblers. I told him that as far as I had been able to find out, that they were a joke. His answer was typical, 'Find me something that isn't.' The Journal of the A.I.E.E. Feb 1926 pp 109–115 had an article by G. S. Vernam of what later was to become Bell Laboratories, on the subject

of Cipher Printing Telegraphs. This came out at the time that I was installing a network of Teleprinters for the Canadian Pacific Railway, and had aroused my interest. I couldn't find Vernam but it mentioned Capt W. F. Friedman, cryptanalyst of the U.S. Signals Corps. I persuaded 'Wild Bill' Donovan of O.S.S. to find him for me and I visited him at his home in Washington. He was naturally not very forthcoming, but told me that Western Union had developed such a machine called a Telekrypton. We found that they had made two of these machines and had stored them as there had been no commercial acceptance. We bought them and rapidly found the troubles. A small cipher tape of about 200 characters, dependence on synchronization at both ends and a hopeless method of starting such 'togetherness'. As their circuits had an average of a hit every ten minutes this meant a communications speed of zero and a security rating of slightly less! A hectic weekend with Hoover of Western Union led to a table model, continuous code tape, perforated tape at the receiving end so the operator could set the code tape at the proper point. The machine was an instant success on the grounds that it was all we had. The code tape was made by putting two girls on hand perforators and telling them to punch complete random nonsense. It soon turned out that once a girl had worked to produce nonsense for a couple of days she unwittingly started a cycle of up to 200 characters that occurred over and over. I then went to shaking steel and glass balls and then feeding them into five tubes with contactors. This gave me a very high grade randomness but unmerciful wear and tear. The final solution was a very high frequency oscillator of poor stability beating against a low frequency oscillator also of low stability. I judged randomness by the ratio of the tape holes to blanks. It worked very well.

Bayly and Welchman became involved with Alan Turing in his work along with people at Bell Laboratories to develop an effective phone scrambler. They were both very fond of Turing and were of the view, years later, that much nonsense had been written about him. Bayly recalled their time together in New York:

Alan Turing lived with me in NY for several months while helping with the famous or infamous phone scrambler. Amazingly I didn't know from Turing what he was doing, but I learnt it from a US source in a casual conversation on security. Turing was a marvellous fellow and we got on very well. I couldn't understand any technical thing that he said, he gave his descriptions in shorthand, but he could write them down so that I at least knew what he was talking about. I was always amazed at his ability to think in terms of a 26×26 matrix. On one occasion they wanted him back in London urgently. By sending one man to the state department, one to the US customs, one to US emigration, and having Bill Stephenson pull wires in the Port of NY Security Committee, we got Turing on board the Queen Elizabeth about half an hour before sailing – all of this in a period of one day. Turing's parting remark to me was 'I hope this hasn't put you to any trouble.'

To create the Rockex, Bayly had used the existing patented Telekrypton enciphering device and modified it in such a way that while the letter characters A–Z stayed as before, when the other six characters appeared on the enciphered tape (the teleprinter alphabet is made up of thirty-two characters), the figures one to six were used. One problem with the Vernam one-time teleprinter cipher system was that the cipher text included many occurrences of operational (also called stunt) characters such as line feed and carriage return. They would preclude the cipher text being given to a commercial telegraph company for transmission. It also proved to be prohibitively expensive to use this over standard cable facilities as the use of a number doubled the cost of transmission and proved difficult for the cable-Morse operators to handle accurately. Two of the modified printers were sent to BP where the little group of cipher clerks who handled the MI6 encryption work were stationed. They soon learned to use the machines at about five times the speed of hand processing. According to Welchman, Travis named the new encryption machine while he was visiting the laboratory where it was being designed and built. The lab was in the Rockefeller Plaza Complex and after observing members of the famous Rockettes sunbathing on the roof of the adjoining Radio City Music Hall, Travis came up with the name, Rockex. Another story is that the name Rockex was chosen after the designers saw a performance by the Rockettes. Parts for the Rockex were supplied by the Teletype Corporation of Skokie, Illinois.

The problems eased when, at a later date, Bayly insisted that they have their own cable terminal and use teletype across the Atlantic. The daily load was running at almost 1.5 million words a day and the supply of teleprinters soon became a problem. They were usually acquired through Lend Lease, the programme under which the USA supplied Allied countries with materials during the Second World War. At one point, Travis and Welchman needed a great quantity of teleprinters worth millions of dollars. As the head of Lend Lease was a friend, Bayly was able to bypass the normal negotiations which could take months.

During his 1944 visit to the US, Welchman began to warm to the energy the Americans showed in their willingness to exploit new ideas. He was able to work with such luminaries in American cryptography as Frank Rowlett of the US Army and Howard Engstrom of the US Navy. However, as he relates in *The Hut Six Story*:

> In our liaison work in Washington, Pat Bayly and I found ourselves in a curious position. The technical staff of the U.S. Army and U.S. Navy organizations were only too willing to discuss their activities and ideas with us. Yet they could not exchange ideas with each other directly. They would have liked to do so, but interservice friction made this virtually impossible. So Bayly and I found ourselves acting as go-betweens. It may seem foolish that we were just about the only means of contact between the leading cryptanalytic experts on Enigma of the U.S. Army and Navy, and indeed it was foolish.

Welchman only found out the real role and influence of Bayly's boss, William Stephenson, during his trip to the USA:

> I did not become aware of Stephenson's existence until I went to America on the Queen Mary in February, 1944, and found myself sitting at the Captain's table with several well-known people, including a minister in the British cabinet, the head of the British National Physical Laboratory, and film producer Alexander Korda. During the voyage it became apparent that the cabinet minister resented the presence of this Gordon Welchman, who didn't seem to be doing anything important. However, when we reached New York, and the passengers were waiting instructions, we heard a broadcast announcement: 'Will Mr Alexander Korda and Mr Gordon Welchman please disembark.' I happened to be standing near the cabinet minister and saw the look of amazement on his face!

He was indeed in august company. As well as the famous producer Korda, the head of the National Physical Laboratory at that time was Sir Charles Galton Darwin, grandson of the evolutionary biologist, Charles Robert Darwin. Korda, apart from being a personal friend of Stephenson, was one of the many people whom Stephenson had recruited to take advantage of their talents and contacts to help win the war.

Not least among Stephenson's accomplishments and contributions to the war effort was the setting up by BSC of Camp X in Whitby, Ontario, the first training school for clandestine wartime operations in North America. Rockex first saw service at Camp X in 1943 to pass messages across the Atlantic, and soldiered on in military and diplomatic applications until 1975. Stephenson's story has been told in some detail and inaccurately by several authors.[7] His initial directives for BSC were to investigate enemy activities, institute security measures against sabotage to British property, and organize American public opinion in favour of aid to Britain. Later this was expanded to assuring American participation in secret activities throughout the world in the closest possible collaboration with the British. Stephenson's official title was British Passport Control Officer. His unofficial mission was to create a secret British intelligence network throughout the western hemisphere, and to operate covertly and broadly on behalf of the British government and the Allies in aid of winning the war. It is generally believed that he also became Churchill's personal representative to US President Roosevelt.[8]

Stephenson was also a shrewd businessman, according to Bayly's former assistant, Kenneth Maidment:

> Again he helped me to (very anonymous) fame in 1944–45 by calling me to his office and handing me a primitive ball-point pen. He wanted me to invent an entirely new name for it, as he had shrewdly bought the patent for it. All the names for pen, I told him, had already been used: so I asked who had invented the thing. He said a Hungarian refugee called Biro, who worked in an aircraft factory in Buenos Aires. So I said: call it a BIRO. Which he did, and hence the name.[9]

This was how the word 'biro' subsequently became synonymous with the ballpoint pen in Europe.

Maidment also had views on the surprising lack of direct contact during the war between Stephenson and GC&CS. According to Maidment, it was because of his close relationship with Bill Donovan, the wartime head of the OSS (Office of Strategic Services) and the growth of OSS, whose ideas of security worried Travis. Even more worrying was the US Army and Navy's antagonism to OSS. Stephenson had been a close adviser to President Roosevelt, and had suggested that he put his good friend, Bill Donovan in charge of all US intelligence services.

Welchman's trip to the USA in 1944 coincided with a secret joint US/ British conference on intelligence at the SIS's headquarters at Arlington Hall on 13 March. While he was busy working with Bayly in Washington and New York, Welchman spent a day at Arlington Hall when Travis attended the conference. He was able to catch up with two former BP colleagues as Philip Lewis and Tony Kendrick were now based in North America and also in attendance. Lewis had been working in Washington, with full access to the Pentagon, visiting Bayly in New York and addressing the Canadian Combined Chiefs of Staff in Canada to describe in outline British intelligence work. GC&CS had sent a high-powered delegation which included, apart from Travis, John Tiltman, Joe Hooper and Edward Crankshaw. The American representatives included William Friedman, Abe Sinkov and Solomon Kullback. At the end of the conference a photograph was taken of the participants on the steps of the main building at Arlington Hall.[10]

Welchman returned from his American trip in the summer of 1944 bearing gifts for the family. He had chocolate, peanut butter and dried bananas but warned the children that the bananas would not be as good as fresh ones. In wartime Britain, the children had never tasted fresh bananas and had only heard how wonderful they would be when the war ended and real life began again. For now they had to make do with dried fruit which was compacted, a brown colour and tasted like dried figs.

On 30 April 1945 Adolf Hitler, besieged in his bunker in the centre of Berlin by the advancing Red Army, placed a gun to his head and pulled the trigger. His closest ally, the Italian Fascist leader Benito Mussolini had been executed by communist partisans on 28 April and his body strung upside down in a petrol station forecourt in Milan. On 7 May, General Eisenhower, the Supreme Allied Commander sent out a brief message which simply said 'The Mission of this Allied Force was Fulfilled at 0241, local time, May 7th.' For the British, the real victory arguably came with the signing of the unconditional surrender of all the German forces in northwest Europe to Field Marshal Montgomery in a large tent at his headquarters at 1830 hours on Friday, 4 May.

At BP, senior managers were seriously concerned about security and in particular, gossip about key wartime personalities gained from decrypts. On 29 April, staff in Hut 3 were instructed to avoid issuing decrypt information about 'large German capitulations' and 'the activities of prominent German personalities'. On 4 May, Travis gave an order that he personally would have to clear any VE-Day congratulatory telegrams sent from BP. The war with Japan was still going on and BP's involvement in Japanese codebreaking had increased. At the same time, senior staff at BP were already planning the peacetime work of the GC&CS organization. It would emerge from the war as GCHQ, first at Eastcote and eventually at Cheltenham. To mark VE-Day, Travis sent every member of staff a note thanking them for their efforts. He also reminded them that the work continued and of the dangers to security of careless talk that could disclose the work that they had been engaged in.

GC&CS staff numbers had approached 9,000 by the end of the war in Europe. At its peak in November 1944 Hut 6 had 575 staff while Hut 8's numbers peaked at 154 in July 1943. While some staff left quite quickly, others were moved on to Japanese and Russian work, particularly those from Hut 8. In each of the huts, senior managers were tasked with writing official hut reports. The Hut 6 report was authored by several individuals never formally identified, but Milner-Barry had final editorial control over the resulting three-volume document.[11]

Strict controls were placed on the demobilization of service personnel based on a points scheme with a shorter delay for those with the longest service. Civilian staff went through a similar process although academics were allowed to go earlier so that universities could cope with the large intake of students returning to complete their education. By the end of August 1945, most of those who had come from the universities had left BP and staff numbers were down to 5,500. Although a small GCHQ team would remain at BP for more than forty years, BP would finally be closed down as the headquarters of GC&CS/GCHQ in the spring of 1946.

And what of Turing, Welchman and Keen's wonderful bombes? It is believed that all but 60 of the 211 built were dismantled in the summer of 1945.[12] It is also believed that of the 60, all but 16 were stored, the rest being used after the war. No official document which provides details of their ultimate fate appears to be in the public domain. The women of the Royal Naval Service (WRNS) who had skilfully operated the machines throughout the war were tasked with dismantling them. Wiring and components were removed and sorted for future use.[13]

Even before the war had ended, Travis had asked Welchman to join a small planning group to look at the future and the Government Communications Headquarters (GCHQ) which would emerge from the wartime GC&CS. After thinking about this for some time, it occurred to Welchman that the triumph of Hut 6 and the reasons behind it could help inform the structure of a future intelligence organization. His views were extremely radical for the time yet resonate in the world of today. He strongly believed that people's salary and prestige should reflect success in their particular field. So the top cryptanalyst at BP should have been able to command a higher salary that the Director. Today, the leading stars in sport, entertainment, banking and, to some extent, IT are top earners who enjoy the trappings of their success. This was certainly not the world of the 1940s! He also felt that cryptological staff at GCHQ should not claim to be experts in related fields unless justified. Technology experts should be part of the early conversation about what the technology can do and how best it can address certain problems.[14]

The planning group produced a paper on 17 September 1944 titled 'A Note on the Future of GC&CS'. Its authors, Welchman, Harry Hinsley and Edward Crankshaw, recommended the following:

- The creation of the Foreign Intelligence Office, which will include Signals Intelligence and Signals Security as part of its sphere of activity.
- The remoulding of G.C. & C.S. in the framework of the Foreign Intelligence Office as an organization which will compel the respect of the Services and take its proper place as the unchallenged headquarters of all Signals Intelligence.
- The development of a first-class Signals Security organization with an expert and professional understanding of communications and communications engineering.[15]

On 1 January 1945 Welchman submitted his personal thoughts in a report titled 'The Place of Cryptography and Traffic Analysis in Signals Intelligence'. The report was considered by a government committee looking at the future of GCHQ. Welchman wrote:

In writing this note the question that is uppermost in my mind is whether it is going to be possible to keep alive in peace time an organisation that is fully prepared for war. There are very great difficulties, which after careful consideration may be considered to be insuperable. But I am trying to analyse the sort of organisation that is required in wartime and to foresee the difficulties involved in keeping at least the framework of such an organization alive in peace time, with the idea in my mind that we should make a very determined attempt.[16]

Some years later he was told that his recommendations had been largely ignored. In any event, a man with a wife and young children needed to start making his own plans for a post-war career. Some BP veterans would remain within the new peacetime GCHQ but the majority of the more technical staff quickly dispersed to other occupations. For his part Welchman was already wondering if the Americans, with whom he had been so enamoured, would be more receptive to his ideas.

Chapter 8

Post-War and the Birth of the Digital Age

In the years leading up to the Second World War, Welchman and Katharine had enjoyed a good life in Cambridge. They had many friends and could enjoy some of the perks which came with being Dean of Sidney Sussex. However, they had always felt like fish out of water there. He had been a clergyman's son at Cambridge on a scholarship and without significant funds at his disposal. The men in Katharine's family were in the military on her father's side and in the clergy on her mother's side. She was a descendant of Elizabeth Fry, the English prison reformer, social reformer and Quaker. Very powerful women were a feature of her family. She would not have access to financial support through her family until later in their married life. After almost six years of working in the exciting and pressure-filled environment of BP, Welchman knew that the academic life was no longer for him. With a wife and three young children, Nick, Sue and Ros, aged six, four and one, to care for he needed to decide on his future without delay.

BP was winding down quite quickly in the summer of 1945, but before he could depart, Welchman had one final matter to deal with. He had become a temporary civil servant at the beginning of the war but eventually he received notice to report for military duty with a unit of the Royal Artillery. He contacted his new employers, the Foreign Office, who said that they would resolve the matter with Army administrators. At the end of the war, Welchman was still classified by the Army as having being called up but never enlisted. So in the eyes of the military, he was in effect a 'draft dodger'. To be discharged, he would first have to enlist and this he duly did. Within twenty minutes he was discharged and once again a civilian. As he remembered in *The Hut Six Story*:

Then, having arranged my discharge, the sergeant gave me a few appropriate papers, one of which I treasured for many years. It urged me to join the Home Guard, where my experience in the Army would be extremely valuable.

So like many thousands before him, Welchman handed in his pass at the gate and left BP, never to return.

While pondering on his future at the end of the war, it is unlikely that Welchman ever seriously considered taking on a role in the research and management of business. However, such an opportunity came along through his old BP friend and colleague Hugh Alexander. Before the war, Alexander had held the position of Director of Research for John Lewis and Co., then as now one of Britain's largest groups of department stores with a staff of about 10,000 at that time. Alexander recommended Welchman as a candidate for his former post and the chairman of the company, Spedan Lewis, made him a very attractive offer, which he duly accepted. As the job was based in London, it was not practical to commute daily from Great Gransden. The Welchmans had to sell their beloved Rippington Manor and moved to a new house in Cookham on the Thames. The road through the village led to Maidenhead which had its own railway station on a branch line about an hour from London. From there, Welchman began the daily commute to London and his new job. John Lewis was not BP and now that he was working normal hours he had more time to spend with his family. His son Nick later remembered his sister Ros being christened around this time and a seaside holiday in Swanage where the family stayed at a hotel with a swimming pool close to an area with an amusement arcade. Katharine could now take steps towards her musical career as a soprano and pianist. She had studied at the Royal Academy, and was thinking about giving recitals, which quite soon she did, at a grand cinema, the Odeon, in Maidenhead.

The man who had run the John Lewis business throughout the war, Michael Watkins, also lived in Cookham. In discussions with Watkins, Welchman realized what a privileged position he had been in during the war:

Discussing our respective experiences, Michael Watkins and I found many differences. I lived in quiet surroundings that were never subjected to anything more than trivial accidental bombing. (I do not remember hearing of anyone being hurt.) When I had to travel any distance on business, I was provided with a car and a female

chauffeur. Because of the importance of my work I was excused from
Home Guard duty. Watkins, though a man of some prominence
doing an important, exacting job, was shown no such consideration.
He lived at Cookham on the Thames, in normal times a railway
journey of about an hour from London. At the end of each day's work
at his office in Cavendish Square near Oxford Circus, he had to
struggle across London to Paddington Station in the hope that a train
would take him home. The journey was often nightmarish, delayed
either by bomb damage or by actual bombing attacks. Yet when he
got home to Cookham he would do his full share of Home Guard
duty.

Welchman found the next three years very interesting as he was able to
study a wide range of business problems and see them from the point of
view of top management. He was Acting Director of Personnel for about
nine months and Acting Director of Expansion for about the same period,
while other directors were ill. He had the opportunity to represent the
company on the committees of a number of national trade organizations.
Welchman was very impressed with the vision of Spedan Lewis, whose
father, John, had founded the business in 1864. Spedan Lewis had
developed power-sharing policies by sharing the profits the business made
with the employees. The democratic and profit-sharing nature of the
business was developed into a formal partnership structure and, in effect,
Spedan Lewis bequeathed the company to its employees.

In June 1946, it was announced that Welchman along with his BP
colleague Alan Turing had been appointed to the Order of the British
Empire for their war services. The OBE was standard for civil servants of
the rank that Welchman and Turing had officially held. There were
rumours that both had been considered for a higher award but that their
rank within the Civil Service limited them to the OBE.[1] Welchman took
his family with him to Buckingham Palace to receive the award but he never
felt compelled to use the letters after his name.

The following year, the Welchmans decided to move to London and
they purchased a house at 29 Holland Villas for £7,500. While life was good
in London, Welchman began discussing with his wife the possibility of
moving to the USA. He had been very impressed with the Harvard Business
School Case Study Program as part of his work for John Lewis. This looked
at real outcomes while he felt that British universities studying business
tended to be more concerned about theory and less about application. The

UK was slowly trying to return to normality while in America major advances were being made and opportunities were opening up in fields of interest to him. He also felt that Britain was not expanding its ideas, while due to his wartime experience his head was full of possible innovative projects. The rigidity of the class structures in Britain made it difficult to propose new ideas in fields such as engineering. He confided to a friend years later that, during that time, he felt as though he was hitting his head against a brick wall. Welchman was very interested in the American education system and felt that his children might get a different kind of education there than in Britain. In fact, the only negative thought he had ever harboured about the USA was the delay in its entry into the First World War. His brother Eric had died very early in the conflict on 24 August 1914 at the age of twenty-one.

In anticipation of persuading Katharine that their future lay in America, Welchman began to contact some of the Americans whom he had worked with during the war. Many of them were now involved in the fledgling computer industry. As he was doing so, an excellent and unsolicited letter of reference arrived from the Director of the Government Communications Headquarters. GC&CS had formally become GCHQ after the war and Travis had stayed on as its Director. The letter, dated 28 October 1948, revealed Travis's high regard for Welchman:

Dear Welchman,

I have recently been reviewing the wartime work of this organization with particular reference to the contribution of individual members of the organization and I should like to place on record my appreciation of the important and outstanding part you played. Your quick mastering of a number of different aspects of the work of which you had no previous experience was most noticeable and your inventiveness and ability in the field of applied mathematics and electronics provided a notable contribution to the success of the organization. From 1943 to the end of the war your services as an Assistant Director gave you an opportunity to display your organizing and administrative ability of which you took full advantage.

I hope your wartime experience will be of real value to you in Civil life in which I wish you every success.

Yours very sincerely,
Sir Edward Travis, K.C.M.G., C.B.E.

Somehow, Welchman had managed to persuade Katharine to take the plunge and move to the USA. As for many families emigrating to another country, it must have been a difficult and painful decision. It meant abandoning many friends, connections and people and, in Katharine's case, the foundations that she had been laying for her own career. Welchman flew, on his own, to America in the autumn of 1948. He wanted to establish himself professionally and find a suitable location for the family to settle in. Back in England, the family received postcards from a succession of American cities. Katharine and the three children boarded the *Nieuw Amsterdam*, a Dutch ship, in December 1948, accompanied by a pedigree Staffordshire terrier. On 19 December they sailed into New York harbour where Welchman was waiting to greet them. They boarded a train for Boston at the beginning of a considerable snowstorm that raged for the entire journey.

The family's financial resources were now under some pressure as exchange rates between the dollar and the pound took away more and more of the value of their money and holdings, and the currency controls delayed the transfer of assets from one country to the other. The move was also expensive. Katharine owned two grand pianos and a clavichord, which she had shipped to America at considerable cost. Welchman had rented a large house for them in Cambridge, Massachusetts, and the children were enrolled in private schools. Nick and Sue started going to Shady Hill School, which was within walking distance of their new home. The school was a standard bearer for progressive education, guided by principles drawn from John Dewey, the American philosopher.

Welchman's wartime 'opposite number' in the US Navy had been Dr Howard Engstrom. Before the war he had been a mathematician at Yale University. After the war, Engstrom had founded Engineering Research Associates (ERA), a pioneering computer company which ultimately became a division of Remington Rand. When Welchman arrived in America, Engstrom was one of the first people he contacted. However, in 1948, the ERA contracts were too highly classified for a non-citizen, so he had to look elsewhere. After considering a number of possibilities, he decided to take up a research post on Project Whirlwind at MIT under Dr Jay Forrester.

Project Whirlwind had emerged from the early wartime computer developments in the USA.[2] At the same time as the Colossus computer was being developed in Britain, work was also under way in America on an electronic and programmable computer for military purposes. An engineer called Luis de Florez, Director of the Special Devices Division of the Navy's Bureau of Aeronautics, had approached MIT to build a new kind of machine to help train naval bomber flight crews. The machine that he asked for was not the machine which MIT ultimately built.

De Florez had wanted a dual-purpose flight simulator, not a digital computer. In 1943 it was taking far too much time and money to train flight crews to man the increasingly complex aircraft in production. British engineers were addressing the same issue and had built a pneumatically operated trainer, the 'Silloth'. In America, the Navy and MIT came together and using Navy funding and MIT technical expertise, embarked on the development of the Airplane Stability and Control Analyzer (ASCA). MIT's Servomechanisms Laboratory was tasked with developing the ASCA system. The lab had been set up in 1940 by the Department of Electrical Engineering to develop a servomechanism to link a computing sight to 37-mm guns mounted on merchant vessels to repel attacks from German dive bombers. By 1944 it had around a hundred staff including thirty-five engineers.

The ASCA project was formally launched on 18 December 1944 and the director of the lab, Gordon Brown, appointed one of his assistant directors, Jay Forrester, to head it up. Forrester had gone to MIT as a research assistant after graduating in 1939 and he eventually spent his entire career there. He in turn brought in Bob Everett to share the responsibility and the technical direction of the project.

The ASCA development was not going well by the summer of 1945 due to the limitations of analogue computational machinery. Forrester had discussions with Perry Crawford, a young electrical engineer whose 1942 master's thesis had been called 'Automatic Control by Arithmetical Operations'. Before leaving MIT to take up a post with de Florez in the Special Devices Division of the Navy, Crawford had told Forrester about digital calculators and a new breed of controlled-sequence devices. At the University of Pennsylvania in Philadelphia an elaborate valve (vacuum-tube in the US) calculator, the Electronic Numerical Integrator and Computer (ENIAC) was under development at the Moore School of Engineering under the direction of John W. Mauchly and J. Presper Eckert Jr. As the development of Colossus in Britain was classified, the two men mistakenly believed that their machine would be the first to use valve-based circuitry to carry out highly complex calculations. The intended application was processing ballistics data for the US Army. A successor to ENIAC was also under development, the Electronic Digital Variable Automatic Computer (EDVAC). Forrester was intrigued by these developments and, years later, both he and Everett would credit Crawford with moving them towards digital numerical techniques.

Like Colossus, ENIAC was designed for a particular use rather than as a general-purpose machine with wide application. It had 18,000 valves compared to the 2,500 in the Colossus Mark II, and 1,500 electrical relays. The electronic computer tradition that followed on from ENIAC was based on wartime developments in the pulsed circuitry of radar, and the well-developed state of the art in radio valves. It would ultimately be transformed by the invention of the transistor and solid-state circuitry. It would incorporate the mathematical ideas of Charles Babbage, Edward Boole, John von Neumann and Alan Turing. So, by the end of the Second World War, computing pioneers on both sides of the Atlantic were forging ahead, pre-eminently Eckert, Mauchly and von Neuman in the USA and Maurice Wilkes, F. C. Williams and Turing in Britain.

Forrester attended the historic first 'Conference on Advanced Computation Techniques' at MIT on 30–31 October 1945. He also visited the University of Pennsylvania and afterwards was determined to take a digital approach to his project. Forrester was attracted to the fact that patterned arrangements of energised valves symbolized numbers and that these patterns were built up from modular units of two valves. This design could be repeated over and over again like bricks in a wall to build a computer. He started to expand his staff and sought talented graduate students of doctorate degree calibre, experience and ingenuity being deemed more important than the degree itself. This was the team that Welchman would join in 1948 having easily met Forrester's recruitment standard.

The Navy raised a new contract with MIT in March 1946. In Phase I, the researchers were tasked with the construction of 'a small digital computer involving investigation of electric circuits, video amplifiers, electrostatic storage tubes, electronic switching and mathematical studies of digital computation and the adaption of problems to this method of solution'. Phase II of the project would be to design an electronic computer and aircraft analyser based on the outcomes of Phase I. The project was given the name Whirlwind, one of a group of projects funded by the Special Devices Division, the others being Tornado and Hurricane. Forrester set out his vision for the Whirlwind computer in a paper delivered on 29 July 1948 at the Modern Calculating Machinery and Numerical Methods Laboratory at MIT:

Project Whirlwind is directed primarily at computer applications though it will continue to carry a heavy responsibility in machine development. The problems which will receive greatest attention are those requiring high-speed machines of some 20,000 arithmetic operations per second giving high computing efficiencies. The Whirlwind I computer, assembly of which is now under way, will permit such applications and studies and will be a proving ground for trouble location methods and circuits in order that improved high-speed computers may follow. One of the first applications for high-speed computers which will be developed will probably be the high-speed traffic flow network. This is chosen first because it is one of the simpler system applications and one which can be achieved in the near future. The lessons learned can be applied in the problems to follow. While computers appear to be capable ultimately of accomplishing most of the functions with which they are credited, it is almost certain that they will not do so at as early a date as anticipated. Many years and large sums of money lie between this audience and the realization of many of their hopes.

By 1948, interest in the analyser was waning and the overriding question being faced by Forrester and his team was 'What is the computer good for?' To Forrester, the key was finding the right people to take the project forward. As he wrote to a colleague 'The general type of man whom we need should have originality and what is often referred to as 'genius'. He should not be bound by the traditional approach . . . I do not know of suitable prospects.' Another major issue to be resolved was the problem of 'internal storage', known today as memory. For a computer to be general-purpose, memory was essential. Forrester considered a number of options including a mercury acoustic delay line which could store data in a linear arrangement. A two-dimensional storage arrangement was possible by making use of the electrostatically charged surface of, say, a disk in a vacuum tube. A number of insulated 'spots' could be placed on such a surface, with each given a positive or negative charge by focusing an electric beam on it. The so-called 'electrostatic storage tube' was first tested successfully in Britain in June 1948. Its inventor, F. C. Williams, integrated it into the University of Manchester's Mark I computer. However, Forrester had concerns about the speed and reliability of Williams's solution.

In 1947, Andrew Booth had delivered a lecture at the University of London in which he discussed the possibility of using magnetic cores as an alternative to storage tubes. Forrester realized the possibilities that this offered and assigned one of his staff, William Papian, to investigate further.

There were shortcomings with all of the available storage technologies available to the Whirlwind team. They had recognized two broad areas of application for computers: scientific problem-solving, requiring large storage capacity and real-time control, and applications, requiring speed. As Forrester said:

> The fundamental storage problem is not so much that of discovering an element which will retain information; it is the far more difficult problem of switching or selecting among the large numbers of individual elements which make up the storage system.

During 1948, Forrester had been in discussion with the US Air Force about it providing finance for a theoretical study of the technical problems involved in introducing a computer into air traffic control. This was one of many computer applications envisaged by Forrester. In the autumn of 1948 a new group was set up in the Servomechanisms laboratory with Welchman at its head. The group's initial remit was 'to study the mathematical background and coding procedures that will be put on Whirlwind when it is running'. In a memo to staff joining the group, Welchman said that the purpose of the group was 'to do original work on problems of computer applications'. By the end of the year, Welchman and Forrester had prepared and submitted a proposal for a two-year study of air traffic control problems. In a covering note, Forrester had made it clear that the project would be the first phase of a longer-term project to provide an interim and then a target air traffic control system. Testing of the interim system might be possible by 1952. While the construction and installation of operational equipment was not part of the project, laboratory trials using the Whirlwind computer would explore coding problems and their solutions. Welchman would head the project group with Forrester, Everett and Philip Franklin of MIT's Mathematics Department operating in an advisory capacity.

In early 1949 MIT was awarded a contract to begin work on the project. Success would depend on the collaboration of engineers, mathematicians, physicists and air controllers. After nine months' work, the team had published detailed descriptions of how to program, step by step, a computer of the Whirlwind design to control the positions of up to 100 aircraft more than ten miles away by means of a private-line communications system and a rotating antenna.[3] A basic introduction to the available 'machine language' techniques was also provided. In January 1950, Welchman and his team were asked to consider air problems of a military nature that would be suitable for computer application. In other words, as Welchman noted in his routine bi-weekly report to project members: 'We were asked to begin to look at the problem of tracking while scanning.'

To Forrester it was clear that they would soon be looking at problems of a greater military value. By the end of March 1950 a higher priority Air Force programme had pre-empted the Air Traffic Control Program. The goal would no longer be to control friendly aircraft, but instead to detect and, if necessary, destroy hostile aircraft. This didn't change the mathematics or programming activities as both goals had similar requirements. In either case, for the first time, a digital computer, in this case the Whirlwind, would be connected to radar equipment. Radar pulses would be converted to telephone-line signals and sent to the computer for processing.

While Welchman was engaged at MIT he gave the first lecture courses on computing in the Department of Electrical Engineering. He did this in parallel with his work on Whirlwind which continued to be wide and varied. He was also a member of the Valley Committee and took part in the early studies that led to the creation of the Semi-Automatic Ground Environment (SAGE), an air-defence control system, for the US Air Force. During the early and middle 1950s, the Whirlwind computer became a fully operating machine but, by then, Welchman had moved on.

While Welchman was busy at MIT Katharine started to make friends and had ventured into dog breeding. She had located the owner of an American Pit Bull Terrier, with pedigree papers issued by the United Kennel Club, and mated the animal with Lucy, the bull terrier she had brought with the family from Britain. Unfortunately, the American Kennel Club was the more prestigious dog breeding organization and the resulting offspring were not deemed to be pedigree animals.

As an English family abroad, the Welchmans sought salt water beaches and they soon found several along the coast north and east of Boston, around Gloucester and Ipswich. In 1950, the family moved to Lexington, Massachusetts, about ten miles from MIT. They bought a house at 26 Hancock Street for $12,000. Welchman had also found time to complete the book on algebraic geometry that he had been writing before the war. In 1950, Cambridge University Press published *Introduction to Algebraic Geometry*.

*

The following summer, the British government organized the Festival of Britain. It was a national exhibition with the purpose of giving Britons a feeling of recovery in the aftermath of war and to promote the British contribution to science, technology, industrial design, architecture and the arts. Welchman took his family back to England for much of the summer, travelling the northern route from Boston to Liverpool in a ship that carried cargo as well as passengers, stopping in Halifax, Nova Scotia, and St Johns, Newfoundland. Nick remembered walking with his father up to the headland above St Johns, site of the Marconi short-wave wireless station. Over a few weeks they managed to visit almost all their English relations, as well as the main Festival grounds in London. The family returned to America by air, a new experience for the children.

Back in Lexington, the children were all in good public schools and the girls were able to renew their friendship with two sisters whom they had known in Cambridge and who now lived in Lexington. Katharine started teaching music at Dana Hall School in Wellesley, another suburb of Boston. She also played the organ and directed the choir at the Unitarian church of Lexington. In preparation for the following summer, Welchman and his son began to learn to fish, with the help of the Unitarian minister of Lexington, who happened to hail from northern Vermont. The Reverend Floyd Taylor taught them the rudiments of fly fishing, and they all happily enjoyed their summer holidays in Vermont. The Reverend Taylor had been a very successful Fuller Brush salesman and was quite a potent speaker. His sermons were widely admired and published. Although Welchman was the first man in his family for some generations not to become a clergyman (apart from his brother who was killed in action in the First World War) and churchgoing was routine for him, he did find meaning in church ritual and was interested in discussing theological issues with clergymen. He had once been called upon to say grace at Cambridge in Latin because of his church background. He proceeded solemnly to recite several verses of Ovid, a Roman poet best known as the author of the three major collections of erotic poetry. Not surprisingly, his recital was greeted with stony silence. At one time, Welchman and his son would go to the Episcopal Church in Lexington and then rush over to the Unitarian Church where Katharine, Ros and Sue were working with the choir (Katharine was choir mistress and the girls sang). He was a devout reader of the Bible and claimed to have read it through from cover to cover three times.

*

In 1951, Welchman decided to leave MIT as he had had an offer to join Howard Engstrom at his pioneering new company Engineering Research Associates (ERA). The story of ERA is a fascinating one and perhaps best encapsulates Welchman's views on opportunities in post-war Britain and the USA.

During the Second World War, a group functioning under the title of Communications Supplementary Activity – Washington (CSAW) had been part of the US Navy. Like a number of people at BP,[4] they had been engaged in early computer developments for cryptanalytic purposes. The staff had a mix of skills familiar to BP: cryptanalysts, chess and bridge masters, mathematicians, physicists and engineers. Two key members of this group had been Howard Engstrom, a professor of mathematics from Yale and Bill Norris, a sales engineer from Westinghouse, the large electronics manufacturing company. As the war neared its end, Engstrom and Norris, who had become good friends, started to think about their return to civilian life. Their counterparts at BP had of course faced the same situation. The more radical recommendations made by Welchman and a few colleagues had been rejected. In the US, the Navy was keen to keep CSAW intact and offered the staff civil servant appointments. This was as unappealing to Engstrom and Norris as a return to their former employment, a sentiment shared by Welchman in the UK.

Engstrom suggested to Norris that they continue their CSAW work by setting up a private company. Since they had no capital or business experience, this seemed fanciful but, much to their surprise, they found that a number of key civilian members of CSAW were interested in their ideas. The Navy was also interested because, while keen to keep CSAW intact, it had found former technical staff members reluctant to join the civil service. Senior officers responsible for the work of CSAW recommended to the Secretary of the Navy, James Forrestal, that he make every effort to keep the group and its expertise together, even if it meant organizing parts of it outside of government. With the go-ahead from Forrestal, Engstrom and Norris began the process of creating their company in the autumn of 1945.

Suggestions that the new venture be run within a public sector body such as a university or research foundation were quickly rejected. While the Navy continued to offer civil service appointments, it unofficially endorsed a private venture, even though it could not officially help to set it up or guarantee that it would receive government business. By late 1945 funding still had not been secured and the venture risked losing its main asset, the skilled CSAW personnel. Finally John E. Parker, a wealthy entrepreneur, agreed to finance the new company. Parker had taken over a failed aircraft company in late 1941. He merged the company with Northwest Airlines to form the Northwestern Aeronautical Corporation (NAC). The company began building wooden gliders for the Army Air Corps. After the war ended, he was encouraged by high-ranking naval officers to finance Engstrom and Norris's venture and run it in parallel with NAC. In January 1946, Engineering Research Associates, Inc. was born, half owned by Engstrom, Norris and another colleague and half by an investor group headed by Parker.

Remarkably, in June 1946 the Navy Department issued contracts to both ERA and NAC without making them go through a competitive bidding process. By having the same management and headquarters, they overcame the problem of ERA as a new company not yet being eligible to receive government contracts. The US Government had in effect acted in an entrepreneurial manner to establish ERA and retain the services of over forty of CSAW's most skilled staff.

ERA's initial work was in the development of special digital machines and ongoing research and development on both data-handling and data-storage technology. Its researchers recognized that reliable data storage was essential for the evolving computer developments. In August 1947, ERA was funded to design a general purpose stored program computer. The design was approved in March 1948 and completed in the autumn of 1950. It was called 'Atlas'[5] and described by ERA as 'a large scale 24-bit parallel magnetic drum, selective sequence calculator'. The machine contained 2,700 valves, 200 more than the Colossus Mark II which was operating at BP in June 1944, but without any memory. At the end of 1951, ERA announced the development of what it hoped would be its first commercial computer, the 1101. It was also starting to develop special purpose computers for customers with applications such as one of the first electronic inventory systems for a wholesale mail order house. Another system delivered in 1953 offered the storage, searching and processing of aircraft flight plans.

Welchman joined ERA in 1951, and became a personal assistant to Engstrom, who had become Vice-President for Planning. Welchman worked on computer applications for a wide range of systems such as wind tunnels, missile control, airborne fire control, war games and inventory control during the Christmas rush for the mail order house. After ERA had become a division of Remington Rand in 1952, he took part in joint planning activities covering both the ERA and the UNIVAC divisions. Remington Rand had already acquired the Eckert–Mauchly Computer Corporation, founded by the makers of the first American electronic computer ENIAC, in 1950. So by 1952 Remington Rand had become one of the biggest computer companies in the USA. It was acquired by the Sperry Corporation in 1955 to form a company then known as Sperry Rand, subsequently shortened to Sperry.[6]

Welchman had joined ERA's Washington branch at the time that a triangular war had developed between ERA, Eckert-Mauchly, and Remington Rand's own research laboratories, all with a wealth of punched-card systems experience. He worked hard to find out what each group had to offer and how their efforts could be co-ordinated for their common good. He was impressed with what the UNIVAC people were doing, but remained an ERA man until he left in 1954. It did mean, however, that he had to commute along a gruelling triangular track, going from Boston to Minneapolis/St Paul, then to Washington and back to Boston.

ERA did little original work except for the physical design of reliable equipment. Because of the combination of security and priority of the work to be performed by the systems after their installation in Washington, ERA was supplied with reports from almost every concurrent development effort everywhere. That this kind of technical espionage was taking place was a carefully guarded part of the whole ERA effort. It resulted in much copying of the better ideas from innumerable sources, and the benefits of 'second guessing'.

The American military had shown itself to be quite forward-thinking as its Navy sought to preserve continuity in its development capability for cryptologic equipment and it encouraged the formation of ERA to deliver this continuity. In Britain, many of the brilliant engineers who had designed and built an electronic and programmable computer two years before the Americans would play no further part in the fledgling British computing industry which started to emerge at the end of the war.

In 1952, the Welchman family was on the move again, this time to Washington, DC. They bought a house at 3401 Porter Street in January for $27,000, which created financial problems as they had not been able to sell their house in Lexington before the move. It was not until June that they finally managed to sell it for $18,000, which at least yielded a 50 per cent profit on their original purchase. That summer the family decided to go on a road trip in their new Plymouth station wagon. They set off from

Washington going south through Virginia to North Carolina, where they stopped for a while at Cape Hatteras. They then went west to the Blue Mountains, on to Kentucky, then up to Illinois and Wisconsin, where they reached the Sperry Rand offices. At this point Welchman left the family to do some work and then rejoined them in New England a few weeks later. Throughout the journey they pitched tents and camped out in state parks. Some of them were very scenic and had good facilities, but it placed a great strain on Katharine, particularly when she was left on her own with the children. They crossed into Canada and then back across the border into Vermont where Welchman rejoined them at the home of Floyd Taylor and his family. Finally, they returned home to Washington. Nick had come to his last year at Shady Hill, and he was planning to go to Philips Exeter Academy, a very good and reputable boarding school in Exeter, New Hampshire.

By 1954, Katharine Welchman had decided that she wanted to return to England. This was a common experience for a number of expatriate families, wherein they would find it difficult to enjoy living in America and would run out of patience with it after five years. However, the danger was that they would then go back to their old country, only to discover that it no longer suited them, either. Nick's second year at Exeter had gone well and while he generally supported his mother's wish to go back home, he was less fervent about it. Welchman came up to Exeter for a couple of days and stayed with Nick in his dormitory room. He lived in the school and met his son's friends and teachers. They cycled together and took out a canoe on the river. Welchman was impressed by what he saw, and was interested to learn that Exeter was half a century older than Marlborough, his old school in England.

Welchman finally agreed to repatriate his family and find employment in England. In the spring of 1954 Welchman returned to Britain and, in April, he bought Milford House in the village of Chobham, Surrey for £3,285. The village was within easy reach of London by train; Katharine had lived there when she was single and had a number of close friends in the village. Schools were soon found for the children. Sue was to go to St Mary's School in Calne, Wiltshire, not far from Marlborough. Ros would go to Hanford, a little school near Blandford Forum run by an elderly friend of Welchman's, and Nick to Welchman's old alma mater, Marlborough.

Before the start of the new school terms, Katharine and the children went to a co-educational summer camp in New Mexico, a few miles north of Taos. The camp was run by Eleanor and Sandy Orr, school teachers in

Washington, DC, and its campers and staff assembled and proceeded in loose convoys to the site of the camp over five days or so. It would prove to be a busy summer with much outdoor life and scenery. While the family was on holiday, Welchman took up a post as personal assistant to the Manager of the Computer Department of Ferranti Ltd. At the time, Ferranti was one of the pioneering manufacturers of electronic computers in Europe. Ferranti and Powers Samas Accounting Machines Ltd were trying to work out how they could combine their resources to cut down the lead time involved in getting a British commercial computer on the market. Welchman worked closely with the research engineers of both companies and led the liaison for applications studies and equipment specifications. From working with the Commercial Research Branch of Powers Samas and taking part in negotiations with its sales organization, he learned a good deal about the methodology of accounting and tabulating machines. His final task for Ferranti in the UK was to start a computing service for them in London.

The Welchman family never lived in Chobham. It seems that not only did Katharine not care for the house her husband had chosen for them, she no longer wished to live in England either. For years she had been scornful of the various American dialects and behaviours, although never in front of American friends. Now that same scorn was directed at hidebound English attitudes and stilted diction, a relic of the Victorian era in Britain. So, after landing at Heathrow and dropping the children off at their respective boarding schools, Katharine returned to New York. Welchman took up lodgings with his old BP colleague and friend Houston Wallace and his sister Hope, in Canonbury, north London.

Nick left Marlborough in the winter of 1955 and a room was found for him in South Kensington with a landlady who provided meals while Welchman continued to live with the Wallaces, in another part of London. Father and son later lived in a *pied à terre* flat just off the Embankment, and when Katharine finally came back to live with them, Nick moved to an upstairs room. By 1956, Welchman had rented a flat at 44 St Petersburgh Place, W2 to provide a base for the entire family when Sue and Ros were home from school. The family were also able to enjoy the pleasures of a small house, built at the end of a row of coastguard cottages at Westgate-on-Sea. Katharine's mother had lived there for a while near the end of the war and for few years afterwards. Westgate was an unpretentious, old fashioned holiday place with many attractions for children, including long seaside walks. In the summers the family sometimes visited Dreamland, an amusement park in Margate, with a pier and a small fishing harbour. At Christmas time there were pantomimes in Margate and impressive services at Canterbury Cathedral. Westgate itself was the inspiration of several of John Betjeman's poems about church bells. He had been at Marlborough at the same time as Welchman and both were commemorated by the school as distinguished old boys.

Welchman particularly enjoyed visiting Quex Park, a unique country park of 250 acres on the Isle of Thanet set within an estate of 1,800 acres around Birchington, Acol and Richborough. The property was an oasis of parkland and trees, all planted in the nineteenth century by John Powell-Powell and his successors. It was also a haven for birdlife with numerous species recorded there. In the 1950s it was the home of the Powell-Cotton family.[7] Katharine's mother and Mrs Powell-Cotton had been good friends for many years, and Katharine and one of her cousins often visited Quex in childhood. Welchman and Mrs Powell-Cotton became friends when she got him interested in dowsing. He would hopefully follow the pipes that conveyed water underground to an ornamental pond in the extensive garden, dowsing stick in hand. As with anything that interested him, he was relentless in pursuing the subject. This personal drive had served him well at BP.

In 1957 Welchman and his family were on the move yet again, this time repeating the journey they had made more than eight years earlier. They arrived back in New York in May and took a two-year lease on an apartment at 15 East 75th Street. Always one to plan ahead, Welchman had secured a job as manager of a new Electronics Division in Ferranti Electric Inc., a New York subsidiary of the British Ferranti Company. His main task was to build up a manufacturing business in the US based on the achievements of the Ferranti research teams in the UK. He was also able to help develop a US market for British-made Ferranti products starting with a type of magnetostrictive delay line that had been developed for the Ferranti Pegasus computer.[8] He subsequently met people at the US Navy, Army and Air Force research labs about possible applications in systems such as radar, sonar, IFF (an identification system designed for command and control) and multipath communications. Welchman's meetings led to contracts for further development to meet specific requirements and, subsequently, quantity orders.

Towards the end of 1958, an old MIT associate, Norman Taylor, invited Welchman to help him build up the electronics division of the ITEK Corporation based in Lexington, Massachusetts, where he was vice-

president. Welchman duly joined ITEK in 1959, taking over the management of an Applied Technology department that combined system studies
with mechanical, optical and electronic engineering. His team was able to
take advantage of ITEK's considerable research activities in photography,
optics, chemistry and information sciences. The core of the business was
the storage, retrieval, reproduction and distribution of information
recorded on photographic film, particularly documentary information. His
department developed a number of new techniques for handling sheets of
film for the Patent Office, the Library of Medicine and the USAF.

The years of moving the family back and forth between the US and
Britain had taken their toll on the Welchman marriage. Welchman's long
absences from home during the war had convinced Katharine that he was
having an affair. The couple had been living separate lives for several years
but had stayed together until their youngest child Ros reached a suitable
age. In 1959 they were finally divorced. As a couple they had mixed socially
in the artistic New York scene and both would soon find new partners.

Later the same year Katharine married Francis Bitter, a physics
professor at MIT. Bitter's father, Karl, had been a noted sculptor. Welchman meanwhile had become friendly with Fannie Hillsmith, a fairly
prominent New York artist and friend of Katharine. Fannie's grandfather,
Frank Hill Smith, had been a painter and one of the founders of the Boston
Museum School, where she had trained for four years. In 1934 she moved
to New York, became inspired by vanguard art, and developed an abstract
style. Her work had been exhibited in a number of New York galleries.
Welchman and Fannie Hillsmith were married on 4 August 1961. Fannie
kept her New York apartment but the couple moved to a house that
Welchman had purchased on Middle Street in Lexington, the same town
he had lived in almost a decade earlier. While the house was a modest one,
Fannie filled it with her painting. Welchman's domain was the garden. He
had read a book about the stone statues on Easter Island by Norwegian
scientist Thor Heyerdahl and how the ancients were able to move such
heavy megaliths. He used the same technique with the help of friends and
family to place large stones around the garden. While undertaking this
work friends and family would be entertained by classical music which
constantly emanated from the house.

By 1962, it became clear that ITEK management did not share either
his or Taylor's vision for the future of data storage. He therefore left the
company to join the MITRE Corporation, based in Bedford, Massachusetts.
MITRE had been founded four years earlier and one of its founding

members was Bob Everett,[9] Welchman's former colleague on Project Whirlwind.

As has been explained, MITRE, ERA and Project Whirlwind all had similar origins as examples of the military and private sector working together to deliver technological solutions to military problems. Around the time Welchman left to join ERA, the focus of the Whirlwind project changed and by September 1951 funding was available to support further computer development. The project was also moved from the Servo-mechanisms Laboratory to become a separate administrative unit under Forrester and Everett's direction. Six months later the laboratory had become Division 6 of the newly established Lincoln Laboratory based at Hanscom Air Force Base near Bedford, Massachusetts.

The Valley Committee, formally called the Air Defense System Engineering Committee (ADSEC) was chaired by MIT physics professor, George Valley. He had worked in MIT's Radiation Laboratory during the Second World War and was greatly concerned about the lack of 'effective co-ordination between the operational and technical personnel' and the need for technical guidance in systems research. These were themes which would resonate with Welchman for the rest of his working life. The Air Force was also troubled by the inadequacy of continental air defence as well as a perceived lack within the Air Force of an appropriate research and development effort.

Most British accounts of early computer developments have ignored Project Whirlwind. Welchman summed up Forrester and Everett's achievement in a letter to Turing's biographer, Andrew Hodges, on 25 June 1984:

> Almost all the early computer people had narrow views of mathematical and computational applications. But Forrester and Everett, with no knowledge of Turing's ideas, were also fighting for the concept of a universal machine. And their objectives, from the outset, included real-time control. Their machines had to be fast enough for the purpose, and could not be allowed to fail. Other early computers were categorised by 'Mean Time Between Failures'.

Forrester and Project Whirlwind were unpopular with most of the computer community, which was mainly concerned with mathematical and scientific problems. He was fighting for a fast universal machine that would operate without failures, and this cost a lot of money. That he got away with it was due to the urgent need for an effective defence against nuclear air attack. His project led directly to the SAGE computers, built by

IBM to his specifications. And he himself developed the first reliable fast-access storage – his magnetic core memory. This was a remarkable series of achievements.

In April 1953, the US Air Force accepted a proposal from a small group which included Forrester, Everett and Valley for improvements to be made to the ground environment of the US Air Defense Command. In the summer of 1954 the proposed system was named the Semi-Automatic Ground Environment (SAGE). Division 6 had started design work on the Whirlwind II while IBM was commissioned to build a computer for the SAGE system.[10] In 1956, Forrester left Lincoln to return to MIT as a Professor of Management and Everett became head of Division 6.

Throughout 1957, the Air Force had been unable to find a contractor to take on the integration of the myriad of weapons and sensors into SAGE. It therefore decided to create a new, not-for-profit corporation that would become the Air Force's centre of technical advice on SAGE and its future development. The core of the new company was Lincoln's Division 6 and Bob Everett became Technical Director. The new company, called MITRE, had the daunting task of integrating a long-range surface-to-air missile system (Bomarc), a line-of-sight missile system (Nike), and the SAGE system. The first SAGE command centre became operational on 1 July 1958.

The work at MITRE represented the beginning of a permanent technical revolution in weapon systems. The US military became ever more dependent upon advanced technology and the engineers who implemented it successfully, much as the Germans had become dependent on the Enigma system and its operators. Who better for MITRE to hire than the man who had led the attack on Germany's tactical communication system during the Second World War? Welchman joined MITRE in 1962 at the request of his former colleague from Project Whirlwind. Bob Everett wanted Welchman to contribute to tactical programmes in development and to explore some open-ended questions such as the application of digital technology to battlefield communications.

Welchman had first-hand knowledge of Germany's innovative use of radio communications to support battle plans. Blitzkrieg, the rapid, disruptive penetration of enemy lines, often achieved by racing around entrenched positions, depended on interconnected radio networks. Commanders in the field could call in air support and maintain constant contact with headquarters.

Welchman's first assignment at MITRE in 1962 was a small project related to USAF operations during a nuclear attack. As project leader, he

supervised the formulation of a scheme, which was fully approved by
NORAD command. The US was worried about the vulnerability of the
headquarters of NORAD's Commander-in-Chief (CINCNORD). The
Canadians had already constructed an underground headquarters for the
North-Eastern Region, for which they were responsible. A system was
sought that would allow this facility to act as an Alternate Command Post
(ALCOP) if CINCNORD became inoperative. MITRE was asked to
establish Project SNOCAP (Survivable NORAD Capability) to look into
the matter.

In the same year, Welchman opted to become an American citizen.
Having decided that his future now lay permanently in the USA, he felt
that it was appropriate to pledge allegiance formally to his new country.

In early 1964 he was transferred to a department studying air operations
on a conventional battlefield outside Europe, specifically offensive missions
against ground targets. He completed and published an analysis of future
limited war environments in the summer of 1964 which became MITRE's
authoritative statement on limited war environments up to 1980. This was
followed in August 1965 by a lengthy analysis of the characteristics of
offensive air missions against ground targets in various possible limited
war situations.

During the following year he became involved in advanced planning
for the overall command and control of tactical air operations and set out
to deliver a system concept which would offer improved capability in a
number of associated problem areas. From August 1966 to August 1967
his assigned objective was to identify areas of Air Force development that
could lead to significant improvements in Joint Task Force capabilities in
the post-1980 time period. At the end of the year's study, he had decided
that tactical communication stood out as a problem of paramount
importance.

As Welchman wrote in *The Hut 6 Story*:

> The planning of battlefield communications gradually deteriorated
> into little more than methods of applying telephone-system thinking
> and switchboard technology to provide a rigid structure of point-to-
> point communications.

Welchman believed that this mode of operation was long since obsolete
in light of what modern communications technology could bring to the
battlefield. In 1966, he had realized that 'digital packets' containing short
bursts of information and broadcast over high-capacity common-user

radios could provide attackers with a tremendous advantage. By 1968, his ideas had evolved into 'a general-purpose battlefield communications system that could handle teletype, digital data, digitised voice and digitised pictures'. He illustrated the workings of this system with an inverted 'U' or horseshoe to represent an 'information pipeline' or bus.[11] Eventually refined under an architecture known as 'time division multiple access' (TDMA), this bus was divided into small, sequential intervals called time slots. Aircraft and conceivably ground or naval forces would be assigned a discrete time slot in which to feed in position and status information in digital packets. This information would be updated at precisely defined intervals in a continuous cycle – a characteristic that led Welchman to describe the entire system as a 'cyclic information system'. Welchman's studies of military engagements across a wide sweep of history reaffirmed a problem labelled by the Prussian military strategist Clausewitz as the 'fog of war'. MITRE's Eric Ellingson attributed battlefield communications failures to people with information not knowing who needed it, people needing information not knowing who had it and there being no means for them to find each other.

The proposed digital radio system appeared to rectify these problems because it relied on broadcast rather than point-to-point communications. Up-to-date information would be available to all subscribers at all times. Welchman labelled this concept, 'selective access to information' or SATI.

The work coincided with other MITRE work on a transportable, long-range navigation system called Loran-D that was designed for tactical operations in Vietnam. This led to a demonstration system known as PLRACTA (Position Location, Reporting and Control of Tactical Aircraft). The system was demonstrated during the winter of 1970/71 and by the end of 1971, MITRE had shown its feasibility. However, the system's success required the support of other branches of the service and it was resisted by pilots and aircraft programme managers.

With retirement from MITRE looming on the horizon in June 1971, Welchman attempted to sell the concept in Washington. His 200-page document, M70-97, was prepared under US Air Force contract F19(628) 71-C-0365, Project 603C. A shortened version appeared in the February/ March 1971 issues of *Signal*, the journal of the Armed Forces Communications and Electronics Association in the USA. In *The Hut 6 Story*, Welchman described the outcome of his attempts to win over senior military authorities in Washington to his proposals:

> The idea of command responsibility for communications was revolutionary, contrary to doctrine, and therefore unacceptable. And that was that!

However, vindication came in 1972 when PLRACTA became part of a bigger Air Force programme called Seek Bus, which aimed at specifying prototype hardware and software for the installation, test and evaluation of the SATI concept. In 1974, the US Secretary of Defense, James Schlesinger, expanded the programme for use by all branches of the military, merging Seek Bus with a related Navy programme to form the Joint Tactical Information Distribution System (JTIDS). The US Department of Defense formed the Joint Service Program Office to administer the plan.

In *The Hut 6 Story*, Welchman gave his final thoughts on these developments:

> The US Army is very interested in JTIDS not only for its own use, but also as a means of achieving more effective co-ordination of ground and air forces in combined arms operations. In view of all this, it is hard to understand why progress has been, and still is, so slow.

Once again, Welchman's vision was to be realized. After more than forty years of evolution, JTIDS is now a fully operational command and control system, providing information, distribution, position location and identification capabilities for the Air Force, Army, Navy, Marine Corps and British, French and NATO forces. Its elegant system design allowed for future expansion and adaption and has stood the test of time.[12]

One former colleague who still works at MITRE recalled his first day there in 1968. Having joined the organization straight from college, he was given an office next to Welchman who was working on an air defence system. Welchman greeted him with a question: 'What do we have for accurate time sources. What have you learned?' He then took the young man under his wing and mentored him through his early days. They also became friends and their families would often spend time together. MITRE seems to have been designed to facilitate this type of interpersonal relationship with its interconnected buildings creating a campus-like environment. Another colleague attended a number of meetings with Welchman and was impressed with his grasp of the problem at hand – the need for a vast data communications system. It was clear that Welchman was the man to deliver it and his contribution would be significant. Yet

MITRE colleagues knew little if anything about Welchman's wartime work at BP.[13]

It wasn't just his job with MITRE which was coming to an end. His marriage to Fannie was in terminal decline and had been for some time. At the beginning of July he began the painful process of telling his children that the marriage was over. Perhaps Fannie wasn't cut out to be the sort of wife that Welchman thought she should be. She kept two houses, one for looking after her mother, and the couple were often apart pursuing their own careers. A psychologist advised them they should divorce as the Arts and Science didn't mix! Given that Welchman's two marriages, one to a musician and the other to an artist had failed, there may have been some truth in the advice, at least in Welchman's case.

After his marriage to Fannie ended, Welchman started to look for somewhere to spend the rest of his life in retirement. He travelled across the country and, after visiting a second cousin once removed in Westchester, Pennsylvania, he considered settling in Sarasota, Florida. On his way back to the home he had shared with Fannie in Lexington, he happened to pass through Newburyport, Massachusetts. Located on the southern bank of the Merrimack River where it reaches the Atlantic Ocean, the city had a long and rich history. The area was originally inhabited by the Pawtucket Indians. It was first settled by Europeans in 1635, prospered and became a city in 1851. Newburyport was best known as a seaport and as a shipbuilding centre in days gone by. Welchman was captivated by its New England charm. He drove through the city and continued on the causeway and drawbridge over the Plum Island River to Plum Island. He knew almost immediately that this was where he wanted to spend the rest of his days.

He fell in love with Plum Island, a barrier island off the coast where the Parker River and the Merrimack River flow into the Gulf of Maine. The island was best known as an outstanding birding spot and was a stop-off on the migration paths of numerous species. Bird watchers came from all over the world to photograph and document birds and other forms of wildlife on Plum Island. There was also a lovely sandy beach running around the north side of the island. By August he had found a house which suited him and put in an offer. After some legal problems were resolved, he purchased the house at 167 Water Street for $5,300 with the rear of the property overlooking the Merrimack River and towards Plum Island and the Atlantic. When he moved to Newburyport in June 1971 he didn't know anyone in the area, but according to friends, was considered to be very eligible. However, he was very much the English gentleman and friends used to tease him about being an old-fashioned one at that. When he was courting his second wife Fannie, his daughter Ros would often accompany them as a chaperone, much to her bemusement. Apparently a lady neighbour, who was a member of a very socially acceptable family, often invited him to her house for parties. At one such event he was at the bottom of the stairs and to his horror, she was removing her knickers. He excused himself and refused further invitations. He even once told his wife not to invite a woman friend around again because she wore eye shadow. However, friends suspected that it was just as likely to be due to her topics of conversation which were not as wide-ranging as the rest of Welchman's friends. His own definition of a gentleman was 'someone who would like to but doesn't'.[14]

On 24 July 1971 the second cousin whom he had visited earlier in the year in Pennsylvania came to see him along with her two young sons and her American husband Bill. Teeny Wimer had an English mother and an Austrian father. Her great-grandfather on her mother's side, Henry Welchman, had been the brother of Gordon Welchman's grandfather. In 1969 she had ended up in the local hospital in Newburyport as a result of a car accident. On that occasion she was helped by Diana Lucy and they had continued to correspond. On this visit, they were able to meet under pleasanter circumstances and of course, at the same time, bring Welchman together with Diana, who would become a close friend for the rest of his life.

One of the problems with life in Newburyport was going to be the winter snows and difficulties in parking his car at the back of the house. So, once again, he considered buying a second home in Sarasota where he could spend the winters in the Florida sunshine. However, Teeny had kept in contact with him after her visit and had found him an apartment in Westchester, near her and her family. Welchman was becoming quite close to Teeny. She had lost her father shortly after the end of the war and initially he thought it would be good to bring her into his family and perhaps be the father that she never had.

Teeny was a very practical and down-to-earth woman and before long events took a different turn. Despite an age difference of thirty years, they had fallen in love. It was hardly surprising that Teeny's husband was not very happy with the impending break-up of his marriage. In any event, Teeny and her boys moved into Welchman's house in Newburyport in April 1972. Ever the gentleman, he promptly took a room in a nearby hotel and would not stay the night until they were married. He did not want to damage her reputation! In early May 1972 he flew to England and then on to Paris to visit his youngest daughter Ros, who was living there with her husband. Welchman told her of his wish to marry Teeny and sought advice on how best to broach the subject with the rest of the family in England. After returning to England, he took the opportunity to meet his old BP colleague Sir Leonard (Joe) Hooper, now the Director of GCHQ. He made enquiries about when the embargo on discussing his wartime work at BP might be lifted. It appears that he was already considering the possibility of writing something about his time at BP.

In July 1972 Welchman and Teeny flew to Haiti where they were married. Returning after a brief honeymoon, they soon settled into life in Newburyport. His MITRE work was going well and taking up much of his time. He had completed a fifty-page document on Soviet weapon deployment in Europe before leaving for Haiti.

MITRE had offered Welchman a consultancy contract which had been ideal for him. MITRE's Bedford, Massachusetts, headquarters was only fifty miles from Newburyport and he wouldn't have to make the journey every day. He quickly became involved in various projects concerning technical solutions for weapon systems being used in Vietnam. In early 1972, he was asked to study Soviet capabilities for military operations in and around Europe. From 1972 to 1978, his studies were centred on anticipating what the Soviets, with their Warsaw Pact allies, might try to do in the first few hours of a conventional attack against West Germany. He would then switch to designing suitable tactical communications for possible future battlefields. In this last study he noted that:

> Our military thinking of today shows the same types of doctrinal inhibition and compartmentalization that were so disastrous for the British [in the North Africa campaign in the Second World War].

In the summer of 1974 Welchman and his wife decided to celebrate their second wedding anniversary in England. It was towards the end of this trip that Welchman came across an article in the 28 July issue of the *Sunday Telegraph* previewing Winterbotham's book, *The Ultra Secret*. This book was the beginning of the gradual release of information about the work of Welchman and his colleagues at BP throughout the war. It would impact significantly on the path that Welchman would take for the rest of his life.

Chapter 9

Writing *The Hut Six Story*

Welchman had thought very little about the Second World War until he joined MITRE in 1962. That changed once he became 'involved in studying the information flow needed for co-ordination of ground and air forces in battle'.[1] It is likely that he started to think about writing about his wartime activities at that point. In any event, in 1974, spurred on by the *Sunday Telegraph* articles, Welchman had tried to contact one of his old BP colleagues, Peter Calvocoressi, while in London. Calvocoressi had been head of the Air sub-section of Hut 3 from 1942 to 1945 and worked closely with Welchman in co-ordinating the flow of decrypts from Hut 6 to Hut 3. Failing to make contact directly, Welchman decided to write to him after returning to Newburyport in late August 1974.[2] While he found the Winterbotham articles irritating, it did seem to him that their publication might result in others being allowed to talk openly about their experiences and to write their memoirs. He also felt that Calvocoressi might be well placed to provide him with advice on this matter. In his letter he told Calvocoressi about some of his work at MITRE. He made it clear that his primary motivation for writing a book was the deeply held belief that an open discussion of the insight into German communications philosophy that BP acquired during the Second World War could be of real value in advanced planning for NATO.

Calvocoressi replied several weeks later and by coincidence, had received Welchman's letter on the very day that he had acquired a proof copy of Winterbotham's book. He had found it disappointing, believing that after an initial account about how BP learned the details of the Enigma machine, it was no more than 'a chapter by chapter account of the principal campaigns and battles of the war with Ultra thrown in'. Calvocoressi had already written a book about the Second World War for general consumption and had approached the authorities for permission to refer to Ultra material.[3] He had been refused but when he asked the same authorities what they might do if he did, in effect, 'blow the gaff', he had been told that they would do nothing because they would look silly in doing so. Nonetheless, he decided to abide by the official ruling, feeling bound by the personal undertaking he had given under the Official Secrets Act. He believed that there was room for the sort of book Welchman suggested but it would probably need to be put together by three or four people. He was well placed to make this judgement as he had been appointed Editor-in-Chief of Penguin books in 1973 and Publisher and Chief Executive the following year. His reservations about being involved himself were due to work commitments and the fact that he did not feel able to write an account of Hut 3 without access to documents, which would probably be refused,

In reply, Welchman told him that he was keen to ask Stuart Milner-Barry to help in the project because he was the principal Hut 6 liaison with Hut 3 while he was in charge and took charge of Hut 6 when Welchman became Assistant Director for Mechanization. At this stage Welchman believed that a combination of himself, Milner-Barry and a Hut 3 man such as Calvocoressi could cover the essential parts. His own contribution would probably be a simple account of the early days, explaining how a huge operation grew out of the early work of Dilly Knox, supplemented by his own initial studies of call-signs and discriminants. He would probably take his story up to the point when the Americans joined the staff of Hut 6, and the Central Party was merged into the rest of the operation under his supervision.

Welchman wrote to Winterbotham on 22 January 1975, saying that he had a fascinating story to tell and hoped to do so before long.[4] In his reply the following month, Winterbotham said that the real object of writing his own book had been to put pressure on the authorities to release all available documents so that history could be properly written. He believed that Welchman had:

> the most fascinating story of all those who took part and one which everyone is trying hard to find out. I cannot go an inch further than the book. Security here are very nervous at present and have warned me not to go beyond the book, since TV & films are likely to follow, and it is all the cryptographic tricks you got up to in order to give the 'Bronze Goddesses' their breakfast that the ferrets are after. Fortunately, I don't know much about them but Milner-Barry tells me you were the driving force in that field.

Winterbotham claimed that his British and Commonwealth publishers, Weidenfeld & Nicolson, were very helpful in getting his book published as Sir George Weidenfeld was a close friend of Harold Wilson who had the final word. He also extravagantly claimed that 'if my own book is any criterion, maybe make you half a million $'s over about 3 years [*sic*]'.

While Winterbotham was certainly the first to make the general public both in the UK and the USA aware of BP, others had previously made references to it. The journalist and author Malcolm Muggeridge had been recruited by MI6 in 1942. In the second volume of his memoirs, published in 1973, a year before Winterbotham's book was published, Muggeridge mentioned BP on numerous occasions.[5] He described 'cracked cipher material' as being the staple product of MI6 which provided the basis of most of its activities. He went on to say that:

> The establishment which produced this precious material was located at Bletchley, in a manor house in which I spent some days familiarising myself with the place, its staff, its output and manner of working. As might be supposed, in view of the business at hand, the staff were a curious mix of mathematicians, dons of various kinds, chess and crossword maestros, an odd musician or two, and numerous wireless telegraphy experts.

Another example can be found in an episode of the classic 1970s BBC television series, *Colditz*.[6] The series followed the lives of Allied servicemen imprisoned at the supposedly escape-proof Colditz Castle. In Series 2, Episode 3 the prisoners are trying to get a message to British intelligence services. One sends a coded letter to his wife who, being good at crossword puzzles, recognizes it as such and takes it to MI5. One of the MI5 officers says to a colleague 'We could try sending it to Bletchley.' The programme was broadcast on 21 January 1974, well before Winterbotham's book appeared. One of the creators of the series had previously drawn on his Second World War RAF experiences to produce, in 1963, a drama about an RAF squadron which ferried agents in and out of occupied Europe. Could it be that he knew about BP and was tempted to drop the name into the script?

By February 1975, it was becoming clear that, while Welchman could write an interesting book without access to GCHQ documents, Milner-Barry and Calvocoressi would find it difficult to do so. Therefore, at a meeting in Newburyport, Calvocoressi agreed that Welchman's book could lead up to a second volume, written jointly by the three of them, when, they hoped, records would be available. Calvocoressi believed that a direct approach to GCHQ or NSA would result in a refusal and leave them in an even more difficult position. He also thought that Winterbotham's idea of going straight to his publishers and letting them fight the battle was naive. He regarded Winterbotham's story of personal influence with Harold Wilson as nonsense.

Calvocoressi strongly recommended that at this point Welchman concentrate on getting a major part of the book written. He might avoid some of the technical details by referring to as yet unwritten appendices. The decision about what to do about publication could be left until he had the material ready. Calvocoressi was willing to help and Penguin was definitely interested in the book. Penguin would handle the British edition, and would arrange for an American hardcover edition by some other publisher. He was certain that a number of publishers would be interested, and it would be a great mistake for Welchman to tie himself to any one publisher, even Penguin, at this point. Calvocoressi agreed to talk to Milner-Barry when he returned to the UK. It was important that neither he nor Milner-Barry do anything rash at this stage. Welchman was keen on selling a paper model of an Enigma machine with the book but Calvocoressi thought it would be too difficult to produce. They were both keen, however, to include a picture of an actual message, pictures of Welchman's original traffic analysis sheets, the 'female' sheets, the alphabet squares for the Herivel Tip and the teletype registers. Welchman was pleased that a non-technical person like Calvocoressi, albeit a very intelligent former solicitor, journalist and academic, was so quick at picking up the technical details. Much to his surprise, that even included his great invention, the diagonal board. This gave him some confidence that his story would be both understandable and intriguing to a wide audience.

Calvocoressi suggested that Welchman contact their old BP colleague Joe Hooper to press the case for access to wartime material which both Calvocoressi and Milner-Barry had previously sought. Hooper now served as Intelligence Co-ordinator in the Cabinet Office, where he acted as a general overseer of the UK intelligence community. Following a meeting with him in early April 1975, Calvocoressi wrote to Hooper, summarizing what he sought as follows:

> Finally, remember that Gordon, Stuart and I are all in our sixties –
> two of us close to seventy. There are people whom we would wish to
> talk to, and they are no younger. Some may be ailing, One or two are

already dead. Postponement in this case is nearly tantamount to killing the whole project.

I would therefore urge that what we seek to do be not prohibited by the authorities but blessed – in, dare I say it, the national interest. Clearly there must be limitations but we do seek facilities for embarking now on the planning and writing. And please do not be misled by the word 'now'. I believe it would take us about two years to write the book from the moment when we can disentangle ourselves from other commitments. The publishing processes take another year. So what we are talking about is publication about the beginning of 1979.

In their meeting Hooper had told Calvocoressi that in 1974, 2,000 volumes of Air Intelligence files had been deposited in the Public Records Office (PRO).[7] He had also said that virtually all Ultra material sent to the Air Ministry was included in the files sent to the PRO.

One late evening in March 1975, Welchman found himself alone at home, looking after his stepsons while his wife Teeny was away. With both his MITRE work and the book on his mind, he had become very quiet at home, often retreating for long periods to work on the book and letters. He was first and foremost an academic and sometimes everything else became secondary. It was also having an effect on his marriage. As was his habit, he wrote a note to himself:

> As I sit down to write, on this Palm Sunday, March 23rd, 1975, at 10.45 pm, I have a feeling that this book, if it ever gets published, has a good chance of being an unusual one. My wife, who as yet knows little about my wartime activities, is away at a friend's wedding. It is odd that she has German nationality, although her mother was English, in fact my second cousin. I am temporarily in charge of her two sons, who, I hope, are now fast asleep, in spite of the fact that I am listening to music. I had intended to go to bed early, with the idea of doing some writing tomorrow, but the urge is on me tonight.
>
> I have several motivations for writing. First of all the big opportunity that I had at Bletchley in the early days of the war resulted in the greatest 'fun' that I have ever experienced. The Hut 6 organization that I developed had a reputation of being the happiest group in Bletchley, the envy of all other groups, but I really believe that no one in Hut 6 had as much 'fun' as I did. It is perhaps rather ironical that many people, like myself, look back on World War II as the most

exciting and rewarding period of their life. I certainly do, and at odd times during my busy and varied post-war life I have longed to share my wartime 'fun' at least with my family and friends.

During the war I had the great satisfaction, denied to so many, of doing a really worthwhile job for my country. It had the disadvantage, however, of being a highly secret job. I bore the heavy burden, familiar to people who worked in 'intelligence', of trying, in my ordinary life, to distinguish between what I knew about the war from Ultra, and what I had learned from newspapers and radio broadcasts. After the war, to be on the safe side, I did not think or talk or read about the war in Europe and Africa for almost 26 years, in fact until my retirement from the MITRE Corporation.

When I joined MITRE in 1962, after a varied experience, I soon found myself involved once again with military problems, but in non-European theatres. At that time it was felt that any war in continental Europe would go nuclear at once. However, I did find that my Bletchley experience had a valuable contribution to make in planning for operations in other theatres.

Not until my retirement from MITRE, at 65, was I asked to pay serious attention to the problems of the continental European theatre, and to the lessons that could be drawn from the experience of World War II. As I studied the NATO/Warsaw Pact confrontation, it became more and more obvious that the true story of what happened at Bletchley would be of immense value, not only to the military planning of the NATO alliance, but also to the general public in each NATO country.

Another facet of the Bletchley story that has been in my mind all these years is the fact that we drafted a lot of young men into the game. Many of them pleaded to be allowed to take an active part in the war, for instance as RAF pilots. But their knowledge of what was happening at Bletchley made this impossible. I have been haunted by one particular young man who was recruited for Bletchley because of his ability, and was doing a magnificent job. He received a vile letter from his former headmaster, implying that he was a disgrace to his school!

In my work for MITRE, both as an employee from 1962 to 1971, and as a consultant, I have become more and more aware both of the major problems that face NATO in the area of battlefield communication, and also of the value to forward planning by the lessons that are implied by the Hut 6 story.

In early April, Welchman received a letter from Robin Denniston of Thomson Publications. Formerly at Weidenfeld and Nicolson, Denniston had been responsible for publishing *The Ultra Secret* and Winterbotham had shown him Welchman's letter. Denniston's father Alastair had been the Head of GC&CS, from its inception in 1919 until 1942.[8] Denniston junior was keen to meet to discuss the possibilities of his acquiring publishing rights for Welchman's book about Hut 6. He went so far as to say that he would 'bring a contract with me so that, all being well, we can proceed to practicalities'. While Welchman, following Calvocoressi's advice, had no intention of tying himself up with a publisher at this stage, he was keen to meet Denniston and hear what he had to say about BP.

Welchman was confident that he could, if necessary, tell his part of the story without access to records and what he might not be able to remember about what he regarded as the brilliantly conceived German signals organization, he could get from unclassified sources. He told Calvocoressi in a letter that:

> In my part of the story I intend to bring out very clearly that our success in Hut 6 was by no means a purely cryptographic success. It depended on developing a key understanding of the purposes of the German command communications system, its methods of operation, and its weaknesses. Without this, our cryptographic methodology would have accomplished very little.

He also had a further incentive to tell the story of Hut 6, not shared by Calvocoressi, Milner-Barry or most of his other BP colleagues. After the war, he had taken part in the early development of digital computers, and been involved in several other technological fields. After joining MITRE in 1962, the principal focus of his work had been the proper application of new technology to communications for command and control on a future battlefield. However, a study of information-handling requirements on a battlefield called for a pretty broad understanding of military problems. This he had been trying to provide in a form suitable for participants in military communication studies. After his retirement in 1972, he had been asked to continue to work for MITRE as a consultant. Research on military history and military thinking had already become a major hobby and he soon found himself developing and presenting background information needed for studies related to the Warsaw Pact/NATO confrontation in Europe. This had brought him right back, after thirty-five years, to the unique characteristics of the German military communications of the Second World War. Part of his current work was for a new educational activity called 'The MITRE Institute', which was beginning to offer courses in systems engineering in the field of communications. An underlying purpose of these courses was to bring out all the important considerations that should be taken into account in the design of a battlefield communication system for use by future NATO commanders in Western Europe. He and his MITRE colleagues had been using military history as a guide. They had found plenty of historical evidence that the early German success in the Second World War owed a great deal to the design and implementation of battlefield communication capabilities that were well suited to, and as revolutionary as, the strategy of Blitzkrieg. It now seemed to be highly probable that the association of new technology with the best features of the German communications of the Second World War would lead to another revolution in communication capabilities that would be ideal for NATO. Consequently Welchman now believed that an open discussion of the insight into German communications philosophy that had been acquired during the Second World War could be of real value in advanced planning for NATO. Furthermore, after the Winterbotham publication, it was hard to see why highly relevant historical information on the subject of German battlefield communications in the Second World War should not be developed and made available to planners.

From late May 1975 there was a lull in his MITRE commitments which would allow him to work on the book over the next two to three months. By the beginning of June, the first three chapters – 'The Cottage and Schoolhouse, Summer 1939'; 'Birth of Hut 6'; and 'The Early Days of Hut 6' – were completed in draft form. Several weeks later, he had a draft of two more chapters covering the golden days of the machine room and the proliferation of Enigma keys. His final three chapters would cover related activities, working for Travis and life at Bletchley Park. He also proposed to produce four technical appendices covering the Jeffreys apparatus, the Turing bombe, the spider bombe and manual methods. At this stage, Calvocoressi advised against telling both the Hut 6 story and the moral for today in one book. He felt that they were two very different things and likely to appeal to different audiences. He had also been given a copy of Anthony Cave Brown's *A Bodyguard of Lies* which he thought Welchman should see.

Welchman had now met Robin Denniston and had a three-hour chat. He believed that Denniston had good reason to feel that his father was badly treated: 'It was utterly disgusting – far, far worse than the way I was treated, which was bad enough.'

By the end of July, he was pressing Calvocoressi on whether he was seriously interested in writing a Hut 3/Hut 6 book in collaboration with Milner-Barry. By early August, Calvocoressi admitted that he was not making any progress. He was still interested in writing the sort of book that they had talked about but had got nowhere in his attempts to get hold of material which he regarded as essential. He felt that he had a dual interest as friend and prospective publisher and, in the latter context, warned Welchman off doing business with Denniston. As a publisher, he now wanted to publish the book throughout the world in both hardcover and paperback. He did, however, advise Welchman that Penguin might not be the best publisher for him in the USA.

In the end, Calvocoressi informed Welchman on 6 August 1975 that:

> It becomes clearer and clearer as you forge ahead that you are out-distancing anything that Stuart or myself can do, and this really means that the separate publication of your book is more likely than a joint publication with us.

On 10 August Welchman sent Calvocoressi an unedited preliminary draft of *The Hut Six Story* along with notes for revision and further thoughts about the book. By November, Milner-Barry had also ruled himself out until after his planned retirement in 1977. He had joined the Treasury in 1945 and, apart from a stint in the Ministry of Health in 1958–60, he remained there until 1966, when he had reached the normal retirement age for the civil service. He had been persuaded to carry on as a ceremonial officer administering the honours system and he was planning to continue with this work until 1977. Therefore, as a working civil servant he was too busy to write a history of Hut 6 after he took over from Welchman. He of course would also have been seriously compromised in being involved in a venture which was likely to be frowned upon by senior government officials. So, on 20 November, he wrote to Welchman saying that:

> It seems to me perfectly clear that for the reasons given above, there is really no contribution that I can offer until circumstances change. That being so, I can only withdraw to the side-lines for the present, while taking the keenest interest in the further developments and wishing you and Peter the best of all possible luck.

Right: GW as a young boy in Bristol.

Below right: GW while a student at Marlborough College.

GW's father William Welchman,
Archdeacon of Bristol.

GW's brother Eric, one of the first British
officers to be killed in WWI.

GW playing hockey for Cambridge
Wanderers around 1930.

GW led a Cambridge University expeditio
to Spitzbergen, Norway, in 1932.

GW with his father and sister Enid at his mother's funeral in 1938.

GW's marriage to his first wife, Katharine Hodgson, in 1937. They had three children.

Bletchley Park, home to the Leon family from 1882 to 1937.

Alastair Denniston, first Operational Director of GC&CS. He made several trips to the USA during the war. GW felt he never received the credit he was due.

Edward Travis, who took over from Denniston in early 1942. GW admired his organizational skills. The photo was taken in Pat Bayly's New York apartment in 1944

The standard three-wheel Enigma machine, as used by the German Army and Air Force.

Above: Dispatch riders who delivered Enigma messages to BP from the intercept stations.

Above left: Inside the Enigma machine. It is believed that only the German Navy used letters A–Z on the wheels rather than numbers 1–26. Note the reflector on the left marked as 'B'. Reflectors with other wirings were available.

Left: General Heinz Guderian in his command vehicle in 1940 during the battle for France. Note his Enigma machine and three operators.

Right: A rare wartime photo of the original wooden Hut 6 taken from the Mansion. Note the bomb blast walls around the huts

Above: Hut 6 Machine Room in Block D.

Above right: Hut 6 Control Room in Block D. It provided the interface between Hut 6 and the intercept stations.

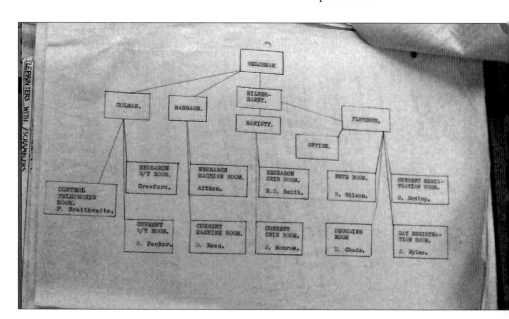

Hut 6 structure chart, *circa* 1942.

Boxes holding some of the 2 million Hollerith punch cards processed weekly in Block C.

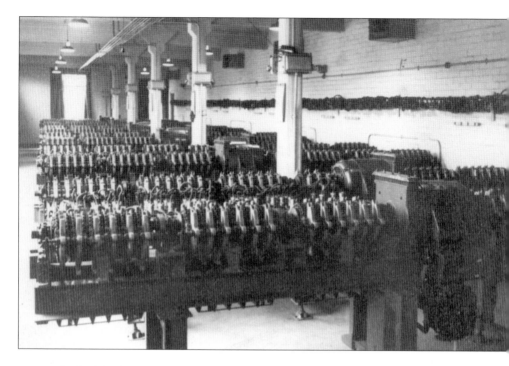

'Cobra' high speed four-wheel bombe attachments later described by GW as 'the monstrosity designed by Flowers'.

Bombes under construction at BTM's Letchworth factory.

The British Typex cipher machine, modified to replicate an Enigma machine. They were produced in large numbers for Hut 6's Decoding Room.

Rare photograph of a prototype of the RM-26, designed by Welchman as a replacement for the Typex.

One of 59 operational four-wheel bombes built by BTM.

Leaders of Allied signal intelligence work meet at the secret J.A.C. Conference on 13 March 1944 at Arlington Hall, Virginia, headquarters of the US Army's Signal Intelligence Service (SIS) during the Second World War. Notable attendees include John Tiltman (1), Edward Travis (2), William Friedman (3), Pat Bayly (4), Philip Lewis (5), Solomon Kullback (6), Joe Hooper (7), Joseph Wenger (8), Abe Sinkov (9) and Tony Kendrick (10).

ove: GW while manager of Ferranti's
w York subsidiary, Ferranti Electric Inc.
ca 1957.

ght: GW with his second wife, Fannie
llsmith, a prominent New York artist, in
69.

GW with his third wife Teeny and her son
Tom in 1972.

GW while visiting his daughter Ros in Paris
in 1972.

Bletchley Park in the early 1970s.

Diana Lucy, a former intercept operator at Chicksands revisits the room in Welchman's former Newburyport house where she first learned of his wartime exploits, and he of her

GW with MITRE colleagues Bobbie Statkus and Bob Coltman following publication of *The Hut Six Story.*

GW with former BP colleague William Bundy at the 1982 convention of the American Cryptogram Association.

GW on holiday in the Virgin Islands at the end of March 1985. He learned of his terminal illness shortly after returning home.

GW's son Nick at lunch with the author in September 2011 and delighted to find a 'bomba' on the dessert menu.

Welchman was very disappointed as Milner-Barry was a highly valued friend, but had not produced anything since they had first started talking about a book. As Calvocoressi had observed: 'He is not nowadays a fast mover, I suspect.' Welchman was also concerned by Milner-Barry's suggestion that he tell GCHQ about the book. He did not want to antagonize the intelligence community and felt that what should be presented to them was a complete version of the book, not a preliminary draft. Calvocoressi was confident that Milner-Barry would not do anything which was against their wishes.

By now, Welchman had received from Penguin in New York a copy of *A Bodyguard of Lies*. He felt that it contributed to the story of codebreaking more generally than books such as David Kahn's *The Codebreakers*. However, he felt that both books were too long and in many places, unreliable. What was needed was a more concise book that would tie up and authenticate the whole story of the cryptological struggle that lay behind the Second World War. By December, Calvocoressi had been to New York on business and shown some of Welchman's manuscript to a senior Viking editor. Penguin had recently bought Viking, a distinguished New York publisher, and Calvocoressi wanted to acquire both paperback and hardcover rights in all markets.

At the end of January 1976, Calvocoressi attended a discussion dinner at the Savile Club in London. Around eighty people were present and the guest speaker was Colonel Tadeusz Lisicki. Lisicki had been in charge of a Polish unit based in Britain in 1942–45 which was working for BP. Two of the three young Polish mathematicians who had initially unlocked the secrets of the Enigma machine in Poland in the 1930s, Marian Rejewski and Henryk Zygalski, joined his unit in 1943. The third, Jerzy Różycki, had gone down with his ship while crossing the Mediterranean from Algeria to France in 1942. The unit had its own 'Y' Service section, cryptanalysts and radio links with Poland, France and many other countries. It also had a direct teleprinter link to BP. In his presentation, Lisicki described the Polish bomba as being similar to the BP Robinson and Colossus machines, in that all were computers with memory, capable of making rapid calculations. He also claimed that the Poles had solved all of the main problems by 1938/39. The discussions at the 1976 dinner threw up some odd views which prompted Calvocoressi to write again to Hooper, urging him once more to permit a well-informed and responsible account of what did happen. In his letter of 2 February 1976 to Hooper, who had not even acknowledged his previous letter, Calvocoressi argued that there is a:

sinister interpretation of history and it can be rectified only by a convincingly truthful and authoritative account of what really happened – in other words by a book, such as I have argued for before, written by an independent writer (not an official historian) with access to the right materials.

Calvocoressi had decided to seek an opinion about Welchman's manuscript at Penguin. Jim Cochrane was the editor-in-chief and had considerable experience and acumen. He was bound to come to the book from a completely different perspective than Calvocoressi and, while he had read the Winterbotham book, he knew nothing else whatever about the story that Welchman wanted to tell. He had been told not to pull any punches and that his comments would be fed directly back to Welchman, not something that a publisher would normally do. Cochrane's view was that they had a marvellous story on their hands and that Welchman was clearly the right person to tell it. He felt that the book was a potential winner but not in its current form. He believed that a professional collaborator was needed who could ask the right questions and pace the narrative, introducing the right amount of anecdote and personality and handling the problems of technical explanation. If the collaborator were a 'name' they might just have a best-seller. The name Cochrane had in mind was the author Len Deighton. Welchman welcomed Cochrane's comments, although he believed that he had most of them in hand. He was working on a redraft and wanted to postpone discussion about a 'big name' collaborator until Cochrane had read that.

Progress on the book had been quite slow during the last five months of 1975. Welchman's wife Teeny had been very busy at work and they had entertained a succession of visitors from Europe. He was also trying to re-establish his consultancy role at MITRE. By February 1976 the situation at home had improved, with Teeny in a less exacting job, no visitors and Welchman fairly well settled in a new consulting job for MITRE.

He had two major changes in mind. The first was a new chapter tentatively called 'The Enigma Story in its Historical Perspective'. A major part of this would be based on his analysis of three books, Kahn's *The Codebreakers*, Cave Brown's *Bodyguard of Lies* and William Stevenson's *A Man Called Intrepid*. The last book had particularly intrigued him because, as Assistant Director for Mechanization at BP, he had come into contact with Bill Stephenson's New York based operation. He hoped to produce a concise but provocative discussion of the importance of Huts 8, 6 and 3, in the general conduct of the Second World War. His second change would involve drawing on his many years of working on computers, communications, military command capabilities and military science in general to project his broad discussion of the Second World War events into the present and future. He seemed to have forgotten that this was exactly what Calvocoressi had advised against, the previous May!

Cochrane visited Welchman in Newburyport in late April 1976 and they got on well. By the following month, Welchman had produced a number of diagrams that he felt were needed to explain the theory of the bombe and in particular the diagonal board, cribs and menus. He tried the diagrams out on colleagues at MITRE and they seemed to find them fascinating and understandable.

During the first half of June, Welchman was completing a paper for MITRE titled 'Military Value of Communications Capabilities'. An earlier paper, 'Survival of the Simplest – Ability to Adapt', had been issued in April. He felt that the success of these two papers was of indirect importance to the book because it would help him get more consulting work and MITRE staff support for work on the book. From recent discussions at MITRE, it seemed likely that he would be given new consulting work by October if not sooner.

On 29 June, Welchman received a letter from Calvocoressi with the surprising news that he was leaving Penguin immediately. He also enclosed a recent exchange of letters with Hooper. Several years earlier, Welchman had spoken to Hooper about the future release of classified material and the discussion had been friendly and positive. His recent response to Calvocoressi was impersonal and formal, however:

> You will recall that when we met in April last year and discussed the official position about access to records, I confirmed that an Official History was being compiled by a team of historians, parts 1 and 2 of which are being edited by Harry Hinsley.
>
> The supporting records, except those of the Service Departments which have already been deposited in the Public Records Office, are at present being used by the historians in their research. There is still quite a long way to go and I cannot say how much longer it will take to meet the requirements of the historians up to completion of the Official work. Nor can I be sure that further records may then become publicly available.
>
> Therefore I must say that unless you are able to find the material

you require among that which has already been deposited in the Public Records Office, we are not in a position to help you further.

In effect, Hooper was saying that as long as official historians were at work, only general material already deposited in the Public Records Office was available to others. In disgust, Calvocoressi wrote a letter to the *Sunday Times* on 28 June 1976 which was duly published. He concluded it with words born out of both frustration and passion:

> My plea is not to throw secrecy to the winds. There was a case for continuing secrecy for many years after the war. But what had to be kept secret was the single simple fact that we could crack Enigma cyphers. That fact was published to the world by Group Captain Winterbotham, since when secrecy has done no more than ensure that history is being written wrong and that British Intelligence continues to be regarded as a tale of muddle and treason (Philby etc.) instead of as an unparalleled and most exciting success.

Calvocoressi wrote again to Hooper and also to the Prime Minister! In his reply, dated 8 July 1976 Hooper gave one more interesting and official perspective on the whole issue of the release of material:

> You will, I am sure, appreciate that it would be impossible for the Government to allow selective private access to the WW II intelligence records. There would be uproar if some were allowed it and others not. You, and all other interested private writers of the history of intelligence and its use in the war, must be on equal footing, and this means waiting until the relevant records can be put in the PRO. I am hopeful that this will now not be too long.

So Welchman, Calvocoressi and Milner-Barry would have to wait in line along with any writers, whatever their credibility as historical authors, to tell the insider's story of Bletchley Park.

With Calvocoressi's departure from Penguin, Welchman would now be dealing with Cochrane on the publishing side, which he was happy with, and he had also decided to take Calvocoressi's advice and work through an agent. He was keen to speak to someone suitable as soon as possible because he had been approached by the BBC to take part in a programme which was to be part of a series called *The Secret War*.[9] The New York agent that Calvocoressi had in mind was John Cushman and, as he was holidaying in the UK, Cochrane said he would speak to him about the book.

He would be returning to New York on 16 August and Cochrane suggested that Welchman contact him directly. Cochrane also advised him to complete his revised draft before approaching Cushman. Welchman had this in hand and the manuscript was being typed on a new word processor system at MITRE, making future revisions much easier. He hoped to let Cushman have a complete version by mid-September.

He had also been approached by an American, Ernest Bell, who with his son, was writing a book about BP and was involved in a legal battle with the NSA over the release of documents. Bell had also spoken to Admiral Farnhill, Secretary of the D-Notice Committee, and he seemed to have obtained a surprising amount of detail about naval Ultra. The BBC letter and the approach from Bell filled Welchman with a sense of urgency. He had to make progress on the book as quickly as possible.

By early September 1976, he had engaged John Cushman Associates to represent him and Cushman himself would be handling all dealings with publishers. Welchman planned to hand over a completed draft to Cushman in New York by 5 October. It was being typed by MITRE staff who were sworn to secrecy, He also had the services of MITRE's writer/editor Bob Coltman to help him prepare the manuscript. In late September, MITRE had given Welchman a new consultancy contract for forty-five hours' writing per month from October to January. The writing would relate to one of the principal themes of the book. He warned Cushman that they still needed approval from the proper authorities and that some parts of the book might come under fire. He had been careful to omit information which he thought GCHQ and the NSA might feel was too sensitive. Following their meeting in New York, Cushman had read the manuscript carefully by the end of November. His view was that the manuscript was not in a form that was saleable to a general publisher. He summarized his by saying:

> The principal point, then, is to make the book more chronological, more colourful (using illustrative anecdotes) and less technical. The emphasis should be on people; their efforts, problems, and achieve-ments as well as their characters. Then the true worth of Bletchley Park and Hut 6 can be seen through the eyes of one of the chief architects

Welchman responded by saying that he and Coltman believed that the faults in structure could be fixed and he hoped to have a detailed plan for restructuring and completion of a draft within two weeks. Cushman suggested that Welchman send him the restructuring plan first before redrafting the manuscript. Welchman had agreed to be interviewed for the BBC's *Secret War* series and its producer, Fisher Dilke, arrived to do this on 22 December 1976. Dilke was very frank with Welchman, who was a bit irritated to hear that GCHQ had warned Dilke to 'be careful with Welchman, who is a slippery customer'. However, he refrained from commenting on this in his answers to Dilke's questions. Dilke gave Welchman the impression that GCHQ had given the BBC approval to discuss matters previously considered off-limits. On the day before the interview, Dilke tried for hours to get him to talk about how the sheet stacking method worked but Welchman just kept on reading him extracts from Goodall's letter from 1974 (discussed above in the Prologue and in Chapter 10). He absolutely refused to go beyond the boundaries implied by that letter until he had received specific clearance from GCHQ. In the end, he persuaded Dilke to let him talk about things that would be of general interest but not offensive to GCHQ.

Both Calvocoressi and Milner-Barry had also been filmed at Bletchley Park and the programme was transmitted at 9.25 p.m. on 9 February 1977. According to Milner-Barry, the whole programme had been done by the BBC in close consultation with Admiral Farnhill of the D-Notice Committee and through him with GCHQ. His view was that anything that appeared would have, if not GCHQ's approval, at least its passive acquiescence. In any event, much to his annoyance, Milner-Barry was not used in the programme. Calvocoressi gave an excellent explanation of how a short and quite innocuous decrypted message was used together with information on Hut 3's card index, to produce useful intelligence. Of the three it was Welchman who featured most prominently in the programme.

Harold Fletcher had watched it with great interest and although he had retired from GCHQ in 1971, he was still in touch with the sole Hut 6 survivor in GCHQ, Malcolm Chamberlain, who provided GCHQ's view. According to Fletcher:

> They were rather peeved with the BBC, who, after the preliminary consultation, apparently implied to at least some of the interviewees that GCHQ had widened the door a little more than they had. I don't know what they said to you, but GCHQ was particularly worried by the interview with Max Newman, and tried to put the matter right by a little pruning. So it appears you could say that GCHQ was by

no means outraged but not altogether happy with at least one part
of the programme

The following year the BBC published a book titled *The Secret War* by
Brian Johnson based on the series.

On 11 January 1977, Welchman had received a letter from Ronald
Lewin, an old friend of Winterbotham's.[10] Lewin was a military historian
and had written books on Rommel and Montgomery, Churchill's war
administration and Field Marshal Slim. He was engaged in writing a
general survey of Ultra, covering its pre-history, the whole system of
processing and distributing intelligence that spread outwards from
Bletchley and, in particular, the impact of Ultra intelligence on operations
in the field. He claimed to have clearance from the Secretary of State for
Defence, subject to submitting his final text to the authorities for approval.
Welchman sent a copy to Cushman, who knew of the book as Lewin's
London agent was an affiliate of his. While he had never met Lewin, he
assured Welchman that his book was completely different from the one
that Lewin was writing. Welchman had nearly completed the restructuring
suggested by Cushman and he was in good spirits as his contract with
MITRE for work on NATO's new battlefield communications system had
been extended to 30 September. He had not been impressed with Lewin's
initial approach in which he had used Winterbotham's name but, after
speaking with him, his attitude had changed. Lewin seemed first-rate and
potentially a valuable ally. Lewin visited Welchman in Newburyport on 22
February and they had very profitable discussions. Lewin showed
Welchman an advance copy of Patrick Beesly's book *Very Special
Intelligence* on how naval Ultra intelligence was used, but they agreed that
it covered up disastrous mistakes made by the British Admiralty which
should be publicized as a warning for the future.

By 18 March Welchman had sent Cushman another draft and was busy
making further refinements. He agreed to meet Cushman in his New York
office on 27 April and drop off the new material a day earlier. Parts Two
and Three were now called The First Year and The Rest of the War, names
that would be retained in the final draft of the book.

Lewin sent Welchman notes from his interview with Milner-Barry on
14 April. Milner-Barry had said that there had been great frustration in
Hut 6 about the inability to obtain sufficient staff and equipment and that
Welchman had written the letter to Churchill, on the basis that it was no
good addressing it to anyone else. Milner-Barry and his counterpart in

Hut 8, Hugh Alexander, signed it along with Turing. While yielding results, it had also produced a not inconsiderable rocket from Alastair Denniston and Stewart Menzies of MI 6. However, Milner-Barry had got the impression that they were in fact rather amused and rather pleased in spite of the by-passing of the chain of command. In his interview with Lewin, Milner-Barry expressed the view that, by the winter of 1940, Denniston was a 'busted flush' and incapable of the organizational effort that was necessary if BP was to be put on a war footing. This was certainly not Welchman's belief. In his reply to Lewin's letter, dated 7 May 1977, Welchman took great exception to these comments. He had checked with a former secretary in GC&CS management before and during the war who had confirmed that Denniston's departure from BP was due to a serious illness. He then went on to say, quite surprisingly, given the sharpness of his memory, that: 'Oddly enough I have no recollection at all of having written a letter to Churchill.'

In early June, Welchman had a phone call from Fisher Dilke of the BBC. *The Secret War* series had been sold to IBM who intended to sponsor it on major American TV networks. Dilke believed that it would now be much easier to get permission to write a book as a result of the reactions to the series. Meanwhile, Welchman and his MITRE colleague Bob Coltman were trying to create clearer mental pictures of some of the technical details of Welchman's story such as the Jeffreys apparatus, the 'brush' sensing of standard punched card equipment and the use of this equipment in Harold Keen's bombe. The mention of the term 'female' in connection with the Jeffreys sheets reminded Welchman that he had not yet mentioned any of the real females who worked in Hut 6, particularly the early recruits in the Registration Room. He remarked to Cushman that it was 'sad that I was far too busy to take advantage of the society of so many attractive and intelligent young women'.

Welchman decided to send the latest draft of the book to Cochrane at Penguin and, by September, Cochrane had informed Cushman that he wanted the book and had made an offer for the hardcover (Allen Lane) and paperback (Penguin) rights. This coincided with some other good news – MITRE had offered him a contract for another year. He also started to be concerned about his tax position if the book was a financial success. According to US tax law, any income earned before he reached his seventy-second birthday in June 1978 would be heavily taxed.

In November 1977, Welchman was having heart problems and he had to go into hospital. He required a pacemaker but by December was back hard at work on all fronts. Unfortunately, Viking had declined to make an offer for a hardcover version of the book for the American market. However, Cushman had already sent it to McGraw-Hill. Bruce Lee, an editor in their General Books division, was enthusiastic about it.

In March 1978 Welchman was contacted by Andrew Hodges, a British mathematician, who had been commissioned by the publishers André Deutsch in London and Harper and Row in New York to write a biography of Alan Turing. He had been told about the bombe and the diagonal board in confidence by someone who had worked at BP during the war and had some idea of the individual contributions of Welchman and Turing. However, he didn't want to write anything without checking its accuracy with Welchman. As the first volume of Hinsley's Official History was known to be in preparation (and was to be published in November 1979), Hodges did not think he would be too constrained by official secrecy. He was not to know that the Official History would be almost devoid of technical detail. Hodges subsequently visited Newburyport in early October 1978 and was greeted warmly by Welchman, whom he later described as being very charming. Hodges was surprised by Welchman's vitality and by his young family. As he said in a follow-up letter to Welchman after the visit: 'I had a sense of time-warp in your house, it was hard to believe I was with someone who was Turing's senior.'

At the end of 1978 Welchman at last was offered a contract by an American publisher, McGraw-Hill, which he decided to accept. Lee encouraged him to develop his last part on lessons for today. He also assigned a young writer, Neill Rosenfeld, to work with him on the manuscript. While this wasn't quite what Cochrane from Penguin had had in mind in 1976, it did offer Welchman a general reader's perspective, because Rosenfeld was not a technical expert. It also allowed a professional writer to help craft his narrative. After reading the manuscript, Rosenfeld submitted a number of questions to Welchman which irritated him. Rosenfeld had taken on the role of the 'dumbest reader', a standard editorial technique. There was a slight lull in the work as Rosenfeld was getting married in January 1979 and Welchman had a very bad bout of flu. They agreed to meet when Rosenfeld returned from his honeymoon in Jamaica. Welchman did produce some notes about Rosenfeld's attempt at producing a 'technical draft', covering the description of the Enigma machine and some related technologies. He believed that the draft was full of technical errors and could not be used. Rosenfeld had also described Knox's reaction when Welchman told him about his rediscovery of the Polish 'Netz' method being accompanied by a 'slightly amused smile'. This was out of character for Knox as Welchman went on to explain:

> He was furious, and most unpleasant. He didn't even have the courtesy to tell me about his plans, or about whatever progress Jeffreys had made at that point. I had said something of this in an earlier draft, but deleted it because I did not want to run Knox down. However, in view of what has been written about him fairly recently, I think I can reveal that, on this occasion, he behaved badly.

As with Denniston, Welchman would not let a particular episode with a colleague distort his overall view of them. He would spend the rest of his life giving due credit to both Denniston and Knox for their magnificent achievements. However, as a result of books such as Penelope Fitzgerald's *The Knox Brothers*, published in 1977, he felt that he could now give an account of his dealings with Knox.

McGraw-Hill had drawn up a list of questions to put to 'Bletchley alumni'. In the main, Welchman wanted to avoid compromising former colleagues, so the questions were of a general nature and intended to solicit colourful anecdotes. However, he felt that it would almost be insulting to pose such questions to former colleagues whom he had worked so closely with. For example, question seven was:

> What was your office like? What were the decorations, the desk, the atmosphere? If there was a window, what was the view? Were there any smells or leaking pipes or anything annoying or endearing about the place? Were there any pets kept at BP by you or others, such as a cat that might have wandered around the work area? Did you share the office with anyone and, if so, with whom: how were your relations? Did you or your co-workers have any particular work habits – coffee drinking, doodling, pencil chewing, humming, whistling, pacing, paper clip twisting, etc?

In early January Welchman confided to Fletcher, who was not at all surprised, that he was writing a book and that hardly anyone in Britain knew about it apart from Milner-Barry and Calvocoressi. He did not want to approach former colleagues for comments on the technical parts of the book until he had approval from Admiral Farnhill and his committee. He did hope, however, that Fletcher would be able to help with non-sensitive matters and with recollections that would add colour. One particular problem he was having was remembering names and their exact spellings.

He was also having trouble remembering the sequence of events which led to the bombe which could deal with the German Navy's introduction in 1942 of a four-wheel Enigma machine. Welchman's own diaries revealed that he had a series of meetings with Frank Birch, the head of the naval section at BP, between 7 December 1942 and 5 April 1943. Birch had been grilling him about whether everything possible was being done. He also had been to Dollis Hill on 29 March 1943 to talk to Radley and Flowers, but he couldn't remember at what point Keen was brought into the picture about the four-wheel problem.

On 3 April 1979, Fletcher sent Welchman a thirty-four-page handwritten letter. It was as if Welchman had pulled out a plug and released thirty-four years of memories, some technical, some personal, which had been bottled up inside for all those years. Fletcher ended with a few personal thoughts:

> You ask if I can remember anything about you or your behaviour which made me mad. If there were, they must have been trivial, because I don't remember any. There were, however, two things which I found trying, though they are not quite what I think you are looking for. The first I have already mentioned viz your tendency to credit me with a better brain than I possessed. You were far too busy for me to protest too violently, and in any case, I must have got there in the end, despite some nasty moments. The second stems from the fact that you always had more stamina, mental and physical, than I had; there were occasions when I was just about done and itching to get home and rest, but no! there was just one more problem to discuss.
>
> If you would like to know my feelings about BP which built up over the years, it goes something like this. There is no doubt that BP made a very big, sometimes possibly even decisive, contribution to the successful prosecution of the war; and we were part of this organisation. On the basis that no one is indispensable, there must have been someone who could have done the job that you did, though there can't have been many. For me, there must have been many thousands who could have done the job I did, but the point is that they didn't do it – I did, and I know that I did it reasonably well. And I have never ceased to be thankful.

Welchman used Fletcher as a sounding board until the end of the year and, for his part, Fletcher read early drafts and made comments where appropriate about the accuracy of names and dates. As Welchman had been keen from the start to give Denniston the credit due to him, he must have been startled by one comment made by Fletcher:

> Denniston was still in post as Director when I arrived in August 1941. I had several dealings with him when doing my stint as Hut 6 Duty Officer. He left during the winter of 1941/42, but I do not remember the exact date. I have a clear recollection that you told me that Travis had told 'C' 'Either he goes or I go.'

Another former colleague, Houston Wallace, was able to shed a little light on some of Welchman's tasks as Assistant Director Mechanization. After being recruited by Fletcher, with Welchman's approval, he had served as Fletcher's assistant in Hut 6. When Welchman moved into his new job in 1943, Wallace became his assistant. He had fond memories of the house in Woburn Sands that he and his sister Hope shared with James Wardrop and his wife. Wardrop worked in Hut 8 as an Italian linguist but left BP in 1943. For the rest of the war, the Wallaces shared their house with Bob Amys and his wife. Amys was at BP throughout the war and set up Hut 8's Registration Room. They were all still good friends, over thirty years later. Unfortunately, Hope was quite ill at this point (and would die in April 1979) and Wallace did not have much time to devote to recalling wartime events. Despite this, Welchman, as tenacious as ever, kept gently prodding Wallace.

In August 1979, one other former colleague proved to have a memory almost the equal of Welchman's. In a long detailed letter, John Monroe was able to provide a remarkable amount of information about the multiplicity and handling of Enigma keys, life and work in the Hut 6 watch, and mechanical adaptations to the Enigma machine which the Germans had introduced in the last year of the war.[11] Monroe had arrived at BP around the same time as Fletcher. A qualified lawyer, he had been recruited by Milner-Barry from the Army and interviewed by Welchman and John Tiltman. He went on to serve as a head of watch and a member of the research section in Hut 6 until the end of the war.

In early February 1979 Welchman told Calvocoressi that Cushman had secured a contract for him with McGraw-Hill and that one with Penguin was on the way. His work in MITRE had also taken a direction that would make the book more interesting and help with obtaining approval from Admiral Farnhill. Twelve years earlier, he had been one of the pioneers in the development of a revolutionary concept of battlefield communications that had evolved into JTIDS. The British forces were buying this system for their Nimrod aircraft. Welchman had a good rapport with the assistant director at the Ministry of Defence who was responsible for the procurement. He also happened to be a Second World War veteran who had served in North Africa with Major General Richard O'Connor. In the spring of 1978, Welchman had shown a draft of his book to some of the key players in the JTIDS project and they had agreed that it could aid their planning for the 1980s and 1990s. He thought this would help convince Farnhill that his book should be published and that further investigations be undertaken, based on the experience of Hut 6 and Hut 3 activities.

Welchman had carefully avoided approaching former colleagues for input until he had approval but at this point he decided to ask some of them for help in non-sensitive areas. He had already written to Fletcher, Wallace, Monroe and Milner-Barry for anecdotes about individuals and life generally in and around BP. Fletcher and Monroe had provided him with much more than that. He asked Calvocoressi for suitable photographs and any other relevant information. Calvocoressi was planning his own short book, devoted to the recruitment and organization of BP as well as its practical impact on the fortunes of war. Documents were becoming available at the PRO but many eager authors were swarming around them. Calvocoressi duly published his book, *Top Secret Ultra* in 1980. Most historians regard it as a valuable addition to the literature about BP, but he avoided any mention of Welchman or other BP colleagues.

With McGraw-Hill pressing him for a new draft and MITRE work also keeping him busy, Welchman managed finally to get what he felt was close to an acceptable draft of the book ready by the end of 1979. However, it would take almost a further year and continual editorial revisions until a final draft of *The Hut Six Story* was in the hands of McGraw-Hill and Penguin.

All in all, 1980 was not a good year for Welchman. He worked up until September on two further revisions of the last part of his book dealing with military communication problems of the day and the relevance of his BP experience to them. But, at seventy-four years of age, the work was starting to tire him. In addition to his own health worries, Teeny was very ill and depressed. Eventually she was diagnosed with anaemia and a course of iron tablets helped considerably.

With a final draft of his book safely with the publisher and Teeny's son Tom off to university, the Welchmans departed for a holiday in Europe. They were temporarily free from parental duties as Tom's older brother Michael had departed for university five years earlier. They travelled to the village of Aschau in the province of Chiemgau in Germany where Teeny had been born. They rented an apartment in the old family home and enjoyed the beautiful surroundings and walked every day. Teeny's old 'housemother' from the school she went to in a nearby village was still a good friend and almost a second mother to her. She took them on several trips by car to even more beautiful walking country. After three relaxing weeks they arrived in England. They visited an aging relative of Welchman's in Chippenham and spent two days in London before returning to Newburyport.

When they arrived home it seemed that they had put all of their troubles behind them. However, the family finances were in bad shape. Welchman was already planning another trip to England, this time to take Teeny to Cornwall, but his MITRE contract would end in September and would not be renewed until the end of the year and he still had not received the advance on royalties that he had been promised by McGraw-Hill. He had finally decided to slow down. It was the MITRE work that was tiring and he was worried that his ability to do worthwhile work was bound to deteriorate. Then, in early 1981 in quick succession, a property that he had inherited from his Aunt Lilian was sold, his new MITRE contract, which ran up to September was going well, and McGraw-Hill finally came through with an advance and assigned an editor to his book.

He now hoped that he could bow out of MITRE at the end of his current contract and live off the royalties from his book. Perhaps the large sums mentioned to him by Winterbotham in 1975 were at the back of his mind. So he started to plan his next trip to England with Teeny from 27 April. They would visit London, Wallace Houston in Brighton, an elderly relative in Chippenham and then relax at a hotel in Watergate Bay near Newquay. Teeny had to be back in Newburyport on 26 May, but Welchman hoped to stay on to visit his old college in Cambridge, an old friend at Quex Park and perhaps other relatives.

In late November 1981, Cushman was able to inform Welchman that the bound book date for the American edition was 1 February 1982 at the latest. Penguin also proposed to print 2,000 copies at the same time as McGraw-Hill. Welchman's UK agent, John McLaughlin, was also happy with the final proof of the book and was holding off offering serial rights until copies of the American edition had been sent to key people in the UK. Welchman was keen to send copies to William Bundy, his former BP colleague and now a distinguished figure in American politics, and to the eminent historian David Kahn. Other people on his list to receive advance autographed copies included Harold Fletcher, John Monroe, Jack Good,

Ronald Lewin, Peter Calvocoressi, Harry Hinsley, Brian Johnson, Jean Stengers, Stuart Milner-Barry and Brian Randell. All of these had provided input to the book in one form or another.

While working on his book, Welchman had been delighted to renew his wartime friendship with William Bundy who had commanded the small American detachment at BP for the last twenty-one months of the war. As Bundy had gone on to become a very significant figure in American political life as foreign affairs advisor to two presidents, Welchman was worried about compromising him in any way. He therefore decided not to name him personally in *The Hut Six Story*. Despite his hugely successful career after the war, Bundy, according to his daughter Carol, had always regarded his work at BP as the greatest achievement of his career. By the early 1980s, his wife had had to put up with his passion for the recent flood of books on what had been done by intelligence agencies during the war, on both sides of the Atlantic. He was finally able to document this passion in a fascinating paper which he presented to the Annual Meeting of the Friends of Princeton Library on 1 November 1981.[12]

The Hut Six Story went on public sale in the USA during the second week in February 1982. As the book was of interest to a wide audience, it was reviewed in the US by journals dealing with computing, cryptography, military history and planning as well as both national and local newspapers. The *Annals of the History of Computing* published a favourable review in their October issue[13] even though they had found that several people would not review the book, fearing 'their Bletchley sources might dry up'. In *Cryptologia*'s April issue Louis Kruh had given the book a favourable review and much to Welchman's delight said, 'Both parts of Welchman's book are fascinating but it is not inconceivable that the second part with its disturbing implication for the future may have a longer lasting effect.'[14] A less than favourable review of both Welchman's book and Hinsley's first two volumes of *British Intelligence in the Second World War* was written for the US Strategic Institute in Washington in the autumn of 1982 but a more favourable review appeared in a US Army newspaper in February 1983. There was also a very favourable review by R. T. Crowley for the *Smithsonian* in May 1982 and in William Bundy's publication *Foreign Affairs, An American Quarterly Review*. The book was very well received by the local Newburyport paper and an autograph party was held at a local bookshop on 17 April 1982.

In his review, Kruh had found it strange that Welchman had either ignored or found untrustworthy, Josef Garlinski's *The Enigma War*, even though Welchman listed it in his bibliography. Welchman had known nothing about the pre-war work of Rejewski and his associates until Jean Stengers sent him his article 'La Guerre des Messages Codes', which was published in *L'Histoire*.[15] Welchman had received it in the summer of 1981 just as the text of his book was being frozen, but he had tried to slip something in about it. Then McGraw-Hill decided to shut down their General Books division and sack his editor Bruce Lee at short notice. The final text had to be settled in a few days, when he had just become aware of the Garlinski book, but had not read it. He realized that it was important, and included it in his bibliography, but did not have time to say anything about it in the text. After the book was published, Lisicki had written to him in August, and they had a brief exchange of letters. By that time he had also seen the Rejewski papers. Already thinking about post-publication projects, Welchman suggested to David Kahn that he write a paper for the January 1982 edition of *Cryptologia* called 'From Polish Bomba to British Bombe'. Kahn was delighted with the suggestion as that issue was going to be dedicated to the Enigma machine. At last Welchman felt that he could tell the true story of what happened in the *Cryptologia* paper. Unfortunately, he would be prevented from doing so.

The book was published by Allen Lane in the UK in the middle of May 1982 and received favourable reviews from Ronald Lewin in *The Times* and Edward Crankshaw in the *Observer*. In his eloquent and insightful review, published on 11 November, Lewin said:

> A reasonably informed reader will be able to follow, at one level of the narration, how speculative intuition and an organized logical attack battened on German procedural errors to achieve a breakthrough. The instructed cryptanalyst, at home amid abstractions which baffle me, is fed by Welchman with tables, diagrams and pointilliste arrays of figures which he will doubtless absorb with the ease of an accountant conning a balance sheet. But in sum, as the elder Mill said after first skimming *Das Kapital* overnight, 'I see what the man is at.'
>
> The first winter of the war was evidently Welchman's 'prime time', and he conveys the sense of urgency, supreme concentration and ultimate success with a passionate brio. When the Blitzkrieg of May 1940 opened, the Germans radically altered their Enigma arrangements. It is clear, now, that unless the most original of the Bletchley intelligentsia had not been working throughout that winter to the

limits of their mental capacity (as others had worked on radar) we should have staggered far behind, in this fascinating aspect of the wizard war.

Harold Fletcher, who was still in touch with top officials at GCHQ, said that while they were sorry that the book had been published, they thought it was a jolly good one. Shortly after the book was published, however, he 'had a reminder from the office to be careful with any approaches which may be made to me by the press or other media'.

Pat Bayly wrote to Welchman after he had read the book several times and made a number of interesting comments. One of his wartime roles had been to take care of purchases of a top secret nature for several groups who did not want some of their requirements to go through the British Purchasing Mission. Typical requirements were for items such as adjustable incendiary devices or quartz crystals of specified frequencies to be used in secret agents' radios on enemy soil. Welchman's book had solved one puzzle for him: 'You finally cleared up a minor mystery for me. We purchased for shipment to England scores of coloured pencils. I never knew why.' Welchman of course had introduced colours to identify different keys for the Registration Room in Hut 6 and coloured pencils were used for this purpose. When the British supply ran out, he had to appeal to America for more.

Bayly also offered some insight into Welchman's remarkable discovery of the diagonal board:

> Your description of the finding of the 'Diagonal Board' as an 'inexperienced recruit from Cambridge'. Your work on Algebraic Geometry which I am sure included modern graph theory was almost exactly the training needed for your monumental discovery, in retrospect one of the most important discoveries of the war.

So, with his book having been received well both by the cryptologic community and general readers, Welchman was looking forward to pressing on with his research at MITRE and to begin the process of drawing out, from the Hut 6 experience, valuable lessons for battlefield communications of the 1980s. Unfortunately, the official reviews from GCHQ and the NSA were not quite so enthusiastic.

Chapter 10

Persecution and Putting the Record Straight

O ver seven years had passed since Welchman first learned about Winterbotham's *The Ultra Secret* and seriously considered writing his own account of events at BP. It had been nine years since he had met with the Director of GCHQ and received assurances that within a few years he would be able to disclose all aspects of his experience, technical as well as personal. When his friends and former colleagues Stuart Milner-Barry and Peter Calvocoressi decided not to author a book jointly with him, he made the decision to go it alone.

By 1980, a number of books had been published which described aspects of the BP operation. However, they had either been written by insiders who had restricted themselves to talking about how Ultra intelligence had been used, or by historians who were dependent, in most cases, on second-hand accounts. The first volume of the authorized history of intelligence activity in the Second World War by Harry Hinsley appeared in 1979 but contained little technical detail and an inaccurate account of the Polish contribution. Several books by Polish and French authors were already in print and described in detail the workings of the Enigma machine.[1] Also revealed in these was how the Poles had gone about breaking it and technologies they had invented to assist them. A British academic, Professor Brian Randell of the University of Newcastle upon Tyne, had managed to get GCHQ to release some details of Colossus, the world's first electronic computer, which had been designed and built to assist BP's attack on the strategic communication networks used by the German high command. Randell presented his findings in 1976, but his interest was in the evolution of computing, not cryptographic applications at BP.[2] Therefore, when *The Hut Six Story* was published in 1982, it was the first book to describe accurately not only how Ultra intelligence had been produced at BP, but also some of the technologies that had been invented to help with the work.

In August 1974, Welchman's former BP colleagues Harold Fletcher and Bob Amys had arranged for him to speak to George Goodall, a senior member of GCHQ. Goodall had responded to specific points in a letter the following month and summarized GCHQ's position as follows:

> Policy with regard to the release of wartime records and the publi-cation of memoirs has been under review for some time and the Winterbotham book has been a stimulus towards this. But the official policy line has not changed yet. It is likely that there will be some relaxation, but that this will apply to the existence of our material and use made of it, not the means by which it was obtained; and I think you can take it for certain that the B.P. records themselves will not be released to the Public Records Office.
>
> Since you do not seem to be in any hurry as regards reminiscences, I hope that you will be content to wait and see what new policy emerges: I will happily undertake to inform you of this. I expect that ex-members of the 'producing' agencies will be advised to clear any plans and publications with Admiral Farnhill, the Secretary of the 'D Notice' Committee.

Regrettably, Goodall failed to honour his undertaking to keep Welchman informed about developments.

Goodall had seemed, though. to be very positive about Welchman's use of his knowledge of German battlefield communications in his consultancy work for the USAF. Welchman wrote to Goodall again on 15 October 1974, explaining more precisely what he had in mind for his proposed memoir:

> I would like to write a simple account of how a vast co-ordinated effort grew from very small beginnings. I would like to concentrate in the early days and would end at the period during which the American group under Bill Bundy joined my Hut 6 staff, the Central Party was brought fully into the picture under my management, and Milner-Barry took charge of Hut 6 on my appointment as Assistant Director for Mechanization.

Welchman understood the dilemma of former colleagues who lived in the UK and were still bound by the Official Secrets Act that they had signed when joining BP. Many, like Welchman, had conditioned themselves to avoid all conversations about their work both during and after the war. In a similar vein, visitors to BP today frequently ask why local people in Bletchley did not suspect what was going on there. This must have been a concern of Denniston, because, in 1941, he asked BP's Security Officer, James Bellinger, to look into the matter. His report did not raise major security concerns but did suggest that the task had its rewards: 'During the course of my investigation I have visited nearly every hotel, public house and club in Bletchley and the surrounding districts.'[3]

Even though Welchman corresponded extensively with former colleagues while he was writing the book, he made a point of only soliciting anecdotal material from them. He also sought assistance with people's names and when they had first arrived at BP. When a few colleagues did volunteer more technical information, he was careful not to attribute it directly to them. As an American citizen, Welchman believed that he could not be prosecuted if his book was published in the USA. Peter Hilton was a former colleague at BP who had also moved to North America and believed that if he chose to write anything, he would be protected as he lived abroad. As he wrote in 1985

> I find it inconceivable that any information I could reveal about our methods over forty years ago could be of the smallest value to a potential enemy today or in the future – but that would be no defence if I were arrested for breach of the Official Secrets Act on stepping onto British soil.[4]

Peter Twinn, one of the first to join Knox's team, had been in correspondence with a series of Directors of GCHQ for years seeking, without success, permission to write the history of the solution of the Enigma. He had been somewhat disappointed to see Welchman's book describing the breaking of the Army and Air Force Enigma traffic and Andrew Hodges's biography of Turing, describing the breaking of the naval traffic, appear in print. Twinn felt that he could have filled in considerable detail about GC&CS's relations with the Polish cryptanalysts from February to September 1939. He could also have written the whole of the Abwehr Enigma story, which was quite different from that of the German military Enigma. He asked GCHQ why Welchman and Hodges had been able to publish their accounts. The answer he received was that as Welchman was now an American citizen, they could not stop him and Hodges had never signed the Official Secrets Act and they did not know his sources. Twinn would not publish his own brief account until 1993, in the same book as Stuart Milner-Barry, Hinsley and Stripp's *The Codebreakers*.

Welchman had thought long and hard about the implications of publishing his book without the approval of GCHQ or the NSA. All advice he received from former colleagues who still had close connections with GCHQ, indicated that, even by 1982, it was unlikely to give him approval to publish. Inquiries within MITRE and elsewhere in the American intelligence community failed to come up with a way to approach the NSA which would lead to anything other than indefinite delay. Welchman revealed his thoughts while working with Neill Rosenfeld from McGraw-Hill in a private memo to himself:

> Finally, as I said, I would like if possible to avoid bad feeling with GCCS and NSA. Above all, I cannot risk trouble with MITRE. My book must in no way run against the position of MITRE with military funding. Nor must it result in MITRE being told to get rid of me. (I am too old to get established elsewhere.)

In the end he had to make the decision himself. He believed that the ideas that occurred to him at BP during the first months of the war could not possibly be regarded as classified material in the United States. He passionately believed that publishing his book was doing something that was important for the future national security of the US. The alternative was submitting his manuscript to GCHQ and an almost certain veto. It seemed quite clear that, as a US citizen, the future security of his country must come first. So, late in 1980, he decided to go ahead with publication.

Following its publication in the USA in February 1982 a copy of *The Hut Six Story* was sent to Rear Admiral Ash of the D-Notice Committee in the UK. Ash had one meeting with Welchman's British publishers, Allen Lane, at which he expressed concern, but he made no official comment. Welchman never received any formal complaint from GCHQ about his book.

Shortly after publication, Welchman received a letter from William Stevenson, author of the bestselling book *A Man Called Intrepid*. Stevenson's book about Sir William Stephenson had been a great success and even spawned a miniseries starring the well-known actor David Niven as Stephenson. Welchman had originally found the book an interesting source of information, but eventually became disenchanted with its many inaccuracies.[5] In his letter, Stevenson thanked Welchman for acknowledging Stephenson's accomplishments and expressed a concern about 'the vigorous efforts to diminish his role, especially in the field of communications'. On 23 July Welchman received a telegram from Sir William Stephenson himself offering congratulations on his book.

After arranging for autographed copies of his book to be sent to his son, two daughters and other family members, as well as the long list of people whom he had consulted during its writing, Welchman was planning to develop his ideas further at MITRE. He also had several new writing projects in mind but, before committing to them, he wanted to spend a bit more time with friends and family. However, at the age of seventy-six, he had no intention of giving up just yet. His love of music had led him and a friend, Dick French, to give monthly concerts at three local nursing homes. This was mostly classical music that they recorded on cassette but they usually ended with something light-hearted like 'Yes, We Have No Bananas'.[6]

On 20 April, Welchman was visited at his home by two USAF special agents and an NSA representative. Much to his surprise, he was told that the ideas that had occurred to him in the first three months of the Second World War were still regarded as classified in the USA. They wanted to interview him formally to find out why he had published this information without first obtaining permission to do so. The next day he met the Corporate Security Officer of MITRE and learned that the top security man in the US Department of Defense had written an unpleasant letter to the president of MITRE complaining that one of his employees had published classified information. He also learned, both from his lawyer and from the MITRE security man, that there was an old agreement under which any cryptological information that was classified in Britain was automatically regarded as classified in the USA.

The interview was held on 22 April, with his lawyer John Stevens present, and Welchman gave an on the record account of how the book came to be written and published. It was a very pleasant discussion and he had the strong feeling that, by the end, all three interrogators were in sympathy with his contention that he had acted in what he believed, with good reason, to be in the best interests of US national security. One of them even asked him to autograph his copy of the book. After the interview, Stevens felt quite confident that there was very little likelihood that the US Government would pursue criminal charges against him. His own impression was that this enquiry had been triggered by a request from GCHQ based on the old international agreement. They were told to expect a decision on the matter by 6 May.

On 29 April, Welchman's security clearance was rescinded and he could no longer enter MITRE's premises without an escort, which severely interrupted his work. He began preparing statements that might be needed if he had to defend himself. From what his interviewers had said and from the fact that McGraw-Hill had not been approached by the Department of Defense, it seemed that, if any action was to be taken, it would be against him personally. There seemed to be no intention of interfering with publication of the book.

The investigation by American special agents was under an international agreement that British ideas on cryptologic security could be enforced in the United States. This document, 18 USC §798, had been drafted in the late 1940s and, if convicted, Welchman could face a fine of not more than $10,000 or imprisonment for not more than ten years, or both. It was part of a US code titled 18 USC Chapter 37 – Espionage and Censorship. Section §798 covered 'Disclosure of Classified Information' and prosecution was possible because he had published material 'concerning the nature, preparation, or use of any code, cipher, or cryptographic system of the United States or any foreign government'.

When Welchman had joined MITRE in 1962 he had signed a statement to the effect that he had been given an initial security briefing. He felt quite certain, however, that this briefing had not included any mention of 18 USC §798. As his work for MITRE had never required a special clearance for cryptological matters, there would have been no need to do so. When he had made his decision to publish *The Hut Six Story*, it was without knowing that in the field of cryptography, information regarded as classified in Britain would automatically be regarded as classified in the United States

At the end of his first interview, Welchman was told to be on the lookout for enemy agents who might try to extract from him additional information on matters discussed in his book. In view of his long experience of handling secret information, it seemed highly unlikely that he would be caught out in this way. To be on the safe side, he decided to ask for a definition of what the authorities were afraid he might reveal. In response to this request, the Chief of the Information Security Division, Central Security Service, National Security Agency, M. J. Levin, sent MITRE a one-page document on 21 May.

18 May 1982
Guidance for Mr.Gordon Welchman

If questioned or interviewed by the media or others relative to the information contained in The Hut Six Story:
    You may discuss:
        – the history, organization, geographic setting of Bletchley Park;

- the identities of persons involved in the wartime effort at Bletchley;
- the 'Enigma' machine in broad generalities;
- the effect of the 'breaking' of the 'Enigma' on the war effort;
- cryptologic collaboration between December 7, 1941 and May 8, 1945;
- the significance of communications in military or other operations.

You may not discuss:

- technical details of the structure, logic or operation of the 'Enigma' machine, or other similar machines;
- weaknesses of German or other communications systems and the methods of exploitation of such weaknesses;
- methodologies which cryptanalysts use to successfully exploit code or cipher systems, except for those which have been officially declassified by the United States;
- methodologies used to provide protection to U.S. or Allied communications;
- details of any cryptanalytic or cryptographic methods, except for those officially declassified by the United States.

Initially, Welchman thought that it was the NSA who were the 'trouble-makers' and concerned about the last section of his book. This dealt with lessons which military forces of the day could learn from the BP story. Ironically, senior staff at MITRE had encouraged him to write this part of *The Hut Six Story*! Most of the cryptological material in the book was already in the public domain in some form or other, apart from his description of menus for the bombe and the diagonal board. He had invented the diagonal board at a crucial stage in BP's battle against the Enigma machine and his account of it was the first to appear in print. If this was the cause of concern by the intelligence people, it struck him as highly ironic. Before he had become ill Alastair Denniston had called him into his office, congratulated him on his achievements, particularly the diagonal board, and assured him that he would be rewarded. Denniston's successor, Edward Travis, had also promised that he would be rewarded after the war. He was approached by Travis in 1948, who said that he was very worried about Turing, as well as Welchman, and that he was determined to do his best for them. Unfortunately, Travis got ill at that point and the matter was left in the hands of a deputy, whom Welchman only knew by the name 'Willy'. The man arranged a meeting at which Hugh Foss and Harold Fletcher were to persuade him that he did not deserve any reward. Travis had recommended that his claim be based on the diagonal board. The original drawing that he had shown to Turing was produced, and it clearly demonstrated that the idea was his. However, 'Willy' told them that he would not be given a reward for two reasons. First, an award had already been given to Harold Keen for inventing the diagonal board. Second, his idea was the sort of thing that could be expected from a Foreign Office employee at his salary level, which was £600 a year. Foss had pointed out that this idea was by no means his only contribution, but it had no effect. Later on, Welchman asked to see his original drawing again, but was told that it had disappeared.[7]

May 6 came and went and the promised decision by the US intelligence services did not materialize. What really upset Welchman was that throughout the investigation, there had been no mention of the value to the US of what he had done during the war, what he had done since and what he could still do. After being interviewed again on 28 June, he decided to document the testimony that he had given and completed a paper called 'The Story of My Story' on 30 July.

Previously, on 1 June 1978 he had sent B. J. Workman, his line manager at MITRE, two memos: 'Wartime Experiences and General Background' and 'Tentative Ideas for Further Study'. He decided to send copies to MITRE's Corporate Security Manager, Robert J. Roberto, to show the origins of his MITRE research and the relevance of his wartime work to it. Levin at the NSA wrote again on June 30, saying that his guidance did not apply to a government-approved classified environment. He claimed that it had not been intended in any way to inhibit his contacts or discussions with appropriately cleared MITRE personnel, subject to whatever ground rules MITRE might apply. In view of this official statement from the NSA, it was hard to see why he was still prevented from continuing his work as a MITRE consultant. In exasperation, he wrote to Levin again and cited an incident which showed up the absurdity of his situation.

In January 1975, Welchman had received a letter from Brian Randell. Randell was researching the history of computers and had attached a list of questions which he hoped Welchman could answer. One aspect involved a study of the role played by Alan Turing in the development of the stored-program concept.[8] Randell's problem was that this facet of Turing's work seemed to be entwined with his work at BP during the war. He had no interest in accessing classified information about the cryptanalysis work undertaken, but just wanted to clarify the early history of electronic computers and computer-like devices. In his reply, Welchman acknowledged that he had collaborated with Turing on several technological developments at BP during the war. In his role as Assistant Director for Mechanization, he knew about Turing's wartime contacts in the US and he had made a trip himself for the purposes of technological liaison. However, he told Randell that he was still not allowed to give a complete account of what he, Turing and their American counterparts were doing at that time. Welchman had to decline further invitations from Randell to contribute to his work apart from providing some detail about his post-war career. Randell went on to write a significant paper which, for the first time, described in some detail, the development of the world's first electronic computer, Colossus and some aspects of its role at BP.[9]

Randell wrote again in November with the news that there had been significant changes in UK Government policy concerning the classification of Colossus. GCHQ had made available a set of photographs with explanatory captions and arranged for him to interview Max Newman, whose section at BP, the 'Newmanry', had commissioned Colossus. Randell had also been able to interview Tommy Flowers, the lead engineer and creator of Colossus. He had, however, been told that: 'The details of the use made of Colossus, or such details of its logical design as might reveal the processes it automated, are still regarded as confidential.'

Once again Welchman had to say that he was unable to help Randell because of the 'increasingly ridiculous clouds of secrecy which still shroud my wartime activities'. In the end, Randell restricted himself to a brief description of Welchman's post-war work. A number of years later, shortly after Welchman had published his book, Randell was visiting the US. They arranged to meet at the opening of the Digital Computer Museum in Marlboro, Massachusetts, on 10 June 1982. As Welchman said in his letter to Levin:

> Early in June, while attending a function at the Digital Computer Museum near here, I was examining the two German Enigmas that they have on public display for anyone to play with. Someone, knowing that I had written 'The Hut Six Story', asked me what the plugs in front of the machine were for. I had to explain that I am not allowed to discuss details of the Enigma, even though the answers to simple questions such as this can be found in my book and elsewhere in open literature. Brian Randell, who has written about Colossus,

was there and answered the question with more detail than I could have supplied. He has his own German Enigma, a 1940 model, at his home in England and has taken it apart, whereas I had not seen an Enigma since the war, and even then was not too familiar with details. (The description of the Enigma in my book was based on my memory and I now find that it is incorrect in some matters of detail.) I had to cancel a seminar at the Museum, scheduled for June 27, because I was expected to make some remarks on their Enigmas.

In early August 1982, Welchman showed his paper 'The Story of My Story' to Bob Everett, President of MITRE, in the hope that he might be able and willing to set up a development overview team to work in the area of communications, intelligence and security. He soon came to realize that this was quite impossible. Any team of highly-qualified people would come up with suggestions that would not be welcomed by the establishment, and MITRE's very existence depended on pleasing its sponsors. It then dawned on him that the same difficulty would apply to other organizations engaged in military research, and where else would one find people with the necessary background?

In late August, the head of the MITRE department for which he had been working asked him to complete a task that he had begun before he lost his security clearance. The work was unclassified and could be done at home. Its purpose was to draw lessons from his research and development project from what had recently become known about intelligence in the Second World War. The resulting paper 'Intelligence Aspects of the Joint Surveillance and Target Attack Radar System (JSTARS)', drew on Lewin's *Ultra Goes to War* and *The American Magic*, Kahn's *Hitler's Spies*, Hinsley's *British Intelligence in the Second World War* Volumes I and II and Calvo-coressi's *Top Secret Ultra*. He worked hard to complete the task before his consultancy contract expired at the end of September. With the work completed on schedule, MITRE Security Services showed its thanks by writing to him on 15 October to remind him that the Department of Defense required that terminated employees should return all picture badges. He had now abandoned all hope of working with a team in MITRE, or in some other establishment engaged in military research and development

Once again, he was on his own and, as six months had passed since the NSA began its investigation, he decided to start offensive action. In October he began working on two documents that he intended to use in an approach to the United States Congress. The first, dated 30 November was entitled 'The Urgent Need for Development Overview Teams Reporting to Congress' and its central argument was:

> A deeper understanding of the problem and of the objectives of the proposed development of overview teams can be derived from the story of intelligence in World War Two. This story was suppressed for a long time, but in the last few years a good deal has been revealed to the public, and there is now no excuse for neglecting this important aspect of military history. It should be taken into account both in our overall planning for the future and in the direction of our R&D projects. We need, both in peacetime and in battle, to know as much as possible about a potential enemy's method of fighting, his capabilities, and his intentions. We also need to prevent him from discovering what we do not wish him to know about our peacetime defence planning and wartime objectives.

The second document, dated December 1982, was entitled 'The Neglected Claims of Intelligence in Today's Defence Spending'. It was based on his last piece of work for MITRE and supported, he felt, by a number of recent books on intelligence in the Second World War. Their authors had all pointed out the importance of interplay between forms of intelligence derived at different times and from different sources. Welchman felt strongly that lessons from actual combat were being neglected by the people who controlled research and development projects.

On 21 August 1982 Welchman had been guest of honour at the annual convention of the American Cryptogram Association. David Kahn, one of the first authors to write about the history of cryptography, had met him in New York and driven him to the convention. One of the keynote speakers was his old BP colleague Bill Bundy, who was effusive in his praise of Welchman's contribution to the success of Hut 6 specifically and BP in general. Kahn introduced Welchman to James Bamford, an author and journalist who was about to publish a book about the NSA. Not surprisingly, the NSA had been trying to prevent Bamford from issuing *The Puzzle Palace*, because it regarded the book as an exposé of its organization. Welchman thought that Bamford's battle with the NSA could prove helpful to him. In fact, it may have been the cause of his problems!

Several years earlier, Bamford had become interested in a clandestine NSA operation to read all international telegrams being sent out of the USA. After repeated attempts to find out more information about this programme, codenamed Shamrock, he eventually received a lengthy document which described it in some detail. The NSA subsequently tried to get Bamford to return the document on the basis that it had been accidentally declassified. Existing American law offered him some protection and he was able to provide details of Operation Shamrock in his book.

Welchman was not the only veteran of Allied cryptographic work to fall foul of the NSA. At the end of 1958, members of the NSA visited the home of William Friedman and confiscated a number of items from his personal cryptographic collection. The years of clandestine work had taken their toll on Friedman and in early 1963 he was admitted to a psychiatric hospital unit suffering from depression. Later in the year, disgusted by the way he had been treated by the NSA, he decided to bequeath the remainder of his remarkable collection of documents, dealing with almost every aspect of cryptography, to the George C. Marshall Research Foundation in Lexington, Virginia. According to Bamford, he managed to gain access to Friedman's papers despite attempts by NSA officials to prevent researchers from doing so. The NSA subsequently tried to prosecute Bamford after the publication of his book.

As computer security specialist Bruce Schneier explained in his review of Bamford's second book about the NSA, *Body of Secrets*:

> 'The Puzzle Palace' was a landmark book, and widely read in circles that knew something of the NSA. Inside the NSA itself, where the agency's secrecy prevents its employees from knowing much about their own history, it was a best seller.[10] The book was a history of American intelligence from 1917 and was both shocking and pedestrian. Operations like Shamrock were exposed for the first time, but Bamford also spent a lot of pages simply explaining how the NSA was organized. Nobody knew anything, so it was all interesting.[11]

In early October 1982, Bamford sent Welchman a copy of *The Puzzle Palace*. Bamford had been helped in his battle with the NSA by Mark Lynch, an attorney for the American Civil Liberties Union (ACLU) specializing in national security matters. Welchman spoke to Lynch initially in November, and sent him his paper 'The Story of My Story'. Lynch agreed to take on his case and offer advice on the best way to proceed. His initial view was that Welchman was unlikely to be in trouble as long as he simply ignored the NSA and used his own judgement about what he said in public. The NSA strategy seemed to be to delay making any decision on the matter while pressuring McGraw-Hill to desist from publishing further editions of *The Hut Six Story.*

Ronald Lewin had been appalled at Welchman's treatment by the intelligence services. He had read *The Puzzle Palace* and found it both ironic and infuriating that a spill-the-beans book of this kind could be published while Welchman was being penalised so heavily for so little. In September 1982 he decided to write an old friend about the situation. His old friend, William Casey, happened to be Director of the CIA.[12]

> PERSONAL
>
> I enclose a sad letter from one old friend about the sad situation of another old friend. No doubt some aspects of the case are already familiar to you, but anyway the letter speaks for itself.
>
> I would only add two points. First, I heard just the other day from the highest possible source that it was Welchman's drive, dedication, and brilliant cryptanalytical flair which, during the first winter of the war, led to the very first breakthrough into the German Enigma cipher. Please do not think it is impertinent of me if I say that I find it shameful that a man of total loyalty and integrity, and of massive achievements, should come to be in his present situation after having made so enormous a contribution to the security and the survival of both our nations.
>
> Secondly, I have it on the personal authority of Welchman himself that at no stage was he ever given a briefing which laid down what he might or might not write about. The book itself is very familiar to me as I recently reviewed it in glowing terms for The Times, and I am bound to say that as one who is constantly alert in security matters I find nothing in the latter portion of the book which could conceivably be held to be a dangerous disclosure of classified material.
>
> Please excuse my making use of our friendship to bring this business to your attention. I can only say that if you were in Gordon's position I should be fighting to the death on your behalf, as I intend to do in his case until some satisfactory solution or explanation emerges – and at least until I can feel that for what seems to be formalities he is no longer in danger of having to stand in the bread line.

From August to November, Welchman had regularly sought the advice of his lawyer, John Stevens. While he had at last realized that he could not achieve anything through MITRE, he still wondered if there was some other way of passing on what he had learned. At seventy-six years of age he was growing tired, and felt that Lewin's comment to Bill Casey on the danger of 'having to stand in the bread line' was close to the reality of his situation.

When Welchman received his copy of Bamford's book, he noticed Frank Rowlett's name in the acknowledgements and decided to contact him. Thirty-seven years earlier, they had worked together when Welchman had visited the US in his role as Assistant Director for Mechanization. Rowlett had been third in command at the NSA before he retired in 1962. During a long telephone conversation, Welchman told him that he was considering a direct approach to the US Government Accountability Office (GAO) whose Office of General Counsel issued legal decisions, opinions, and reports on bid protests, appropriations matters, and other issues of federal law. Rowlett advised against such an approach. Mark Lynch also felt that this would be a mistake as 'it is just another government agency scrapping with the rest of them'. He offered to speak to a friend in the GAO, and suggested instead that Welchman approach Senator Edward Kennedy and Congressman Mavroules. To help with such an approach, Welchman wrote a document titled 'Appeal of an Author', which he sent to Lynch along with his 'The Urgent Need for Development Overview Teams Reporting to Congress'. Rowlett, however, did not think that Senator Kennedy would be much help. His view was that the sort of problem that Welchman was posing was not one which could be effectively resolved in a political arena. Rowlett did offer to prepare a statement regarding the importance of Welchman's contribution to the vital intelligence produced from the Second World War German Enigma intercepts. This statement, dated 17 January 1983, coming as it did, from one of the USA's leading cryptanalysts during the war, gave a good idea of how high a regard he was held in and went on to say:

> In my position in the Army Security Agency, I had full access to the technical information on the processing of the Enigma intercepts conducted at Bletchley Park, including the development of the procedures and equipments used for their exploitation. It was in this connection that I met Gordon Welchman, one of the key individuals involved in the British effort on the Enigma intercepts.
>
> Gordon Welchman's imaginative foresight, coupled with an exceptional administrative capability and an extraordinary

comprehension of the intricacies of the Enigma cipher machine, enabled him to make an outstanding contribution to the successful and timely exploitation of the Enigma intercepts. He deserves credit for a major contribution to the design of a special cryptanalytic device employed in the recovery of the various daily keys used in the Enigma intercepts and for developing organizational and administrative procedures for the expeditious processing of the intercepted messages. Because of the paramount need for secrecy, as well as the technical complexity of the procedures and equipments employed, the full impact of Gordon Welchman's contributions could be appreciated only by the relatively small number of those of us in the U.S. and U.K. who were involved in the technical management of our respective parts of the combined effort.

Welchman pressed on and wrote to the mayor of Newburyport, who apparently had read *The Hut Six Story*. His heart doctor, Dr Leary, was a close friend of the mayor, who in turn was a friend of Kennedy. Leary was convinced that the stress of the persecution was affecting Welchman's health. He thought he had made a strong case and, with high hopes, he submitted his documents with covering letters, to the two senators and one congressman from Massachusetts. He received neither an acknowledgement nor a response. Though this was hard to understand and disappointing, he eventually realized that politicians, like the senior managers at MITRE, had to worry about their sponsors too. What he was proposing would be unpopular with many senior members of the military establishment and with the weapons industry. It would be hard to explain in their constituencies and they would prefer more straightforward issues.

Meanwhile, life had to go on. The Welchmans were having financial problems as Teeny had been laid off at the local hospital where she had worked for the previous seven years. Welchman made enquiries about possible royalty payments and the chance of a second printing of his book. He documented the changes he had in mind for his agent John Cushman's consideration. Ralph Bennett, a Cambridge historian, had contacted him for help on a new book and, in May 1983, he had a visit from Whitfield Diffie, one of the pioneers of public-key cryptography. However, his ever fragile body gave out once again and on 10 June he had a left hip total replacement operation.

His spirits were lifted the following month. Rowlett told him that, in his view, he had made a greater contribution in the Second World War than Turing. He then received a letter from Marcus Shudforth, a Sidney Sussex alumnus and contemporary of John Jeffreys at Brentwood School and Cambridge. Following a report in the *Sidney Sussex College Annual*, Shudforth had read *The Hut Six Story*. He had recently had lunch with the senior maths tutor at Brentwood School, who had never heard of Jeffreys. Shudforth asked Welchman to autograph a copy of his book and send it to the school in Jeffreys's memory, which he duly did. It was somewhat appropriate that the school's motto was 'Here in the past, may the present, find the means to fight the battles of the future.' The dedication in the book, which is held as a showpiece in the school library, reads

> In Memory of John Jeffreys, a
> Most valued friend and colleague.
> Perhaps the story of what he did
> Will be an encouragement to
> Present and future generations
> Of mathematicians at Brentwood.
> Gordon Welchman
> Newburyport, Mass., U.S.A
> October 1983

The events of the previous year had clarified his thinking and he had finally realized that Peter Calvocoressi's publishing instincts had been right when he had advised against trying to write two books in one. As he said in a letter to Robin Denniston, dated 17 January 1984

> The failure of my book, The Hut Six Story, has also been a major frustration. Having shut down their General Books Division, McGraw-Hill wanted to suppress it, and I gather that Penguin/Allen Lane made no real attempt at promotion. But it has at last dawned on me that it was a mistake to include Part Four, which is concerned with military problems of today.
>
> It was an understandable mistake. At the time I wanted to justify my revelations of Hut Six methodology by showing that they contain valuable lessons for today. But I was drawing on a wide range of historical evidence of which the Hut Six experience was only a small part. Moreover my studies since the book was finished have provided new and better material, and my thinking has matured a great deal. Already Part Four seems obsolete, whereas the rest of the book is not.

Thinking on these lines I wondered whether the remainder of the book could stand on its own if Part Four was cut out. It could! Only a few minor modifications would be needed, and the result would be a far more attractive book that would retain its interest.

Returning to the ideas of a new version of The Hut Six Story, I could try to get permission to add two appendices. I can now see the relationship between the Polish Bomba and the British Bombe. And the story of the Stephenson/Bayly development of teletype encryption should be told.[13]

Welchman also wrote again to Sir William Stephenson on 10 January 1984 telling him about Hodges's book and drawing parallels between himself and Turing. Stephenson offered to do anything he could to help. Welchman proposed the creation of a foundation along the lines of the 'Stephenson–Donovan Foundation for the Advancement of Military Communications, Intelligence and Security'. It would be the ideal sponsor for his Development Overview Team idea. Stephenson cabled back on 12 February suggesting that Welchman write to William Casey. He also said 'as Travis would say to Bayly, get cracking'.

Buoyed by the good news from Penguin that *The Hut Six Story* would be published in paperback in the UK on 31 May, Welchman wrote to Casey on 23 February, as suggested by Stephenson. Casey replied on 10 March, saying that he was familiar with Welchman's thoughts on battlefield management and he had read *The Hut Six Story* as well as Lewin's letter in 1982. Casey said 'I will get the views of some people here and think about the people who might participate in the meeting and carry on whatever evaluations might be decided upon.' He requested copies of Welchman's two papers, which Welchman duly sent to him on 19 March. Once more Welchman reached a dead end; he never heard from Casey again.

The year 1984 brought the sad news that his agent John Cushman had died and Jane Wilson was picking up his work at JCA. He also met Linda Malvern who had written a front-page article in the *Sunday Times* about James Bamford and his trouble with the NSA over *The Puzzle Palace*. She had been shocked by Welchman's treatment by the NSA and the Department of Defense but Mark Lynch advised against any kind of public protest on Welchman's behalf.

Following a stay in hospital with a bad bout of flu he wrote to Penguin's Head of Publicity, Dotti Irving, pointing out that they had put the wrong machine on the cover of the paperback version of the book and that the cover information completely ignored Part Four However, in July, Irving told him that they had sold 4,400 copies into bookshops and that a good review by David Darby in *Time Out*, had particularly praised his Part Four.

Throughout his battles with the NSA and his repeated attempts to get his views about battlefield management on to the American political agenda, one other project drove Welchman on. He had learned some of the details of the pre-war work by the Poles on the Enigma machine too late to include them in his book. He had suggested to David Kahn that he write a paper for *Cryptologia* in January 1983 to put the record straight about the Polish contribution. His proposed title, 'From Polish Bomba to British Bombe', delighted Kahn, but it appears that pressure from the intelligence services, prevented the project from going ahead. By the middle of 1984, Robin Denniston was encouraging him to press on with it. Welchman had already written to former colleagues whom he thought could help, including Harold Fletcher, Peter Twinn, Dennis Babbage, Reg Parker and Jean Howard. He had also written to Tadeusz Lisicki, with whom he had had an exchange of letters after the publication of *The Hut Six Story*. Apart from relating an accurate account of the Polish contribution, he was also determined to give appropriate credit to the achievements of Dilly Knox and Alastair Denniston.

The Polish historian Władysław Kozaczuk had claimed in his book *Enigma* in 1979 that none of the Polish ideas had been thought of by the British and that 'virtually all major cryptological techniques that the British used to break Enigma during the Second World War had been thought of and used by the Poles earlier'.[14] The revised (1984) English version had been particularly critical of Welchman. This was no doubt written to counter Hinsley's account in the Official History.

The early part of the story was also incorrectly told in other sources. In a letter to Denniston, in July 1984 Welchman said:

> Hinsley's account of Bletchley Park activities during the first year of the war is wrong in almost every detail, and I do not know why. I believe that he was originally commissioned to write the history as GCHQ wanted it written. He was not at BP himself in the early days, so he must have been told that the first bombes arrived in May 1940. I can only suggest that GCHQ wanted to conceal the methods by which we managed to keep on breaking from the German change of procedure in May 1940 to the actual arrival of the first bombes [i.e. the first production examples] many months later.

In any event, the development of the British bombe involved four new ideas that Welchman described in *The Hut Six Story*: loops derived from a crib, the double-ended Enigma scrambler (a column of three drums on the bombe which simulated three wheels on the Enigma machine), the diagonal board and taking advantage of the 'filling up' of the test-register. Tadeusz Lisicki confirmed that this was the case:

> None of the ideas which you listed were Rejewski's. He was happy with the sheets and discarded the idea of improving his bomba. The loops, the double-ended Enigma, the diagonal board, and the filling up of the test register were all British ideas, and Rejewski in his letters to me several times mentioned that he had no idea how to mechanize the search for the keys and thought that the British mechanized the sheets, but that would be useless after May 1940. In Bruno he had absolutely no time for creative work. The running of a number of Enigma scramblers was the only idea which the Poles first used and perhaps was born from the Cyclometer.[15]

A later version of the Kozaczuk book included an article called 'The Polish Success with Enigma in British Literature' by Zdzisław Jan Kapera which was much more complimentary about Welchman's book:

> By giving in his book the first complete and accurate description of the significance of Enigma's intricacies and of the extraordinary methods needed to break its signals he created a proper standard by which to evaluate the Polish breakthrough in 1932 and the subsequent successes until the end of the 1930s.[16]

Lisicki replied to one of Welchman's letters in early September 1984. He had access to some unpublished Polish documents and papers written during the war by Colonel Guido Langer, head of the Polish Cipher Bureau in 1930–42, and Marian Rejewski. He also had over sixty letters from Rejewski written after the war. He said that Bruno (codename for the French cryptological unit during the campaign in France in 1940) had seventy cryptanalysts and staff working on codes and ciphers on 12 May 1940. He went on to say that:

> How Bruno collaborated with Bletchley was agreed on a conference held in London on December 1939. From France came Braquenie and Langer. I do not know who was on the British side. The main points agreed were: interception, exchange of solved keys and

decrypted messages. All this collaboration was super secret, Mcfarlan[17] acted in Bruno as a cut-off and had a direct line (teleprinter) to BP; all messages passed through him and were enciphered on an Enigma.

By 18 September, Welchman had been able to read a paper sent to him by Professor Jean Stengers and published by Macmillan in *The Missing Dimension* in 1984. As already mentioned, Stengers had also sent him an earlier paper, in 1981, published in *L'Histoire*. Welchman had received this paper, along with Jozef Garlinski's *The Enigma War*, too late to include details in his book. He had also read the English translation of Kozaczuk's *Enigma – How the German Machine Cipher Was Broken and How it was Read by the Allies in World War Two*. This edition had been published in 1984 and in his review for *Parameters*, the Journal of the US Army War College, the cryptanalyst Cipher Deavours had written:

> The book's chief flaw consists of its notably anti-British approach. In particular, Welchman (whose book is quoted at excessive length) comes in for a lot of undeserved criticism. It is the thesis of the book that 'virtually all major cryptologic techniques that the British used to break Enigma in the Second World War had been thought of and used by the Poles earlier'. This statement is simply not true.
>
> In fact, the Poles never did break the actual Enigma machine, but only the ill-conceived German keying methods used with the device. This is, in fact, the true lesson to be learned from the book. It is generally the circumstances of use that determine the security of a cryptographic system and not the actual security inherent in the machinery itself. The use of electronics in cryptography has not changed this situation.
>
> Not until September 1940 when the first British Bombes (codebreaking machines) started recovering daily Enigma keys using only short plaintext cribs was the Enigma obsolete in its then current form.
>
> Without the Polish work, the British would likely never have gotten started in the first place, but once they did get started, British codebreaking was as dazzling as the earlier Polish accomplishments. The British bombes were in no way related to or derived from the earlier Polish bomby (codebreaking machines) nor were Polish methods of cryptanalysis particularly useful after the Germans changed to a better message keying system in May 1940.

At the end of October, Lisicki sent Welchman a list of Enigma keys broken at Bruno. He was also critical of the Kozaczuk book and noted that the translator was not a cryptanalyst and the censor was probably looking over his shoulder. By early December, Welchman was able to send Lisicki a breakdown of his new paper and he promised to ask Denniston to send him a copy of the preliminary draft. Lisicki duly received the manuscript in March 1985 and made a number of comments.

Welchman had heard from Dennis Babbage at the beginning of August 1982 (*see Appendix 3*) and was keen to speak to him and David Rees as both had worked with Knox in The Cottage. He said that he learned nothing from Knox himself but both Peter Twinn and Tony Kendrick had been helpful to him. Babbage passed on Harry Hinsley's greetings and advice to get GCHQ approval before publishing anything else. Hinsley warned against relying on memory but Welchman's view was that Hinsley may have been too much influenced by the history that Frank Birch wrote. In fact, he believed that Peter Twinn's memory was quite likely to be more trustworthy than the Bletchley archives.

Welchman had still not heard from Rees or Parker. In desperation, he asked Fletcher to deliver letters to them personally. Parker had devised the Parkerismus method to show up repeats of keys and Rees was one of Welchman's Hut 6 'wizards'. Alas, not all former BP colleagues were keen to speak about their wartime activities and Welchman never heard from either Parker or Rees.

Harold Fletcher was still willing to help where he could but, as he had not been well, he hoped that Houston Wallace could answer Welchman's questions. Fletcher confirmed that, at the end of 1942, the overall organization of Hut 6 was still based on Welchman's original proposals and that indeed the basic framework remained for the whole war. He also suggested that Peter Marychurch would be a good GCHQ contact if Welchman had further publication plans. This would prove to be a less than successful recommendation! Regretfully, Wallace confirmed that Fletcher was seriously ill with a growth on his pancreas and the outlook was gloomy.

Welchman was hoping that, if nothing else, former colleagues would be able to help him to pin down names and dates. He heard from John Herivel, who provided some helpful information.[18] The difficulty with remembering names was brought home when Malcolm Chamberlain wrote to Welchman. Much to his embarrassment, Welchman had referred to him as John in *The Hut Six Story*. A possible explanation for this was that

Chamberlain and Herivel were inseparable. They had both arrived at BP on 27 January 1940, two days after Welchman had recruited them from Cambridge. They had even attended Welchman's tutorials together. Chamberlain confirmed that the 'sheets' were already in use by the 'girls' when he and Herivel arrived in Hut 6. A bit later, they had two days' training in The Cottage.

In July 1984, Welchman received a letter from Jean Howard who, as Jean Arlington, had worked in Hut 3. She had been asked to research BP preparations for D-Day for a programme on the subject. She worked in 3L in Hut 3. One of her problems was that in trying to research both the 'Y' Service and its traffic analysis activities, she had discovered that GCHQ had decreed that no book could be written about the 'Y' Service. Welchman was amazed by how much wrong information she had been given. She had heard one so-called expert who had worked in signals give a lecture at an Anglo/Yugoslav Symposium at the Imperial War Museum at which he said blandly 'I suppose we just covered frequencies by luck.' It seemed that all those in Hut 3 worked in ignorance of each other's work and the programme never went ahead. Howard also quoted General A. L. Gadd who eventually became head of Sixta:

> The control of interception was never properly managed, in my view, and was effective only because a few people like Gordon and, later, Oscar and 3L, studied the problems. There were both technical and security aspects which added to the difficulties. Hamish B-C [Blair-Cunynghame] and Neil Webster and Philip Lewis, whom you don't mention, were the key figures on the T/A side. SIXTA was a belated effort to rationalise matters and was my particular baby.[19]

Webster had played a key role in liaising with Hut 6's research sections, the Watch and Control. He was very much liked by all of his colleagues and, as Philip Lewis remembered in a letter to Welchman:

> To your question about Neil Webster who was appreciably older than I was. He was indeed one of my officers – a supremely brilliant evaluator living an almost trance-like existence – totally unmilitary but immensely capable. He seemed at times utterly unaware of his surroundings and we would find him in profound and totally immobile meditation halfway up the stairs working out the significance of some message we had received. His thinking was superb and we owed a great deal to him.

Like Welchman, Webster had been scrupulous about not speaking about the war but when the books about BP and Ultra started to appear, he followed developments closely. After he retired in 1976 he began working on a book about his intelligence activities as he felt existing books were short on crucial elements of his work. For example, Welchman had not said much about re-encryption work in his book. As Webster recalled:

> It was my job to see that wireless intelligence gave the cryptographers all possible help in finding cribs ... this aspect has hardly been mentioned in accounts so far ... Yet Bletchley's rapid and regular breaking [of Enigma], a major factor in Allied victory, was based on cribs, and accounts which omit this are simply 'Hamlet without the prince'.

In September 1980 Webster received formal written permission from GCHQ to publish his draft text. Having lined up a publisher and sent drafts to Ronald Lewin, Ralph Bennett and Jean Howard, he suddenly learned that his permission to publish had been withdrawn by the Director of GCHQ, Sir Peter Marychurch. Webster consulted a solicitor and wrote to GCHQ in protest but in August was told that it should not have been cleared and that no amount of editing would make it publishable. He then withdrew graciously and even turned over copyright, voluntarily, to GCHQ. He received a cash payment to cover expenses, disappointment and loss of face with his publisher.[20]

Between 5 August 1984 and 26 February 1985, Welchman had an exchange of letters with Peter Twinn, the first mathematician to be recruited by GC&CS and, arguably, the first man to break a message encrypted by an Enigma machine which included a plugboard. Twinn was also the only living member of Knox's team from the period leading up to the war before the arrival of GC&CS at BP. Welchman was keen to get Twinn's take on Knox and establish once and for all in his paper what the Poles did and the extent of Knox's contribution

As Peter Twinn would not publicly comment on his time at BP until 1993, and even then in the most general of terms, some of his comments to Welchman in a letter dated 25 September 1984 appear below verbatim:

> How was the liaison with Vignolles handled? Very cloak & dagger. Clearly Dilly was involved but he never told me much about it. He was extremely secretive even with me & I was for some time of course before the war, his only assistant!

General discussion of how to cope with Enigma was widespread in the then tiny circle of people concerned (except for Dilly who was always aloof). Indeed I think all the writings about Enigma tend to try to attribute the ideas to specific people in a way that hardly represents the atmosphere correctly. So much was discussed that I think it is not at all easy in all cases, to say where ideas sprung from – often I think they developed in general conversation until someone crystallized them in final form.

I am sorry that I cannot see eye to eye with you on the subject of Denniston. I do not regard him as a success. I think he failed between the wars to get GCHQ (GCCS as it was) the status & facilities it needed. And he was on a pretty good wicket in the years just before 1939. The organization was having stunning success in reading the Spanish Civil War codes & had clearly demonstrated its potential at trifling expenditure. Denniston's posting to the U.S.A. was clearly demotion. Indeed Denniston said to one of my colleagues, when his posting was arranged & Travis took over 'I am not jealous of Travis – what grieves me is the realization that I didn't prove man enough for the job.' These are my own views – naturally not for publication & on no account whatsoever to get back to Robin Denniston.

My own impression is that the drive to set up BP came much more from people like Tiltman & Menzies.

In response to Welchman's question about whether Dilly and the others would have been able to read Enigma traffic without the Poles if they had guessed the connection pattern between keyboard and entry drum – 'Yes indeed – a simple guess. But not only Dilly & I failed to make it – so did Kendrick & Turing – neither of them remarkable for lack of imagination!'

Also in September 1984, Welchman received a rather different assessment of Alastair Denniston than that of Twinn's harsh account. Thomas Parrish was an author who had interviewed him for a book he was writing on the American involvement in Ultra. Parrish attached a letter from William Friedman to Denniston's daughter following her father's death. The letter could not have been more effusive in praising Denniston's contribution. A further testimonial came from Frank Rowlett in a telephone call to Welchman. Rowlett was the first of William Friedman's original employees, hired for the Army's Signal Intelligence Service in 1930. As well as their vital work on Purple, he and Friedman also helped design the Sigaba cipher machine, which was never solved by the Germans during the war. As Welchman wrote to Robin Denniston:

> [Rowlett] well remembers your father's visit before America entered the war and says that both he and Friedman very much admired him both as a person and as an outstanding cryptologist. He also says that the impression your father made on the Army cryptological organization undoubtedly helped to establish the close relations with Bletchley Park that were to develop later.
>
> I asked him about relations with Travis. He said that he and Friedman, and others at Arlington, appreciated Travis as a sincere person whose word could be trusted. But, because he had no feel for cryptology, Travis never won their affection and admiration to the extent that your father did.

On 28 January 1985 Welchman sent a copy of his paper to Twinn to make sure he was happy with it. Twinn made the following further comments in a letter dated 25 February 1985:

> As late as July 1939, GC&CS could not see how to capture the Enigma problem with the information they possessed. An inspired guess as it turned out, would have made the available evidence adequate for a solution.
>
> I can remember reading in the Cottage an account of the construction of the Polish Bomba. That Hinsley was ignorant of this is irrelevant. He was, naturally as it wasn't his job, ignorant of all the technical problems.
>
> As regards the question of whether Dilly gave us a complete picture of what the Poles had achieved, I think almost certainly he didn't because everything paled into insignificance in comparison with the knowledge that the diagonal was A, B, C, D, . . . But we all appreciated the Polish achievement. We did because knowledge of what they had done arrived at Bletchley as the war progressed (by way of the French). Remember that we had the knowledge about the diagonal from the Poles just before the war began & Poland was overrun. Information about the success the Poles achieved came later.

*

Meanwhile, the news from McGraw-Hill was that they intended to declare *The Hut Six Story* out of print and dump an unsold 1,125 copies on the remainder market. Up to 1985, Welchman had received advances totalling

$6,855.74, an amount which author royalty earnings barely covered. Penguin accounts also made depressing reading with royalties just paying off Welchman's initial advance. The untold wealth forecast by Winterbotham had certainly not materialized. And there was also to be one final twist in his ongoing battle with the NSA as he related to Denniston on 5 September 1984:

> Another helpful fact cropped up in my long talk with Frank Rowlett yesterday morning. He told me about the troubles he has been having with Mr MJ Levin, Chief of Information Security Division, NSA. Apparently Rowlett had been asked by the NSA historians to write an article that in their view could be published. But Levin maintains that it must be classified 'confidential' and not published. Rowlett challenged this and attended a meeting in Washington, I think only a few days later. At the meeting, the subject of The Hut Six Story came up, and Levin said that I had really gone too far. At this Rowlett blew up. He told Levin that in his opinion nothing that I said in my book could do any harm today, and that it is shocking that a man to whom both Britain and the USA owe so much, should have been so badly treated. From what he said to me, Rowlett thinks that Levin is the principal, if not the only source of my troubles with NSA.

In early November, Welchman received a letter from Christopher Andrew, Senior Tutor at Corpus Christi College, Cambridge, suggesting that his article might appear in the first issue of a new publication, *Intelligence and National Security*, of which he was editor. Welchman was encouraged that Andrew and David Dilks had been able to publish Stengers's article in *The Missing Dimension*. By now he had sent final corrections to Denniston, who was acting as an intermediary, for his 'From Polish Bomba to British Bombe' paper. He also liked one of the new journal's stated objectives: 'While recognizing that current intelligence operations usually require secrecy as a condition of success, *Intelligence and National Security* will attempt to lift the veils which still pointlessly conceal the past history of intelligence.'

On 18 March 1985, Welchman was informed by Andrew via Denniston that he was proposing to send the article to press on 1 July. Welchman had also decided to send Andrew a copy of the paper he had written about himself and Turing. He had given it to his friend Diana Lucy to take to England along with the final corrections to his paper and photographs of Enigma-related and other documents.[21]

With the paper ready for publication, Welchman enquired about contracts and fees. As it was 16,000 words, his agent Jane Wilson thought that he would be paid for his work. Much to his disappointment Andrew informed him that no payment could be made as it was appearing in an academic journal. He had not been aware of this and was surprised to learn that he would have no financial return for six months' work. Andrew cited the example of David Kahn as an academic who published free but then earned money subsequently from book spin-offs. Welchman still had hopes of publishing the paper in book form but, for the moment, decided to issue it in Andrew's journal. One positive piece of news was that the Penguin paperback could now be sold in the USA because American rights had reverted to Welchman when McGraw-Hill remaindered *The Hut Six Story*.

At the end of March 1985, Welchman and Teeny were able to have a two-week holiday in Tortola, British Virgin Islands. On returning to Newburyport, he became worried that Andrew had failed to clear the paper with GCHQ and the NSA. He had promised Twinn, Herivel, Chamberlain and Babbage that the paper would be cleared before publication and that they would be protected.

Welchman had been suffering from jaundice on his return from holiday in early April and arranged to see a liver specialist in Boston on the 11th. He thought he might need a gall bladder operation. Never one to remain idle for long, he was already working on ideas for a book that his old McGraw-Hill editor, Bruce Lee, wanted him to write. The subject would be the development of computers and information technology on both sides of the Atlantic up to around 1960.

On 7 May, he wrote a letter while a patient in the New England Deaconess Hospital and sent copies to Robin Denniston, Christopher Andrew, Jane Wilson, Bruce Lee, Cy Deavours and David Kahn. The news was not good. A seven-hour operation on 17 April had revealed several tumours. After a few difficult weeks he felt he was making progress and hoping to be home in two or three weeks more. He had been plagued with health problems throughout his adult life and after several heart operations, two complete hip replacements and numerous bouts of debilitating flu, he and his family thought that this was just another problem that he would overcome.

In light of Welchman's concerns about publishing the paper before getting clearance from the proper authorities, Andrew had submitted it to the D-Notice Committee at the Ministry of Defence. On 22 July he was able to write with the good news that the D-Notice Committee had cleared the article and he attached written confirmation from Major General Kay, Acting Secretary. Apparently, this had been achieved after protracted discussions between the committee and the 'relevant departments'. This was interesting news as Welchman had received a letter from the Director of GCHQ, Sir Peter Marychurch,[22] four days before he received Andrew's letter. He had come home from hospital on 5 July and, while still very weak, was improving slowly. The letter was extraordinary for several reasons, the obvious one being that Welchman had in his possession written confirmation from the D-Notice Committee that his paper had been cleared by them. It was also hard to understand how the Director of GCHQ, the successor organization to GC&CS, could use such condescending language to a person of Welchman's stature in the history of his organization.

Several days after writing to Welchman, Marychurch also wrote to Neil Webster, rescinding GCHQ's previous approval for him to publish his personal memoir about his wartime work in traffic analysis. On 9 August, Andrew replied with an explanation which made the Marychurch letter even more reprehensible.

> When I first submitted your article to the D-Notice Committee I received an acknowledgement from Major General Kay promising to get in touch with me again as soon as possible. Some weeks passed. I then had a letter from Major General Kay containing no comment on your article but saying that it was up to you to clear the article directly with your former department. This response clearly derived from Major General Kay's consultations with GCHQ. I duly remonstrated with Major General Kay. He himself seemed unhappy with the bureaucratic reply he had passed on and agreed to have further talks with the 'department concerned'. Following these discussions, he rang me to say on behalf of the D-Notice Committee that no deletions were necessary before your article went to press. He duly confirmed this in writing by the letter which I have sent you. Evidently, he had succeeded in wringing from the 'department concerned' an admission that there is of course nothing in your article which in any way threatens national security. I imagine that Sir Peter Marychurch composed his letter to you in the light of Major General Kay's first response to your article before it had been cleared by the D-Notice Committee. Anyway, though Sir Peter may not like it, the fact is that I have cleared your article with the appropriate authority.

Andrew did not see how there could be any American objection to a paper cleared by the D-Notice Committee in the UK as it was exclusively restricted to British matters. He asked Welchman's permission to publish 'the whole sordid affair' of his treatment in a future issue of the journal. On 22 August, Welchman wrote what appears to be his last letter on the matter. He gave Andrew permission to use the material about his case in any way he saw fit. He felt that it would be nice if the shabby way in which he had been treated could be publicized before he died.

Epilogue

Like that of many of his former BP colleagues, Welchman's later life was defined by his wartime work. BP proved to be a unique experience and one that he would never be able to replicate. The Canadian Pat Bayly and the American William Bundy felt the same, despite distinguished careers after the war. In a letter to Welchman in 1983, Bayly observed that 'In retrospect, the years I spent in your company were the happiest and most productive, years of my life.'

Inevitably, Welchman felt compelled to share some of that experience with the general public through *The Hut Six Story*. He felt that by explaining some of the technical detail that lay behind BP's success, readers would have a better understanding of the magnitude of its achievement. He also believed that the lessons learned at BP could help the United States and Britain develop a more secure tactical communication system. When Welchman began to write his book the Cold War still had seventeen years to run.

Many of the early books about the BP's wartime activities contained inaccuracies or missed crucial details from the story. This was even the case when Harry Hinsley published the first volume of his *British Intelligence in the Second World War* in 1979. Given that access to official technical documents was restricted to Hinsley's team, there was much anticipation that a technical appendix would shed light on how the Enigma messages were actually broken. Alas, neither the long awaited appendix nor the body of the book gave any technical detail of either Polish or British methods.

Welchman vented his frustrations in a letter dated 10 July 1984 to Ralph Erskine, a leading historian of wartime codebreaking. The following are extracts from that letter:

> Hinsley could have avoided his gross errors by talking to people who were involved in the birth of Ultra. Travis, Denniston, Knox, Turing,

Jeffreys and Alexander were dead. But several key members of the early Hut 6 were still alive. For example, Babbage, Colman, Milner-Barry and myself. Perhaps Hinsley was not allowed to consult us.

Hinsley suggests to the uninformed reader that the breaking of Enigma keys was entirely due to the Bombes. This, as I tried to point out in my book, is quite untrue. Our success was the result of German errors and of excellent communication, collaboration and co-operation among the many specialized activities that were involved.

Indeed Hinsley ignores the importance of the high quality people who were recruited in the early days for the many different tasks that would be involved. If Travis and I had not been able to start building up the many-faceted Hut 6 organization and staff before the end of 1939, Ultra intelligence might never have come to bloom. Fortunately, we had built up an embryonic team of new-style cryptanalysts, with supporting activities operating round the clock, before the invasion of Denmark and Norway in April 1940.

Without the early demonstration of codebreaking success in Norway, based on the Polish manual methodology, we would have not won support for the major expansions that proved so necessary. If Turing and I had not come up so quickly with our ideas for a Bombe, the early success would have fizzled out. If I had not come up with an organizational plan before the war was three months old, the early success itself might not have been achieved. These startling facts are not brought out in Hinsley's 'Official History'.

You may well wonder, as I do, why on earth so much nonsense has been talked about the early days of Hut 6. The answer may be that very few people in GCHQ knew what was involved, and that the people who have written and talked, like Hinsley and Good, arrived late in the game and never worked in Hut 6. Even Calvocoressi, who headed the Air Force Section in Hut 3, arrived pretty late. Bundy, who did work in Hut 6, arrived even later. Our continuing success depended on being able to recruit large numbers of top quality men and women, but when they arrived they were rightly concerned with what they had to do; not with how things started.

*

At the end of the Second World War, a number of BP veterans returned to academic life and successful careers while others remained within GCHQ. The first five post-war directors of that organization, Edward Travis, Eric

Jones, Clive Loehmis, Leonard (Joe) Hooper and Arthur (Bill) Bonsall had worked at BP during the war. While it is not appropriate to equate the experience of Welchman and others at BP to that of fighting men and women returning home after the war, the void in their lives must have been similar.

Welchman never seriously contemplated a return to Cambridge, having become disillusioned with academic life there. He had completed research which he believed would have earned him a PhD but had never got around to submitting it formally before putting his life on hold and reporting to BP on 4 September 1939. He thought that lack of a doctorate would have been a barrier to success at Cambridge if he had returned. While he did work at MIT after the war, he tried to discourage his daughter Ros years later from becoming an academic. She did not take his advice and in the end he was proud of her academic achievements.

In its early days, BP was like a research laboratory which eventually put in place an infrastructure capable of turning innovation in cryptanalysis and signals intelligence into real products and systems. Its research activities as described by its wartime participants, particularly in the early days, share many of the elements of what today's IT world calls skunkworks projects.[1] These are typically developed by a small and loosely structured group of people who research and develop a project using processes which encourage radical innovation. Skunkworks often operate with a high degree of autonomy and, unhampered by bureaucracy, are tasked with working on advanced or secret tasks. These projects are often undertaken with a tacit understanding that if the development is successful then the product will be designed later according to more structured processes. BP might well have been the world's first such endeavour and more recent examples include CERN (the European Organization for Nuclear Research)[2] and PARC (Palo Alto Research Center Incorporated).[3]

Of the technologies that emerged from BP, the bombes and Colossus best fit the approach described above: that is research and innovation leading to a real game-changing product which can be produced on scale. The bombes wedded Turing's and Welchman's innovative thinking to existing technologies already being produced by BTM in Letchworth. In January 1944, Tommy Flowers delivered to BP the world's first electronic computer. Like the bombe, this development was based on the innovative research of people at BP such as Bill Tutte. However, its realization at the Post Office's Dollis Hill research laboratory also required research and innovation since many of the components of the end product needed to be invented. Brian Randell, the man who subsequently told the world, in some detail, how Colossus actually worked, claimed that Flowers's achievements were a major and highly original step towards post-war electronic computers in Britain.

Welchman would have initially agreed with Randell but, with his extensive experience of American post-war computing developments, he changed his mind. His view was that while Flowers did a magnificent job for a specific problem, developments in America had a much greater impact on post-war electronic computers, in Britain as well as in America. He believed that the BP experience was more of special-purpose equipment than computer experience. He also felt that the development of the modern computer started after the war by taking advantage of technology developed during it, in places such as the MIT Radiation Lab.

The success of BP was in many ways so astonishing that many German officials who survived the war refused to believe that it had actually happened. In 1983, Welchman's nephew invited him to meet a work colleague in the American aerospace industry. His colleague was a German by the name of Karl Kober. A brilliant man with two doctoral degrees, Kober had been brought over by the young American space programme from a French prison after the war and turned into a space engineer. He had been a leading figure in Germany and here he was, now a respected NASA scientist, sitting across a kitchen table from one of the people who had made a significant contribution to Hitler's downfall. The discussion was lively and quite remarkable. Kober completely denied even the possibility that Britain had ever broken the Enigma machine. According to Welchman's nephew, Kober got quite heated and was adamant and not to be convinced otherwise. Welchman appeared to be quite calm and almost bemused to see his former enemy unwilling to accept the evidence before him.

Towards the end of 1983, while still recovering from a hip replacement operation, Welchman read Andrew Hodges's biography of Alan Turing. He was moved to write a paper, titled 'Ultra Revisited, A Tale of Two Contributors', which contrasted his life to that of Turing. After the war, it was rumoured that both he and Turing were being considered for knighthoods. They were both then led to believe that they could not receive such an award for work carried out as Temporary Civil Servants at a salary of £600 per annum. He summarized his frustration as follows:

Then, not long ago, the Hodges book on Turing came my way and helped to crystallize my thinking. Before doing anything else, I decided to write about the comparison between his life and mine. The contributions to science that he might have made, if he had not been hounded to death, would have been far deeper than anything I could produce. What a waste! Yet, I too, in a more pedestrian way and over a longer period of time, have been able to contribute visionary ideas, many of which could still be valuable. But I find myself with frustrating problems.

I have tried over the years to take advantage of the expertise of others. But changes have been rapid and are likely to continue that way. Much of my acquired knowledge and perception of the future must already be out of date. I still believe that I have something of value to contribute to our military preparedness, but my contribution can bear fruit only if I can pass on my accumulated experience and ideas to an interdisciplinary team of younger men who will keep up to date.

Here again, I run into frustration. What I want to contribute is twofold. First, my evaluation of what is seriously wrong with our military R&D, particularly, but not exclusively, in the area of communications, intelligence and security. Second, my ideas on what could be done to improve our military preparedness. These are highly sensitive matters. We do not want to broadcast our weaknesses to potential enemies. Consequently, the contribution that I am uniquely qualified to make can be made only in an environment in which secrecy can be effectively maintained. Yet, just as Turing was prevented from making further contributions to cryptology because he was regarded as a 'security risk', so am I prevented from contributing to our future national security for the same reason. This, also, seems to be a waste.

Ronald Lewin had written to various officials in the intelligence community in 1982 about their shabby treatment of Welchman. Other authors such as Nigel West and David Hooper would later refer to the matter in books published in 1986 and 1987 respectively. Former colleagues, however, kept quiet after Welchman's book was published and, according to Diana Lucy, he felt a bit let down by them. However, he understood the pressure on anyone who had signed the Official Secrets Act to remain silent. West would go so far as to add the subtitle 'Including the

Persecution of Gordon Welchman' to his 1986 book *The SIGINT Secrets: The Signals Intelligence War, 1900 to Today*. In the book, West gave his view of why GCHQ and the NSA had reacted in the way they did to the publication of *The Hut Six Story*:

> Until his intervention, GCHQ and the NSA had perpetuated the myth that code breaking had won the war and the Enigma machine had been solved. Very few knew this to be a distortion of what had really happened. In consequence public attention had focussed on cryptography and been diverted away from the more sensitive matter of traffic analysis.

He would go on to conclude that the impact Welchman's book had on the intelligence community in the USA and Britain was to compromise the carefully nurtured cover story of the Enigma's vulnerability. Also included in an appendix was some of the correspondence between Welchman and the NSA.

In his 1987 book *Official Secrets*, David Hooper quoted from the letter Welchman received from Sir Peter Marychurch, the Director of GCHQ, dated 12 July 1985. Stuart Milner-Barry waited until 1993 before finally writing publicly about his work at BP and something of Welchman's contribution. He had previously authored a powerful obituary following Welchman's death and written to the press about his outrageous treatment by the intelligence services in the UK and US.

> When we first came to GC&CS, Bletchley Park was a tiny organization, probably not more than thirty strong. It consisted of a few old-time professionals who had worked in Room 40 at the Admiralty in the First World War, such for example, as Dillwyn Knox, a Fellow of King's who died during the war, and A. G. Denniston, and new recruits such as Welchman and Alan Turing. Knox, had, so I understood, been defeated by the Enigma and subsequently exploiting its success, should (subject to the Poles) probably go to the other two.
>
> Turing was a strange and ultimately a tragic figure. But as an admirable biography of him has been written, I shall say no more here. Welchman, on the other hand has, I think, never received his just deserts, quite apart from being ridiculously persecuted on security grounds for revealing, some forty years after the event, how the job of breaking the Enigma had been done. Welchman was a visionary, and a very practical visionary at that. In spite of Knox's

failure, he always believed that Enigma could be broken. He also realized the enormous importance of the success, and took it for granted that, when the phoney war ended, the Germans would rely principally on the Enigma for their military communications. He foresaw much of what would be involved in the way of expansion of staff, machinery (the bombes), and all the other necessary substructure. And he had the fire in his belly that enabled him to cajole higher authority into supplying our wants. If Gordon Welchman had not been there, I doubt if Ultra would have played the part that it undoubtedly did in shortening the war.[4]

So what lay behind Welchman's harsh treatment by GCHQ and the NSA? In 1981, Chapman Pincher had published a book in which he publicized, for the first time, suspicions that a former Director-General of MI5, Roger Hollis, had been a spy for the Soviet Union. He had also described MI5's and MI6's internal inquiries into the matter. Its publication even prompted the British Prime Minister, Margaret Thatcher, to give a statement about it in the House of Commons.[5] She announced that she had asked the Security Commission 'To review the security procedures and practices currently followed in the public service and to consider what, if any, changes are required.' She went on to say that 'My concern is with the present and with the future.' By 1982, Nigel West had already published two books about MI5. In the USA, the NSA had been trying to stop James Bamford from publishing his book about their organization. The material in *The Hut Six Story* was hardly the threat to security that an exposé of the NSA and MI5 might be. Yet the FBI felt compelled to interview Welchman several times, tap his phone and place agents in an unmarked car outside his house in Newburyport.

A recently declassified government document has shed some light on the matter. In a note to Prime Minister Thatcher, dated 30 April 1982, the Secretary of the Cabinet, Sir Robert Armstrong, informed her of the publication of Welchman's book in the USA and its imminent publication in the UK. He also summarized the security and legal issues raised by its release. With regard to security, Armstrong stated that while there was no direct damage to UK–USA sigint co-operation, there was indirect damage. His carefully worded rationale for this was that:

> so long as Sigint and cryptanalysis are kept in the public eye by books of this sort, foreign COMSEC organizations will receive more funds and will be stimulated to greater efforts.[6]

With regard to the legal position, Armstrong stated that the US Justice Department did not think it was feasible to prosecute Welchman and that any legal action to stop publication in the UK offered no guarantee of success.

It seems that Welchman was simply collateral damage at a time when both GCHQ and the NSA were trying to restrict the information being published about themselves and related government agencies. He was a 76-year-old veteran of BP largely unknown to all but former wartime colleagues. Pressuring him might, at the very least, dissuade former colleagues from publishing their own accounts of BP's wartime work. However, it didn't prevent Peter Wright from publishing his insider's account of MI5 in 1987. Pincher and West both went on to publish further books about MI5 and MI6. Sir Peter Marychurch may well have been urged by higher authorities to write his distasteful letter to Welchman in 1985. It is interesting to note that Marychurch was only the second Director of GCHQ not to have worked at Bletchley Park during the war.

By the new millennium, things had changed quite dramatically. As noted above, Christopher Andrew had arranged to publish Welchman's last piece of work, 'From Polish Bomba to British Bombe'. Welchman had also entrusted him with telling the story of his treatment by the intelligence services. Andrew had been outraged by the story but had managed to get D-Notice Committee to approve the paper before its publication. In February 2003, Andrew accepted the post of official historian for the Security Service, MI5. He was asked to write an official history of the service due for its centenary in 2009. At the end of April 2002, James Bamford was writing his second book about the NSA, *Body of Secrets*. According to Bamford, NSA Director Michael Hayden gave him unprecedented access to the NSA campus in Fort Meade, MD, senior NSA officials and thousands of NSA documents.

Throughout his life, Welchman had been strongly influenced by religion and music. He cut a dashing a figure as a young man, excelling at sport, and he certainly had an eye for the ladies. However, he greatly valued the teachings of the Church of England and greatly admired his father. He was also very patriotic and his son Nick remembered him being moved to tears when told of the death of King George VI in 1952. He was also very loyal to friends and former colleagues and tended not to talk about people unless he had something good to say about them. A friend remembers him being very upset and quite emotional after he learned about Turing's suicide.

Apart from recognizing his genius, he remembered Turing as 'a completely gentle soul'.

Music was a constant theme throughout his life and he used to sing madrigals together with his first wife Katharine while they lived in England. They continued to do so when they moved to the USA and on one occasion even included their son Nick, who was a choir boy at the time, in a production of *Three Kings*. A friend recalled him having 'a gorgeous tenor voice'. His stepson Michael remembers him sitting in his music room with headphones on, listening to classical music and conducting along with it. His musical tastes were quite wide and he loved the ragtime music of Scott Joplin. He was always open to new types of music and, on one occasion, introduced Michael to records by Simon and Garfunkel. Michael in turn played him a record by his favourite band. Welchman liked the first album that Michael played him, although not the second one. The fact that he liked the first one was surprising enough as the band was none other than the famous West Coast hippie rock group, Grateful Dead.

Ros Welchman and her family spent the summer of 1985 in Newburyport, renting a house not far from that of her father. Welchman had experienced an extraordinary number of health problems throughout his life and, by the summer of 1985, it was becoming clear to both his family and himself that even he was unlikely to recover from pancreatic cancer. Ros was able to help Welchman complete 'From Polish Bomba to British Bombe', being a mathematician in her own right. He felt very good about finally finishing the paper but still had concerns about sending it to Britain by post. This time, he was determined to get official approval before publication. His close friend Diana Lucy was paying a visit to England and he asked her to deliver the manuscript personally to the publisher. Diana recalls it being all very cloak and dagger and that she travelled in casual clothing with the document stuffed up her jumper. She had a number to call when she got to England to arrange its delivery by hand.

By now Welchman had to spend most of his time in bed but he was surrounded by family and friends. He turned to an elderly homeopath for treatment as it was clear that his doctors could do little for him. At last his prodigious research and writing had come to an end and his working life was over. Now he could devote all of his attention to his family, particularly his grandchildren.

Gordon Welchman did not live to see some of his story told by authors such as West and Hooper or by former colleagues such as Milner-Barry.

He passed away on 8 October 1985 at the age of seventy-nine at Anna Jaques Hospital in Newburyport, Massachusetts. His funeral was held at Linwood Crematory in Haverhill, Massachusetts, on 12 October. Before his death, Welchman and his wife had made enquiries about holding his funeral in Bristol Cathedral but the cost was exorbitant. As the son of a former archdeacon of Bristol, Welchman was quite annoyed by this and would not let the family 'waste' money on a funeral there. The British Government was represented by its consul based in Boston. When he heard about the final years of Welchman's life, he asked, much to the bemusement of the family, why they had not come to him when the problems with the intelligence agencies began. Teeny chose all German music for the funeral initially but then changed her mind. On reflection, she chose the English music that Welchman loved such as Vaughan Williams's 'The Lark Ascending'.

On 12 November 1985, McGraw-Hill signed over rights to *The Hut Six Story* to Teeny Welchman while retaining the right to sell or remainder existing inventory. In January 1986, his final paper was published in *Intelligence and National Security*. When *The Hut Six Story* was republished in 1997, the publisher, with the agreement of the Welchman family, replaced the last section with that paper, 'From Polish Bomba to British Bombe'.

At his request and somewhat ironically, the ashes of a man who, along with Alan Turing and a few others, had made one of the most significant individual contributions to the Allied victory in the Second World War, were interred in his wife's family plot in Aschau cemetery in the province of Chiemgau, Germany.

Appendices

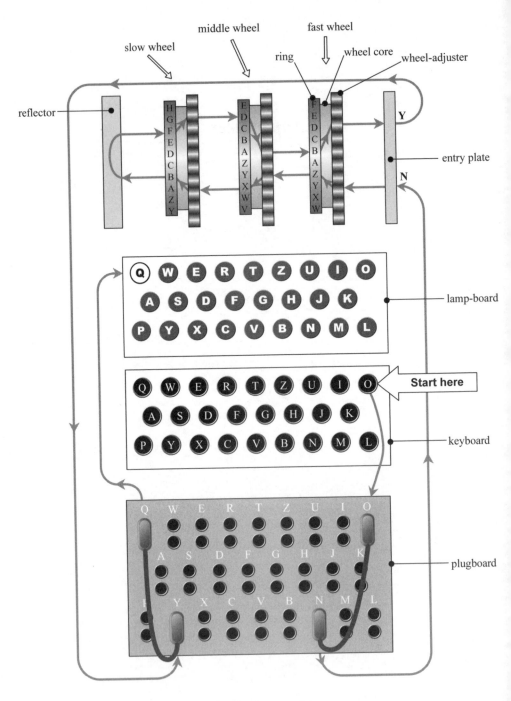

The Enigma machine.
(*Diagram by Dustin Barrett and Jack Copeland*)

Appendix 1

A Beginner's Guide to Enigma and the Bombe

When he arrived at BP on 4 September 1939, Gordon Welchman was initially assigned to Dilly Knox's team in The Cottage. He wrote years later that he didn't learn much there about the Enigma machine but it didn't matter because any reasonably intelligent person could learn all they needed to know about it in an hour or two!

Enigma

The Enigma machine was used to encrypt and decrypt a message. Sending and receiving the message was a separate process. It could run off a battery as well as a mains supply which made it ideal for mobile communications. The machine had a keyboard with 26 keys, one for each letter of the alphabet. laid out in three rows; there were no number or punctuation keys. Above the keyboard was the lampboard which consisted of 26 small circles of glass, each embossed with a letter of the alphabet and laid out in the same pattern as the keyboard. Underneath each circle of glass was a small bulb, much like one in a modern torch. Each time a key was pressed, one of the bulbs switched on and the letter that was illuminated above it was the encryption of the letter on the key that had been pressed. So if the O key was pressed and the bulb under Q switched on, then Q was the encryption of O (*see opposite*).

Inside the standard German military machine were three wheels with 26 contact points on each side wired together internally with strands of wire. At the front of the machine was a plugboard consisting of 26 double sockets also laid out in the same pattern as the keyboard. Pairs of letters were connected with cables having plugs at each end. Around each wheel was a ring with the letters A–Z (Navy Enigma) or the numbers 1–26

(Army/Air Force Enigma) which could be set to any one of its 26 positions. When the wheels were put in the machine and the lid shut, their serrated edges protruded through slots in the lid. Adjacent to each slot was a small glass viewing window and the topmost letter or number on the ring around each wheel could be seen. Each wheel could be turned freely by hand by rotating it to any one of its 26 positions.

From late 1938, German Army and Air Force Enigma operators were issued with a set of five wheels from which they would choose three. Each wheel was wired differently and they could be put in the machine in any order. So when the wheels were clamped together in the machine, you had in effect, a 26-way circuit running through it. When a key was pressed on the keyboard, a current passed from contact point to contact point through the machine as shown in Figure 1. Each contact point represented a different letter so, as the current passed through the machine, the letter on the key pressed could change up to nine times before it reached the lamp-board. To the left of the three wheels was a fixed wheel called the reflector which had 26 contact points connected in 13 pairs. The other ingenious design feature of the machine was that when a key was pressed at least one wheel would move forward one position. The right-hand 'fast' wheel moved at every key stroke while the movement of the middle and left-hand wheels was determined by the ring settings. The result of this was that the circuit through the machine changed every time a key was pressed.

The starting configuration of the machine, consisting of the wheel choice and order, the ring setting and the pairs of letters plugged together, was known as the key. As the Germans had a number of communication networks, each with its own daily key, Welchman devised a naming convention, based initially on the coloured pencils used to mark them up on lists. The main German Air Force key was known as Red. Army and Air Force keys usually changed every twenty-four hours and operators were issued with monthly key sheets.

The Enigma machine was designed to have reciprocal characteristics so that the processes of encryption and decryption were essentially the same. This meant that if O was encrypted as Q, then at the same starting position, Q would be encrypted as O. The machine achieved this by always partitioning the 26 letters of the alphabet into thirteen reciprocal pairs of letters so that for any of these pairs, one letter would always be encrypted as its partner. When the wheels moved to another set of positions (which happened every time a key was pressed), the circuit configuration in the machine changed along with the identity of the thirteen letter pairs, but the reciprocal relationship between the letters in each pair remained.

It was the reflector which delivered the reciprocal characteristic of the machine and thus also guaranteed that a letter could not be encrypted as itself. This was a weakness that the Germans were apparently prepared to accept as it provided the machine with the extremely useful property that the encrypting and decrypting processes were the same and one machine could do both tasks. This would have greatly simplified the training of their Enigma operators.

Once the machine had been set up using the daily key, a final layer of security was implemented. The procedures for this changed several times but, from early May 1940, the Air Force and Army operators were told to choose 6 letters of the alphabet (known as the indicator) at random. The machine would be set to the daily key and then the wheels turned until the first three letters (known as the indicator setting) appeared in the windows adjacent to the edge of each wheel. The next three letters (known as the message setting) would then be encrypted. Finally, the wheels would be turned to the message setting and the plain text of the message encrypted. Both the indicator setting and encrypted message setting would be sent along with other information before the encrypted message. The settings of the machine provided by the key sheet combined with the message setting, defined the starting position of the machine.

The receiving operators would set the wheels of their machines to the indicator setting and then recover the message setting by entering the encrypted message setting letters. They would then turn the wheels to that setting and recover the original plain text by simply entering the encrypted message. The whole encryption and decryption process assumed that both the sender's and the recipient's machines had been previously configured to the daily key.

The Bombe and the Diagonal Board

A more detailed description of how the bombe was used at BP is given in Appendix 2. It has been written by Frank Carter, a leading expert in the field, and includes details which have not previously been published in a mainstream book of this type.

To start, it is worth restating the problem faced by Turing and Welchman as they designed the bombe. In order to decrypt a message sent on a particular German communication network on a particular day, they needed to know the daily key and the message setting for each message. The daily key provided the following settings:

- The choice and location of the three wheels in the machine. There were 10 ways of selecting three wheels from five (in the case of the Army and Air Force) and six ways of arranging the three wheels in the machine. The total possible number of wheel orders was therefore $10 \times 6 = 60$. (three wheels from eight in the case of the Navy yielded $56 \times 6 = 336$)
- The identity of the set of 10 'plug pairs' typically used on the plugboard; the total possible number of combinations was 150.7 million, million.
- The wheel turnover positions which were determined by the ring settings. The ring around each wheel had 1–26 (Army/Air Force) or A–Z (Navy) engraved on it and could be set to any one of the 26 positions. Thus there were $26 \times 26 \times 26 = 17,576$ possible ring settings. More details of the effect of multiple wheel turnovers are given in Appendix 2.

The number of daily keys was therefore 60×150.7 million, million $\times$ $17,576 = 158.9$ million, million, million. As the number of possible message settings was also $26 \times 26 \times 26 = 17,576$, the number of possible ways of electrically configuring the Enigma machine before encrypting a message was the same extraordinarily large number.

The following is a real example, taken from the 'Official History of Hut 6'. Each day German airfields would receive instructions for their targets from Luftwaffe HQ and the signals always began with the phrase

BESONDERE ANORDNUNGEN FUER DIE ...
('SPECIAL ORDERS FOR THE ...')

Using the fact that the Enigma machine could not encrypt a letter as itself, a cryptanalyst hoped to find a position in which the first 20 characters of the German phrase in plain text, were different from a run of 20 encrypted characters from the intercepted message. These could be aligned as in the table below and the letters of the phrase which could be matched sequentially to a different letter of encrypted text was referred to as a crib. x was used to represent a space.

1	2	3	4	5	6	7	8	9	10	11	12	13	14	15	16	17	18	19	20
B	E	S	O	N	D	E	R	E	X	A	N	O	R	D	N	U	N	G	E
S	F	V	X	D	E	B	T	N	G	N	O	I	B	T	G	C	P	D	U

On the Enigma machine the right-hand wheel turned every time a key was pressed but the turnover position of the middle and left wheels was determined by the ring settings. As each ring could be set to one of 26 positions, the middle and left wheels could turn at any point between the 1st and the 26th key stroke. This would create problems for the method of solution that Turing had in mind. Therefore, cribs were usually restricted to not more than 12 characters to give a better than 50:50 chance of avoiding a middle-wheel turnover. In this example, the first 12 letters were used for the crib.

The Crib

1	2	3	4	5	6	7	8	9	10	11	12
B	E	S	O	N	D	E	R	E	X	A	N
S	F	V	X	D	E	B	T	N	G	N	O

The relationship between the plain text and the encrypted text could be described graphically and the resulting diagrams were referred to as menus. While the bombe was not a computer, it had some computer-like characteristics. Therefore, this was arguably the first use of the word menu in association with a computer-like device.

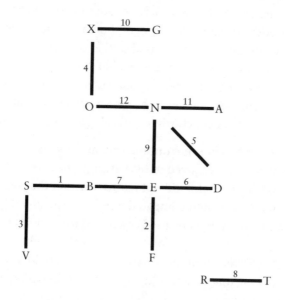

The Menu

Each line in the diagram represented a 26-way cable and showed the relationship between the plain text/encrypted text pairs of letters at a particular position. The menu was in effect an instruction sheet for the technicians (usually members of the Women's Royal Naval Service or WRNS) who operated the bombes. The letters were connected at the back of the bombe with red 26-way cables. 108 round drums were mounted on the front and each was wired internally to replicate an Enigma wheel. They were laid out in three banks of 36 in columns of 3. Each column replicated one Enigma machine and was called a scrambler.

It was obvious to Turing that a head-on attack was doomed to failure if all of the elements of the daily key were taken on simultaneously. The bombe managed to isolate the plug connections and concentrate on finding the wheel choice and their order in the machine, one possible plug pair (one of which Turing called the central letter) and information relating to the message setting. Turing's idea was that once you found these, you could then work out the plug connections and the rest of the key as a separate process. Turing described his brilliant idea of testing for the plug (or stecker) connections separately as follows:

> There is no reason why, when from one hypothesis about the stecker partner of the central letter we have deduced that it must have a different stecker partner, the process should not go on to draw further conclusions about this second stecker partner.
>
> At first sight this seems quite useless, but as these deductions are reversible [i.e. can be used as new hypotheses] it is actually very useful for all of the conclusions that can be drawn will be false, and those that remain will stand out clearly as possible correct hypotheses.

So a letter would be chosen from the crib and a guess made about its plug pair (the hypotheses referred to by Turing). The extraordinary thing about this approach was that it did not matter whether the guess was right or wrong. The machine would come to the right conclusion in either case. A wrong answer would simply be used as a new starting point to find more wrong conclusions, thus eliminating them as possible right solutions and leaving the right answer. In other words, each letter could have one of 26 plug partners and the machine would eliminate the 25 wrong ones.

The early prototype was called Victory and had a serious limitation which was brilliantly resolved by Welchman. Only certain cribs worked effectively and Turing's original design would have struggled to find a solution to the example above. It was also restricted to what he called single-line scanning which meant that for each wheel choice and order, 26 electrical tests had to be carried out, one at a time. The physical realization of Welchman's idea was called the diagonal board and resulted in a huge increase in the power of the bombe. It also delivered the simultaneous scanning feature that Turing wanted, i.e. that at each wheel choice, order and position, 26 electrical tests were carried out simultaneously. A detailed description is given in Appendix 2 but in essence, the device consisted of an array of 26×26 (676) electrical terminals that were connected to each other and to the scramblers in the bombe in such a way as to exploit the symmetrical properties of the electrical connections in the Enigma plugboard. It significantly increased the number of false conclusions arrived at from any false initial hypothesis.

For each of the possible wheel starting positions, the machine automatically carried out an electrical test to determine if the current starting positions were logically consistent with the menu. If the current starting positions satisfied the requirements of the test, then the machine would automatically stop; otherwise it would proceed to test the next set of starting positions. In effect, the Bombe found wrong answers and reduced the impossibly large number of possible starting positions of the Enigma machine when the message was encrypted, to a manageable number. Information provided by the Bombe at the 'correct stop' allowed the cryptanalysts to find the complete key as well as the message setting using a range of manual methods.

Appendix 2

Enigma and the Bombe in Depth

By Frank Carter

The 'military' Enigma machine generates a sequence of cipher text letters from the corresponding sequence of plain text letters that are typed on its keyboard. When a letter key is depressed the movement closes a switch under the key and this completes an electrical circuit that lights a lamp (one on a panel of 26 lamps) that indicates the corresponding cipher text letter. The convoluted wiring of this circuit passes through the interior of three moveable wheels or rotors, and also through a plugboard.

Every rotor (referred to as a wheel in the body of this book) has a set of 26 electrical contacts on each of its opposite sides, with a different internal arrangement of 26 wires connecting the contacts on one side to those on the other, so that when located in the machine every possible combination of the rotational positions of the three rotors will result in a different electrical circuit between the keys and the indicating lamps. The three rotors turn in a way that is somewhat like the motion of the wheels in an odometer fitted in a car, the right-hand rotor turning on by one position for each letter key pressed, and at a particular position, this turning motion causes the middle rotor to turn on by one place. In the same way at a certain position the movement of the middle rotor causes the left-hand rotor to turn on by one place. The design of the machine is such that when a key is pressed the rotors move before the switch under the key closes to complete the electrical circuit and to light one of the lamps.

The rotor orientations where the 'turnovers' take place are determined by the positions of a notch cut into the side of the ring that is fitted round the rim of each rotor, rather like a tyre on a wheel. These rings either have the 26 letters (A–Z) or alternatively the 26 numbers (1–26) inscribed on them (the following exposition will assume them to be letters).

In the initial setting-up of the machine each ring is made to rotate around the inner core of its rotor to a position where a chosen letter on the ring is aligned with a fixed index mark embossed on the rotor, and it is then locked at this position by a spring clip. These chosen positions are referred to collectively as the 'ring settings' of the rotors and as the plain text is 'typed' on the keyboard of the machine the 'turnover' positions of the middle and left-hand rotors are determined by these settings.

The rotor 'turnovers' have the following unexpected characteristic: every time a key is pressed on the Enigma machine the right-hand rotor moves on regularly by one position; once in every 26 of these moves (at the turnover position set on the right-hand rotor) the middle rotor will also move on by one position. If this movement of the middle rotor happens to bring it to its own 'turnover' position then it will move on again by one position when the next letter key is pressed, and also cause the left-hand rotor to advance by one position. This behaviour is known as the 'double stepping' of the middle rotor and it has the effect of reducing the cyclic period of the rotors from the expected value of $26 \times 26 \times 26$ ($= 17,576$) to $26 \times 25 \times 26$ ($= 16,900$).

The three chosen rotors are placed side by side in one of the six possible arrangements. When in position, three small viewing windows allow one letter on each of the rotor rings to be visible to the operator. The rotors can then be turned by hand until the three letters chosen for the initial rotor starting positions appear in the three windows. Then each letter of plain text entered on the keyboard will result in the illumination of one of the lamps on the lamp panel indicating the corresponding letter of cipher, the electric current passing first though the plugboard to the rotors, and then again through the plugboard and finally to the lamp panel.

The function of the plugboard is to enable additional special changes to be made to the electrical circuits connecting the keys to the lamps. For pre-selected pairs of letters this device enables exchanges to be made automatically between the letters in each pair in the electrical circuits between the keyboard and the rotors and again between the rotors and the indicating lamps.

After passing through the three rotors the electric circuits are connected to another device known as the 'reflector'; the internal wiring in this has the effect of returning the circuit back through the rotors for a second time but in the reverse direction and following a different path, returning again to the plugboard where further exchanges between the pre-selected pairs of letters are made.

The Steckers

The pairs of pre-selected letters that were subjected to these exchanges were known at BP as the 'stecker pairs' (*Stecker* is the German word for 'plug'). The remaining letters not paired for this purpose were said to be 'self-steckered' or 'unsteckered'. During the war the standard German practice was to select 10 pairs of letters each day, and one of the tasks at BP was to identify these 10 stecker pairs (by default the remaining six letters would be self-steckered).

The Reciprocal Characteristics of the Machine

The Enigma machine was designed to have reciprocal characteristics so that the two processes of encrypting and decrypting a message are essentially the same. In order to understand how this can be achieved it is necessary to consider the electrical circuits inside the machine connecting the keys on the keyboard to the indicating lamps on the lamp panel. At each set of rotor positions the effect of the design of the machine is to partition the 26 letters from the alphabet into 13 conjugate pairs so that for every pair one letter will be encrypted as the other and consequently no letter will ever be encrypted as itself. It is important to remember that as the rotor positions change the identity of these conjugate pairs will also change but there will always be 13 of them.

Two highly simplified versions of the circuit diagram of the machine are given opposite showing only 4 of the keys and 4 of the indicator lamps. A machine based upon this simple circuit would be of no practical use but the electrical principles of the real machine can be readily understood by considering the characteristics of the electric circuits shown in these diagrams.

The first diagram shows a configuration of the machine for which letter Q is encrypted to letter E. The second diagram of the same Enigma configuration shows the reciprocal process where letter E is encrypted to letter Q.

The diagrams also show the basic electrical design of the double sockets on the plugboard, where the insertion of a two-pin plug moves the spring-loaded shorting bar across the sockets causing a break in the electrical contact between them and thus enabling the required external 'crossed' pair of connections to be made. The diagrams show how the insertion of plugs in sockets 'Q' and 'W' enables the electrical cross connections to be made to form the stecker pair Q/W.

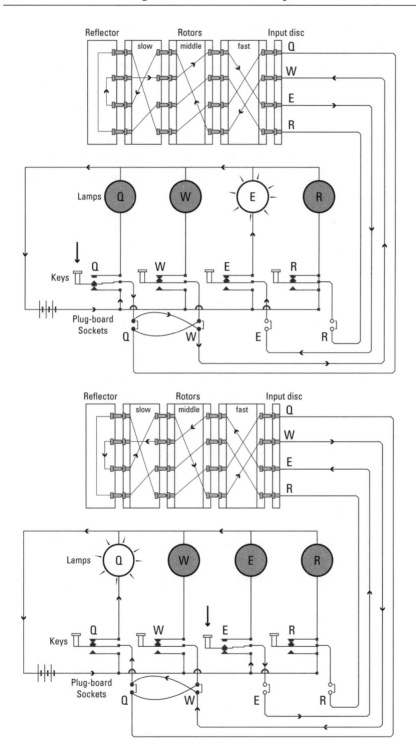

The addition of the plugboard to an earlier version of Enigma transformed it into such a formidable cipher machine that throughout WWII the German authorities never seriously thought that it had been broken. The function of the board was to add to the effects of the rotors the further complication of the transposition of selected pairs of letters. The number of pairs subjected to this process changed over time; initially 6 different pairs were selected each day, but by 1939 this had been increased to 10 pairs. So then each day 10 pairs of sockets from the 26 on the plugboard were chosen and these pairs were electrically connected by means of external cables that had special plugs at each end.

As might be expected the number of possible ways of selecting a set of steckers is a function of the number that are to be selected. Let n represent the number of steckered pairs of letters that are to be selected, so that the number of sockets on the plugboard that will be involved $= 2n$. The first pair of sockets can be selected in $^{26}C_2$ ways. After the selection of the first pair has been made from 26 sockets there will be 24 sockets remaining from which the second pair of sockets can be selected. Hence the second pair of sockets can be selected in $^{24}C_2$ ways. After the selection of the second pair has been made there will be 22 sockets remaining from which the third pair of sockets can be selected and so on. In general, the number of remaining sockets from which the nth pair of sockets can be selected is given by the expression $(28 - 2n)$.

Hence from this chain of values, the total number (T_n) of possible selections of n pairs of sockets is given by the following expression:

$$T_n = {}^{26}C_2 \times {}^{24}C_2 \times {}^{22}C_2 \times {}^{20}C_2 \times \ldots \ldots \times {}^{28-2n}C_2$$

Hence

$$T_n = \frac{26!}{2! \times 24!} \times \frac{24!}{2! \times 22!} \times \frac{22!}{2! \times 20!} \times \frac{20!}{2! \times 18!} \times \cdots \times \frac{(28-2n)!}{2! \times (26-2n)!}$$

After considerable simplification (by cancellation)

$$T_n = \frac{26!}{2^n \times (26-2n)!}$$

In this analysis, the order of occurrence of the selected pairs of sockets is not taken into account and hence the total number T_n of possible selections found includes all of the possible orders of arrangement of the n selected pairs of sockets. The total number of arrangements of n pairs of sockets $= n!$.

Hence if S_n represents the number of possible selections of n pairs of sockets (when no distinction is made between different orders of arrangement) then it follows that:

$$S_n = T_n/(n!) \qquad \text{Hence} \qquad Sn = \frac{26!}{2^n \times (26-2n)! \times n!}$$

Two numerical examples:

If $n = 1$ then $S_1 = 26!/(2 \times 24! \times 1) = (26 \times 25)/2 \; (=325)$

If $n = 2$ then $S_2 = 26!/(4 \times 22! \times 2) = (26 \times 25 \times 24 \times 23)/8 \; (=44,850)$

It is evident that at this stage the number of possible sets of steckers increases very rapidly!

The expression for S_n given above is inconvenient to use when calculating the results for larger values of n. An alternative method is to use the ratio

$$\frac{S_{n+1}}{S_n} = \frac{(26-2n) \times (25-2n)}{2 \times (n+1)}$$

(As an algebraic exercise the reader may wish to confirm this result.)

By using this ratio the results for larger values of n can be more readily determined:

if $n = 1$: $S_2/S_1 = (24 \times 23/4)$
then since $S_1 = 325$, $S_2 = (24 \times 23/4) \times 325 \; (=44,850)$

if $n = 2$: $S3/S2 = (22 \times 21)/6$
then since $S2 = 44,850$, $S3 = (22 \times 21)/6 \times 44,850 \; (=3,453,450)$

This process can be continued for values of $n = 3, 4, 5 \ldots . 13$.

Overleaf is a graph of the results obtained in this way.

It is perhaps surprising that the maximum possible number of stecker pairs is produced when 11 pairs are selected. From the perspective of German security, the greater the number of stecker letter pairs the better, and so 11 pairs would have been the optimal number to use. However the number for 10 pairs is close and slightly reduced the daily task for the Enigma operators when setting up their machines. The value of S_{10} is approximately equal to 1.5×10^{14} (i.e. about 150 million, million). (About 95% of the letters of cipher were affected by the 10 stecker pairs.)

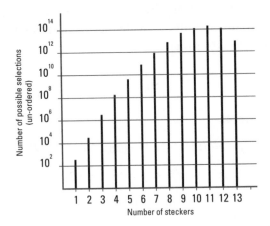

The addition of the plugboard to the Enigma machine gave a huge increase in the number of possible keys that could have been used on a given day, and so greatly increased the security of the system.

Breaking Enigma ciphers

In order to be able to read an Enigma message, it was necessary to find the 'key' that had been used to encrypt the message. This consisted of four component parts.

    (i)   The choice and location in the machine of the three rotors used, referred to as the 'rotor order';

    (ii) The rotor turnover positions for the rotors, given by the 'ring settings' that had been selected for the three rotor rings;

    (iii) The identity of the set of the 10 'steckered pairs' of letters that had been set up on the plugboard;

    (iv) The starting positions of the three rotors that had been used to encrypt the message, known as the 'message settings'.

The function of the bombe was to carry out a systematic search to find the following parts of an unknown Enigma key: (a) the rotor order, (b) the rotor 'core starting positions' (c) the 'stecker partner' of one of the letters on the plugboard.

The expression 'core starting positions' used above is not easy to come to terms with and requires a careful explanation. The 'core starting positions' of the rotors are defined by the respective differences (i.e. the number of places in the alphabet) between the letters of the message settings and the corresponding ring settings. For example the 'message settings' JHL and ring settings DGR taken together define the rotor 'core starting positions'; initially of course both of these parameters would be unknown.

However the 'core starting positions' can be represented by many different combinations of rotor settings and ring settings, and by provisionally assuming the ring settings to be z z z, a bombe could be used to find the rotor settings that represented the same unknown rotor 'core starting positions'. For example with the provisional ring settings z z z, the rotor settings that will give the same 'core starting positions' are F A T.

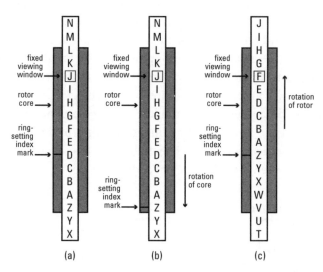

(a)   (b)   (c)

This can be explained by means of the above three diagrams that show the left-hand rotor adjusted in three different ways. In diagram (a) the rotor setting is J and the ring setting is D so the letter D on the ring is aligned to be in registration with the index mark on the core of the rotor. The entire rotor has then been turned so that letter J appears in the left-hand viewing window on the Enigma machine. (Note that the positions of letters J and D in the alphabet differ by 6 places).

In diagram (b) the ring setting has been changed from D to z by turning the inner core of the rotor 'forwards' so that the index mark on it comes into registration with letter z on the ring. Note that the ring itself has not been moved and letter J still appears in the left-hand viewing window.

In diagram (c) the rotor setting has be changed from J to F by turning the entire rotor (i.e. including the core) 'backwards' so that the letter in the viewing window changes accordingly. Note that this has the effect of moving the index mark on the core (together with the internal wiring) to its original position. (Note that the positions of letters F and z in the alphabet differ by 6 places.)

Similar thinking applied to the two other rotors should lead to the conclusion that the rotor positions F A T and 'ring settings' z z z do represent the same set of rotor 'core starting positions' as message settings J H L and 'ring settings' D G R

The penalty incurred by assuming the 'ring settings' to be z z z, is that the true locations of the left and middle-rotor turnover positions will almost certainly differ from those given by the assumed letters. During the war the correct turnover positions had to be found by a sequence of trials that were made at the last stage of the codebreaking process.

The rotors and reflector as used in the Enigma machine were designed as a single-ended unit. In the development of the bombe, an alternative double-ended form was devised which used rotating 'drums' instead of rotors as this was an essential requirement in the design of the machine. Each of these double-ended 'scramblers' had two sets of 26 input/output terminals, and the units could be linked together by 26-way cable connectors in a variety of ways. The following two diagrams show the distinction between the two forms of construction:

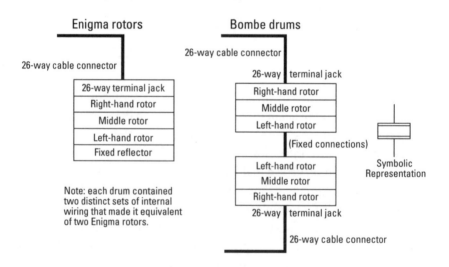

The drums in each scrambler unit were mechanically linked so that they moved from one position to another like the wheels in the odometer of a car. However, they could be independently pre-set to any chosen starting position.

Unlike the adjustable rings attached to the rotors in the Enigma machine, the drums simply had fixed rings of reference letters marked on their circumferences. Consequently the unknown turnover positions of the middle and right-hand rotors of the Enigma machine were unlikely to be the same as those of the corresponding drums in the bombe. This resulted in some restrictions and difficulties in the operational use of the machine.

The Turing Bombe

The fundamental ideas upon which the bombe was based are attributed to Alan Turing, and the first two of them are given here as direct quotations from his wartime paper 'Treatise on the Enigma'.[1]

(i) 'The best data for finding an Enigma key is a crib.'

(ii) 'The method to be used for finding a key will be to take a hypothesis about part of the key and then draw from it all the conclusions that one can, hoping to obtain either a confirmation or a contradiction.'

(iii) The perception that a closed chain of successive Enigma encipherments had a very useful property that could be exploited. (These chains were to be found in some of the cribs as will be explained.)

(iv) His realization that a search for the correct key could be hugely reduced by rejecting all the possible keys which were found to be logically inconsistent with the information that had been derived from a crib.

A Crib

This was a conjecture (an informed guess!) for the letters of plain text represented by a given sequence of cipher letters. The big advantage of finding keys by means of cribs was that the process could not be compromised by any future changes that the Germans might make in their operational procedure. An analysis of some messages broken by earlier methods had revealed that a useful proportion of the messages contained common forms of expression (stereotypes) that could be used as cribs.

The whole basis of Turing's approach was the idea of running a crib through all 17,576 different positions of the drums for a given wheel order, and accepting or rejecting a given position by testing to see if possible stecker pairs could or could not be found for it. This was a very remarkable idea: although in theory the steckers made the identification vastly more difficult, in practice they provided a method for spotting possible positions. Thus the steckers were used to work for a solution and their 'difficulty' was thus neatly compensated for by their ' utility'.[2]

The following illustrative example of a crib was derived from a dummy message encrypted on an Enigma machine. The initial rotor configuration used was specially chosen to avoid the additional complications that would have arisen if a middle-rotor turnover had occurred within the span of the 25 positions of the crib (the problems caused by middle-rotor turnovers will be addressed later):

Position: 1 2 3 4 5 6 7 8 9 10 11 12 13 14 15 16 17 18 19 20 21 22 23 24 25
Plain text: T H I S I S T H E T R I A L T E S T M E S S A G E
Cipher text: C U Q U C D Z X H O B F V M F Y K W R F Q Y V B J

This crib can also be represented in the diagrammatic form that was known as a 'menu':

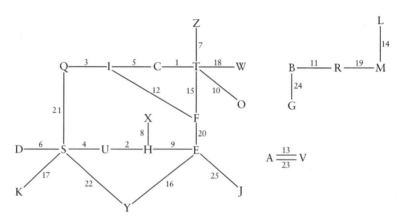

Each 'link' in the menu shows the relationship between the cipher/plain text pair of letters at a particular position on the crib. For example at the fourth position the relationship shown is that letter s is encrypted as u or alternatively, as a consequence of the reciprocal nature of Enigma, letter u is encrypted as s.

Turing found a useful way of formulating a hypothesis about part of a given message key that depended on the sequences of links forming the closed 'loops' that appeared in some menus. The bombe was designed to test these hypotheses in a way that provided parts of the Enigma key that had been used, so that subsequently the complete message key for the day could be found.

The given menu shown contains three such sequences of links forming loops, one for example for the positions: 4, 2, 9, 16, 22. Starting with the letter s this generates the closed letter sequence: S U H E Y (S).

The following diagram gives this sequence of links again now showing only those parts of the encrypting process due solely to the effects of the Enigma rotor system. Starting with the letter α (representing the unknown stecker partner of letter s), the diagram shows how the closed chain of (unknown) stecker letters: α, β, γ, δ, ε, (α) are related to one another.

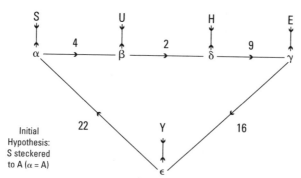

It is very important to appreciate that the identity of the unknown stecker letters β, γ, δ, ε will depend only on the identity of letter α together with the rotor positions *but not on the letters that appeared on the original menu*. It was from sequences of steckered letters like this that Turing was able to formulate his working hypotheses.

Suppose that the rotor configuration is correct (i.e. both the rotor order and rotor core positions are correct), and that the working hypothesis to be used for identifying the stecker partner of letter S is: $\alpha \equiv$ A (i.e. the stecker hypothesis is: S/A). Then as the diagram shows, if this hypothesis is correct, then the final outcome from the closed sequence of successive encipherments, beginning with the chosen letter A must also be letter A as any other outcome would imply a logical contradiction, as the letter s must have a unique stecker partner.

A practical way of testing a working hypothesis like this can be carried out by means of the circuit shown overleaf. Assuming that the rotor configuration in use is correct, then to test the hypothesis: S/A, the switch for letter A on the panel is set to 'on' and the identity of the single lamp on the board that becomes lit is noted.

If the hypothesis S/A is correct then lamp A will be lit, but if it is false then instead a different lamp will be lit, indicating a logical inconsistency and establishing that hypothesis S/A is false. In this event the sequence of alternative hypotheses: s/B, s/C, s/D . . . etc. could then be systematically tested in turn, the final outcome being the discovery of the true stecker hypothesis and thus identifying the correct stecker partner of letter s.

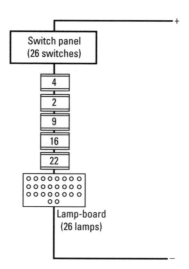

The searching process carried out on the bombe was essentially the systematic testing of these stecker hypotheses. Turing called the basic process 'single line scanning', as the test involved applying a voltage to the input terminals of the scramblers one at a time. However, he realized that this would be much too slow as it would have been necessary to carry out up to 26 of these single tests, for every rotor configuration. Substantial improvements were needed if the bombe was to have any operational value.

There is some evidence that at an early stage in the design of the bombe, an electronic system was considered that would have enabled the 26 individual stecker hypothesis tests to be made at a very high speed. Turing referred to this ideal process as 'simultaneous scanning'. This project was quickly abandoned, after it had been discovered that new ideas (to be considered later) made it unnecessary to resort to the use of complex electronics.

There was also a significant weakness in the test procedure as it has so far been described, that is best understood by means of an example. Suppose that a false stecker hypothesis is under test say s/D and that the rotor configuration being used is also wrong. The identity of the lamp on the panel that is lit now depends entirely on random chance, and so it is possible that it could be lamp D, thus wrongly indicating that the false hypothesis s/D was true. The probability of this happening is 1/26, which is an unsatisfactorily high value.

To reduce the chances of such false conclusions occurring, Turing proposed that the testing process should be carried out with menus that contained at least three closed sequences of successive encipherments. The example menu is of this type containing the sequence S1 = (4 2 9 16 22) already described and also the 2 additional sequences S2 = (21 3 12 20 9 2 4) and S3 = (21 3 5 1 15 20 9 2 4).

These three sequences have the letter s in common (Turing called this 'the central letter', and so in testing any of the stecker hypotheses involving letter s, say (s/D), the condition now required to establish the truth of the hypothesis is the simultaneous lighting of lamp D on all three panels shown in the next diagram.

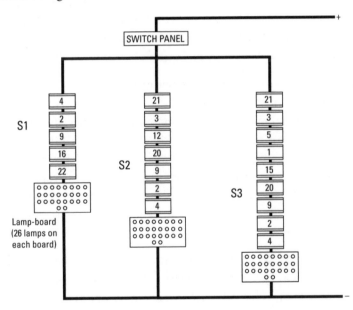

With this circuit if the rotor configuration and the stecker hypothesis to be tested (s/I, the correct hypothesis in this case) are both correct, then lamp I will be lit on each board. If however a wrong hypothesis is tested then it is highly probable that a different lamp will light up on each of the boards.

Suppose for example that the false hypothesis s/Q is tested, and that as a consequence of setting the switch Q to 'on', lamp W is lit on one of the boards. Thus the hypothesis s/Q has led to the inconsistent conclusion s/W, showing that the hypothesis s/Q is false. It is important to appreciate that the conclusion s/W will itself be false. This can be verified in the following way:

If the hypothesis (s/w) were true, then when tested (i.e. by setting switch w to 'on'), lamp w would be lit on all three boards. But it has already been established that on one of the boards lamp w was lit by means of switch Q and not by switch w, consequently the hypothesis (s/w) must be false.

Speeding up the Scanning Process

Turing thought of a highly ingenious idea that enabled the true stecker hypothesis for a chosen letter on the menu to be quickly identified by means of a procedure that eliminated all of the false ones. Provided that a suitable menu was available, this procedure enabled the correct hypothesis to be identified by means of a single electrical test that was carried out with modified versions of the electrical circuits described earlier.

The most important practical outcome of his innovative thinking was that this procedure could be carried out almost instantaneously, so that with suitable menus simultaneous scanning could be achieved.

The following is an extract from Turing's 'Treatise on Enigma':

> There is no reason why, when from one hypothesis about the stecker partner of the central letter we have deduced that the central letter [s in the example] must have a different stecker partner, the process should not go on to draw further conclusions from this second stecker pair. At first sight this seems quite useless, but as these deductions are reversible [i.e. may be used as new false hypotheses] it is actually very useful, for all the conclusions that can be drawn will be false, and those that remain will stand out clearly as possible correct hypotheses.

In the procedure based on this remarkable idea, each false conclusion reached in the way previously described, was to be used as a new hypothesis and so on. This gave rise to a chain of logical conclusions that were almost instantaneously deduced by means of the electrical circuits in the bombe.

A practical way of implementing this procedure is illustrated in the accompanying diagram where the output voltage signal representing the (false) conclusion resulting from the initial (false) hypothesis (s/A) is fed back as a new hypothesis, and the process is repeated until all the possible false conclusions have been reached. These are all revealed by the lamps that become lit, and these are represented in the diagram by the hollow circles.

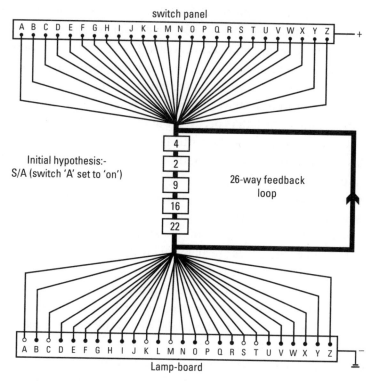

Insight into why the circuit behaves in this way can be obtained by considering the permutation of the 26 letters represented by the switches created by the sequence of scramblers in the circuit.

The pairs of elements from such a permutation can in theory be determined one by one, by setting each switch in turn to 'on', and noting which lamp on the board is lit as a consequence.

For the sequence of scramblers shown in the diagram the permutation is:

A B C D E F G H I J K L M N O P Q R S T U V W X Y Z

C R K Z G F O J I N S H P V X T U E M A L W B Q D Y

Then beginning with the letter A the permutation gives the letter C and likewise from C the permutation gives the letter K, and so on. If this process is continued a sequence of letters will be created that will ultimately terminate when letter A recurs, so giving rise to the sequence (A C K S M P T). This is known as a 'permutation cycle' from the complete permutation.

The reader may wish to verify that the permutation also contains the following other permutation cycles:

C2 = (B R E G O X Q U L H J N V W), C3 = (D Y Z), C4 = (I), C5 = (F).

It will be seen that collectively the five cycles account for all 26 letters of the alphabet, and that there is no single letter common to any pair of cycles, (i.e. the cycles are mutually disjoint). The electrical behaviour of the circuit can now be predicted from the associated permutation cycles. The letter designated by any switch on the panel will also occur in one of the permutation cycles given above. If this switch is set to 'on' then all the lamps that correspond to the letters occurring in this cycle will be lit.

In one special case since the correct stecker hypothesis is s/i, the only conclusion reached will be s/i, so setting switch i to 'on' will result in only the lamp i on the panel being lit.

The structure of the cycles shows that tests carried out on the other 25 false stecker hypotheses will, with the exception of the hypothesis s/F, all result in more than one lamp on the panel being lit, but none would cause lamp i to be lit as the cycles are all mutually disjoint.

The application of voltage feedback to this particular circuit leads to results that considerably reduce the number of possible choices for the correct hypothesis. However the outcomes obtained on the lampboard fail to identify all of the false hypotheses and so it is still not possible to isolate the correct one. In addition there is one totally misleading outcome indicating that the false hypothesis s/F is in fact true!

The full value of voltage feed-back only becomes apparent when a longer crib is used such that the circuit derived from it contains more than one loop. This is illustrated by means of a more complex menu derived from the original crib, containing the 2 sequences S1 and S2. The following diagram shows the 2 loops for S1 and S2 from the original menu, in a circuit configuration that is similar to that used in the first version of the bombe.

The diagram does not include a lampboard as in fact lamps were not used on the bombe; instead a device known as the 'indicator unit' (or the 'test-register') was used, which incorporated 26 indicating relays. A test voltage was applied to the input terminal of one these relays and they provided a visual/tactile indication of the final results.

The input terminal chosen for this purpose was connected to a voltage source by means of the corresponding switch (A–Z) on the panel of switches. The indicator unit was connected to a chosen position on the scrambler circuit by means of a 26-way cable.

The terminals of the relays in the indicator unit that will also 'receive' the test voltage via the scrambler circuit can be identified by considering the permutation cycles for the two sequences S1 and S2.

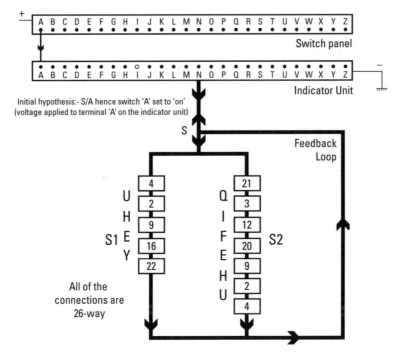

S1 cycles: $C1 = (A C K S M P T)$, $C2 = (B R E G O X Q U L H J N V W)$,
$C3 = (D Y Z)$, $C4 = (I)$, $C5 = (F)$.

S2 cycles: $D1 = (A J U G F W Q L R S C Z M O)$, $D2 = (B H D K Y)$,
$D3 = (E V)$, $D4 = (N T X P)$, $D5 = (I)$.

If a test voltage is applied to terminal I on the indicator unit (i.e. testing the correct hypothesis s/I), then as the permutation cycle (I) occurs in the lists of cycles for both the sequences S1 and S2 the voltage cannot reach any of the other terminals on the test-registers. Terminal I is now the only one with this property so identifying the correct stecker hypothesis to be s/I.

If instead a false hypothesis, say (S/A) is tested, then the test voltage will be applied to relay terminal A, and because of the existence of the permutation cycle C1, the voltage will reach terminals A, C, K, S, M, P, and T via the S1 loop, and likewise because of the existence of the permutation cycle D1, the voltage will also reach the terminals A, J, U, G, F, W, Q, L, R, S, C, Z, M and O via the S2 loop.

Some of the letters in the second list are duplications from the first list, but others are not, terminal G being one example. As a consequence of this, via terminal G, cycle C2, will give rise to voltages on the other terminals B, E, H, N, V and X.

Again as a consequence of the voltage on terminal B, cycle D2 will give rise to voltages on terminals D and Y, and at this stage the terminals of all the relays in the indicator unit, with the exception of terminal I, will have a voltage on them.

As the following table shows, beginning with the false hypothesis S/A, all of the 25 possible false conclusions are arrived at. The reader may wish to test other false initial hypotheses, and should find that they will all produce the same final outcome on the indicator unit where, with the exception of relay I, all of the others will receive the test voltage.

Test register term in all letters	A	B	C	D	E	F	G	H	I	J	K	L	M	N	O	P	Q	R	S	T	U	V	W	X
													Terminals receiving voltages at each stage											
Initial selection for input letter: A	A																							
Voltage feedback due to cycle C1	A		C								K		M			P			S	T				
Voltage feedback due to cycle D1	A		C			F	G			J		L	M		O		Q	R	S		U		W	
Combined effect of C1 and D1	A		C			F	G			J	K	L	M		O	P	Q	R	S	T	U		W	
Feedback via letter G due to cycle C2							G																	
Voltage feedback due to cycle C2		B			E		G	H		J		L		N	O		Q	R			U	V	W	X
Combined effect of C1, D1 and C2	A	B	C		E	F	G	H		J	K	L	M	N	O	P	Q	R	S	T	U	V	W	X
Feedback via letter B due to cycle C2		B																						
Voltage feedback due to cycle D2		B		D				H			K													
Combined effect of C1, D1, C2, D2	A	B	C	D	E	F	G	H		J	K	L	M	N	O	P	Q	R	S	T	U	V	W	X

In the way that has already been explained, if the true hypothesis (S/I) were to be tested, then only the terminal I would receive the test voltage.

The required discrimination between the correct stecker hypothesis and all the false ones has been achieved, and the general behaviour of the bombe characterized by the above example, is summarized in the following statements:

(i) At each possible rotor configuration, the feedback circuit, in effect, tests simultaneously all of the 26 possible stecker hypotheses for a chosen letter on the menu, and if the rotor configuration is correct then the true hypothesis can be identified from a distinctive pattern of voltages appearing on the relay terminals of the indicator unit.

(ii) The distinctive pattern can take two forms: either the test voltage will reach 25 of the 26 relay terminals of the indicator unit, or alternatively only one of them.

The 26 relays in the indicator unit, one for each letter of the alphabet, were used to provide the required logical control of the machine, so that when it was operating with the rotors progressively rotating through all their possible positions, the system would be halted automatically whenever the test voltage failed to reach all of the 26 relays (known as a 'stop').

The introduction of the concept of a feedback loop was of huge importance; providing that a suitable menu was used it enabled simultaneous scanning to be achieved in a remarkably simple way. This enabled part of an Enigma key to be found in a way that avoided having to confront at the same time the severe complications arising from the unknown connections on the Enigma plugboard (the steckers).

As the process of finding the true stecker hypothesis does not depend on which switch is used to input the test voltage, it was a common practice at the time to use an on-menu letter at least two links away from the central letter. The indicator unit was connected by a 26-way cable to the 'best' position in the circuit and this was usually taken to be the one corresponding to the letter on the menu that had the most links attached to it.

Eliminating All the Wrong Rotor Configurations

Clearly a matter of great importance is to consider how this circuit will behave when the rotor configuration is wrong as this will be by far the most common occurrence. In all such cases both sequences S1 and S2 will produce random permutations and a 'random stop' will occur when by chance both of these permutations happen to include a unit cycle of the same letter. The probability of this happening is $1/(26 \times 26)$ implying that the expected number of random stops will be about 26 for every rotor order tested.

However, as a consequence of the feedback processes previously described, a much more likely outcome is that the test voltage will reach the terminals of all the relays in the indicator unit, no matter which input switch is used to 'inject' the test voltage. As all the stops had to be subsequently checked by hand the expected number of random ones given by a menu with 2 loops was inconveniently large. When a menu with three loops was available, the expected number of random stops would be reduced to only one for each rotor order that was tested.

The First Prototype

In the previous circuit diagram, there are duplications of some of the scramblers used at certain positions, and it is possible to eliminate these by making some simple changes to the electrical configuration. The resulting circuit, shown below, has an improved structure that is more suitable for setting up on the bombe, and corresponds to the circuit configurations that were used in the prototype.

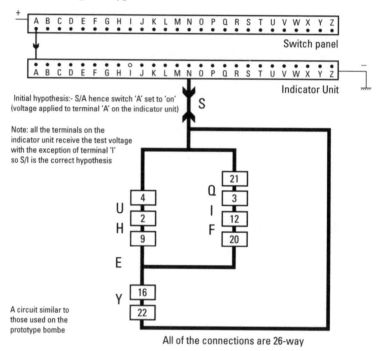

All of the connections are 26-way

The first machine arrived at Bletchley Park in March 1940, and was rather optimistically called 'Victory'; however, the operational performance of the machine was somewhat below expectations. The effectiveness of the prototype bombe was critically dependent on the use of menus containing multiple loops and these were not available as often as had been hoped.

An additional reason for the limited success of the machine was that it was mainly used in attempts to break German Navy ciphers, and this meant that many more possible rotor orders had to be tested than was the case for the messages transmitted by the German Air Force and Army. Consequently a considerable amount of 'bombe time' was expended in attempting to find Navy Enigma keys, using relatively weak menus. German Navy Enigma operators had eight rotors available for use compared to the five for the operators in the other two services. With eight rotors in use there were 336 possible rotor orders to consider!

The Diagonal Board

The invention of the diagonal board by Gordon Welchman was of vital importance in improving the performance of the bombe. It had the valuable effect of hugely increasing the number of electrical connections between the contacts in the circuits that represented valid logical deductions, and enormously increased the likelihood that with a given menu the process of simultaneous scanning would be successfully completed.

This meant that after the addition of the diagonal board to the bombe it became possible to achieve simultaneous scanning using much weaker menus than before. The diagonal board also greatly reduced the number of random stops obtained from a given menu. It enabled menus that covered spans of less than 13 consecutive Enigma positions to be more easily formulated, thus reducing the chances of a middle-rotor turnover (explained below) occurring to less than 50%. In some extreme circumstances the diagonal board even made it possible to achieve simultaneous scanning when using a menu without any loops at all.

The effect of the diagonal board was to enable additional logical inferences to be made about the stecker hypotheses that potentially existed in the original bombe circuits during the course of an operational 'run' but which could not have been foreseen in advance from the menu.

Basically the device consisted of an array of 26×26 ($= 676$) electrical terminals that were connected to each other and to the scramblers in the bombe in a particular way that made it possible to exploit the symmetrical properties of the electrical connections on the Enigma plugboard.

As an illustrative example the diagram overleaf shows the sequence of encipherments S2 previously described, but now set up in the form of a circuit as used on the bombe with the indicator unit connected to position s. The diagram shows an additional row of 26 terminals (A–z), all connected to position s on the menu by means of a 26-way cable, so that they will have the same voltages on them as the corresponding terminals of the relays in the indicator unit.

As has previously been explained, when used with the correct rotor configuration, the voltages on the relays represent the false conclusions for the stecker partner of letter s that follow as logical consequences from an initial false hypothesis. It should be clear that the voltages on the row of terminals could be used instead to represent the false conclusions for the stecker partners of letter s, instead of the relays in the indicator unit.

Additional rows of 26 terminals are also shown connected to the other six scrambler positions in the menu circuit, and likewise the voltages on the terminals in these rows could be used to represent the false conclusions for the stecker partners of these other letters (Q, I, F, E, H and U) also occurring on the menu. (For this particular menu an array of 7×26 of terminals is sufficient for the purpose.)

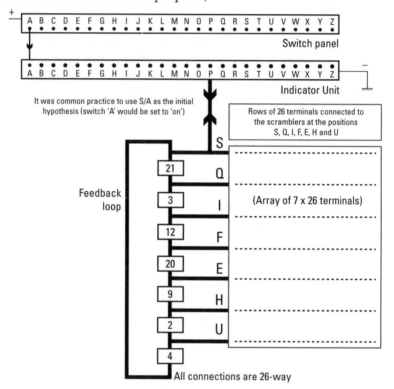

Welchman realized that permanent connections could be made between some of the pairs of the terminals in this array, and that electrically they would significantly increase the number of false conclusions that could be made from any false initial hypothesis that might have been used. His reasons for adding these permanent connections to the circuits in the bombe were based upon the reciprocal relationship existing between the pairs of stecker letters on the Enigma plugboard. For example if say the conclusion s/H is deduced by the electrical circuits in the bombe then as a consequence of this reciprocal stecker relationship, the additional conclusion H/s can also be made.

In electrical terms, this means that if a voltage happens to appear on the terminal H in row s of the array (corresponding to the conclusion H/S), then there should also be a voltage on terminal s in row H (corresponding to the conclusion S/H). This can easily be arranged by simply making a permanent electrical connection between these two terminals to create a new electrical path in the scrambler circuit. If the conclusion H/S is false then so will the conclusion S/H and this in turn is highly likely to result in the generation of further false conclusions (as voltages on other terminals). The same argument can be made for all the other reciprocal stecker letter pairs represented in the array of terminals.

The combined effect of all the connections in the array is to increase hugely the number of false conclusions arrived at from any false initial hypothesis, to the extent that even for some menus without any loops at all, it remains highly probable that all of the possible false conclusions will be obtained, thus maintaining the desired simultaneous scanning that was essential for the correct functioning of the bombes. (The diagonal board had the same powerful effect when the rotor order was wrong.)

A much larger array of 26 × 26 (= 676) terminals is required to provide for all the possible situations that might arise, consequently the wiring of the complete diagonal board is too complex to be given in the form of a diagram, but for purposes of illustration a 'mini' 3 × 3 version of the board for just three letters, is shown below.

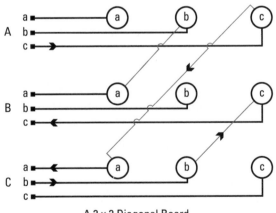

A 3 x 3 Diagonal Board

To avoid confusion lower case letters have been used in this diagram to denote the individual terminals in the array and upper case letters to denote the multiple cable connectors used to link the rows of terminals on the board to the corresponding positions between the scramblers.

This 'mini' board would require three 3-way external connecting cables at the positions indicated by the capital letters to make the necessary electrical connections to the other circuits in the bombe.

As previously explained, the wiring of the diagonal board is based on the symmetrical property of the reciprocal stecker relation between pairs of letters on the plugboard. This means that with the wiring of the diagonal board, if the test voltage appeared on wire c, at position A it would cause the test voltage also to appear on wire a at position C. The arrows in the diagram show how the board provides the required electrical connections corresponding to the following stecker relationships:

A/c implying C/a and C/b implying B/c

(Note: the 'self steckers', for example B/b, do not require any interconnections on the board.)

When the diagonal board is extended to cover all 26 letters, each of the necessary 26 cable connectors, represented by capital letters in the diagram, will have 26 individual contacts, so that the internal electrical connections between the diagonal board and the other circuits in the bombe were made by means of 26-way cables.

The way in which the diagonal board functioned is not obvious, and it is on record that when Welchman first described it to Turing, the latter was 'incredulous' (for a moment or so)!

In order to provide some idea of how it functioned, the following simplified example is given that is based upon an alphabet restricted to the five letters A, B, C, D, E. As a consequence there will only be five connections through the scramblers and only a '5 × 5' diagonal board will be needed.

Then, starting with the false stecker hypothesis A/d, the additional connections through the diagonal board will lead to the following sequence of outcomes:

The voltages on the 'live' contacts, representing the false steckers (A/d, B/e, C/d, D/b and E/c), will be passed to the diagonal board and returned from it to other contacts on the scramblers that represent the reciprocal steckers D/a, E/b, D/c, B/d, C/e, so that these contacts become 'live'.

Each of the five 'live' contacts representing these reciprocal steckers will be on a 'line of electrical continuity' through the scramblers and consequently as well as the contacts on the scramblers these lines will also be made 'live'.

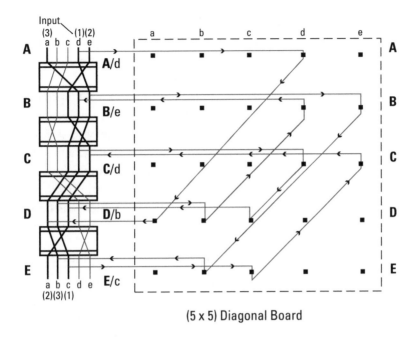

(5 x 5) Diagonal Board

As the diagram shows, two additional lines of continuity marked (2) & (3) are made 'live' by the wiring in the diagonal board. Consequently through these additional lines, more contacts on other scramblers will also be made 'live'. These 'live' contacts will also indicate false steckers, and the voltage on them will be carried back again to the diagonal board to be returned as reciprocal false steckers. This virtually instantaneous process will continue until a stable state is reached.

There are three special circumstances that usually occur that will reduce the number of scrambler contacts involved:

(i) 'Repeats'. It is possible that the voltage representing a reciprocal stecker may be returned from the diagonal board to a contact that is already 'live'.

(ii) 'Self steckers' (A/a, B/b, C/c, D/d, E/e). These have no effect on the process and the 'voltages' are not returned from the diagonal board.

(iii) 'Letter not on the Menu'. In general (but not in this example) a returned reciprocal stecker may involve a letter that is not on the menu. Consequently the voltage from the diagonal board cannot be returned to any of the scramblers.

The complex sequences of events carried out by means of the diagonal board are not easy to quantify. However, the following approximate analysis based on probability considerations may help to provide a better understanding of the role of the diagonal board than is possible from a purely descriptive account.

Consider for example a linear menu (one without loops) consisting of 12 letters, and suppose that the rotor order and current drum settings are both correct. If a false initial hypothesis for the partner of a chosen letter on the menu is used, then in electrical terms the test voltage is applied to a chosen contact on a particular scrambler so that it becomes 'live'. The voltage will be conveyed by means of a line of electrical continuity through the scramblers so that one contact on each of the scramblers has become 'live'. These 12 'live' contacts each represent a stecker partner for the corresponding letter on the menu.

Then, by means of the electrical connections to and from the diagonal board, the voltage on some of these 'live' contacts will be returned and will make other scrambler contacts 'live', these corresponding to the reciprocal steckers. For each of these reciprocal steckers the probability that it will involve one of the 12 letters on the menu = 12/26. So assuming there are no 'repeats' the expected number of reciprocal steckers returned via the diagonal board that will result in additional 'live' contacts = $12 \times (12/26)$.

This, however, is still a slight overestimate, because 'self-steckers' are not returned. The probability that a letter on the menu is 'self-steckered' = 1/26, hence the expected number of self-steckers = $(12 \times 1/26)$, and so a better estimate for the expected number of reciprocal steckers that will be returned from the diagonal board to contacts on the scramblers = $12 \times (12/26) - 12/26$ (≈ 5).

The processes involving the diagonal board can be considered in a number of stages. In the first stage, as explained above, simplified theory shows that a voltage on one line of continuity will cause one contact on each of the 12 rotors to become 'live' and via the diagonal board an estimate of five other contacts on the scramblers will be made 'live'. Hence, assuming there are no 'repeats', the total number of contacts to become activated during the first stage = $12 + 5$ ($= 17$).

However, the possibility of the occurrence of one or more 'repeats' must be taken into account. The diagonal board consists of 26 rows of contacts, one for each letter of the alphabet, and each row has 26 contacts in it (in all $26 \times 26 = 676$ contacts). For a menu with 12 letters, the total number of operational contacts on the diagonal board is 12×26 ($= 312$).

Suppose that at any stage, T represents the total number of terminals on the board that are 'live'. Then the probability that a given terminal is not 'live' $= 1 - T/312$ or alternatively $= (312 - T)/312$. This expression can be used at the next stage as an approximation for the fraction of the predicted number of new 'live' contacts that are not 'repeats' of ones previously counted.

Hence an approximation for the expected total number of new contacts made 'live' by the end of the first stage is: $5 \times (312 - 12)/312]$ (≈ 5) (so at this stage repeats are unlikely). By the end of the first stage a total of $12 + 5 = 17$ contacts will be 'live', (the same approximate value as before).

During the second stage the five additional scrambler contacts that became 'live' during the first stage will have two effects:

(i) As each of them is on a 'line of electrical continuity' through the 12 scramblers this will result in a contact on each of the 12 scramblers becoming 'live', so in all $5 \times 12 = 60$ contacts will be made 'live' in this way. However, taking into account the probable occurrence of 'repeats' this number is reduced to about: $60 \times (312 - 17)/312$ (≈ 57). So the current cumulative total number of 'live' contacts $= 17 + 57$ ($= 74$)

(ii) Probability theory has already shown that the voltage on 5 out of the 12 'live' contacts on each of the above lines of continuity will be returned via the diagonal board and will result in another 'live' contact on another scrambler. Since there are five such lines the total number of contacts that will be made 'live' $= 5 \times 5$. Then taking into account that some are very likely to be 'repeats', the expected number of new contacts to be made 'live' in this way $= 25 \times (312 - 74)/312$ ($= 19$). Hence the cumulative total number of activated contacts at the end of the second stage $= 74 + 19 = 93$. This analysis can be continued for the third stage, fourth stage and so on until no additional new contacts are made 'live'.

The set of results obtained for six stages is shown in the table overleaf.

The 'live' contacts on the diagonal board represent the steckers that can be deduced from the initial false stecker hypothesis that was chosen to start the process. The final number of 305 'live' terminals obtained is only an approximation (about 2% too big) for the total number of (25×12) false steckers that would be expected to be obtained when using an open menu with 12 letters.

New contacts	Number of contacts on the 'live' lines of electrical continuity		Current total number of live contacts	Additional contacts made 'live' via links through diagonal board		Curren numb live co
	Including duplications	Probable number of new live contacts		Including duplications	Probable number of new live contacts	
1	$1 \times 12 = 12$	12	12	$5 \times 1 = 5$	5	$12 + 5$
5	$5 \times 12 = 60$	$60 \times (312 - 17)/312 = 57$	$17 + 57 = 74$	$5 \times 5 = 25$	$25 \times (312 - 74)/312 = 19$	$74 + 1$
19	$19 \times 12 = 228$	$228 \times (312 - 93)/312 = 160$	$93 + 160 = 253$	$5 \times 19 = 95$	$95 \times (312 - 253)/312 = 18$	$253 + 18$
18	$18 \times 12 = 216$	$216 \times (312 - 271)/312 = 28$	$271 + 28 = 299$	$5 \times 18 = 90$	$90 \times (312 - 299)/312 = 4$	$299 + 4$
4	$4 \times 12 = 48$	$48 \times (312 - 303)/312 \approx 1$	$303 + 1 = 304$	$5 \times 4 = 20$	$20 \times (312 - 304)/312 \approx 1$	$304 + 1$
1	$1 \times 12 = 12$	$12 \times (312 - 305)/312 \approx 0$	$305 + 0 = 305$	$5 \times 1 = 5$	$5 \times (312 - 305)/312 \approx 0$	$305 + 0$
0	0	0	305	0	0	30

The final outcome obtained is that all but one of the contacts in each of the connected rows on the diagonal board become 'live'. The remaining 'non-live' contacts will all be on one particular 'line of electrical continuity' that is electrically isolated from the others and these contacts represent in electrical terms the true stecker partners of the twelve letters on the menu. If the initial stecker hypothesis used happens to be true then only the contacts on the isolated line of continuity will become 'live'.

The first machine to be fitted with a diagonal board became operational in late August 1940; it was a considerable improvement on the early prototype and operationally it proved to be very effective. Subsequently a large number of bombes of this type were manufactured, and for a time these were known as spider bombes. The probable reason for this name was that Welchman often referred to bombe menus as 'webs'.

All of the 'stops' given by the bombe are detected by means of a test procedure that is carried out at each of the possible rotor settings, where at each setting the 26 alternative stecker hypotheses for a chosen input letter on the menu are tested simultaneously. In electrical terms the true stecker hypothesis is identified by a particular contact on one line of continuity through the scramblers that is found to be electrically isolated from all the others. Each of the contacts on this isolated line of continuity represents a possible stecker partner for the corresponding letter on the menu. When such a single line of continuity is detected by the logic circuits incorporated in the bombe it will automatically execute a 'stop'. The information provided by a 'stop' consists of the rotor settings together with a corresponding possible stecker partner of the chosen input letter.

A serious problem that had to be dealt with was that in addition to the stop that provided the correct information, additional random stops could also occur. The number of random stops obtained depended on the structure of the menu and clearly it was necessary to be able to predict the number likely to be obtained from a given menu.

Consider a menu consisting of a single open network, (i.e. one without any loops). At each of the possible $26 \times 26 \times 26$ rotor settings for a given rotor order, any initial stecker hypothesis, say g, for the chosen input letter A will lead to one stecker partner for each of the other letters on the menu, and so will satisfy the necessary condition for a 'stop' to occur. Hence the expected number of stops resulting from any initial stecker hypothesis = $26 \times 26 \times 26$. In all there are 26 possible initial stecker hypotheses, so it follows that there are $26 \times 26 \times 26 \times 26$ ($= 26^4$) possible combinations that will all satisfy the condition required for a stop to take place (i.e. 26 'stops' for each of the possible rotor settings)!

Each 'stop' will lead to stecker partners for all the letters on the menu. For example the two letters E and F on the menu will have 26×26 possible different pairs of stecker partners (including 'self-steckers'). The diagram shows the pair (E/c and F/k).

Stecker hypothesis:- g/A

A g ▪ Input

B s

E c ▪ ▪ k F

The Effect of the Presence of a Loop in the Menu

Suppose that the letters E and F are in positions on the menu such that the introduction of a new link between them will create a closed loop. This link has the important effect of reducing the number of possible stops by a factor of 26 which can be explained in the following way:

When the link between the letters E and F is added to the original menu, a restriction is imposed on the number of possible pairs of stecker partners for the letters E and F.

The diagram showing one possible pair of (x n) when letter x is encrypted through the new scrambler to give n, so that E/x $\leftrightarrow$ F/n. consequently the corresponding pair of stecker partners for letters E and F is (x n). Since every scrambler permutation consists of thirteen pairs of reciprocal letter transpositions, the total number of possible pairs of stecker partners for letters E and F is reduced from (26×26) to $(2 \times 13) = 26$.

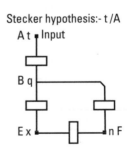

Stecker hypothesis:- t /A

A t ▪ Input

B q

E x ▪ ▪ n F

Thus the introduction of the additional link has the effect of reducing the number of possible pairs of stecker partners by a factor of 26, and consequently there will be the same reduction factor for the number of stops obtained when the new link is added to the menu. Hence the expected number of random stops obtained with a simple menu with one loop = $26^4/26 = 26^3$ (i.e. one for each of the possible rotor settings.)

In general if the links in a menu result in the formation of c loops then the number of random stops S obtained is given by the expression:

$$S = (26^4)/26^c = 26^{4-c}$$

Turing carried out a mathematical investigation to estimate how effective the diagonal board was in reducing the number of random 'stops', and produced a very useful table that enabled an accurate estimate to be found for the number of random stops to be expected from a given menu (he described this work as 'very tedious and uninteresting'). This table was based on an expression for the expected number of random stops in terms of the number of loops c on the menu and a factor F that depended on the number of letters it had:

$$\text{Estimated number of random stops} = 26^{4-c} \times F$$

He derived numerical values of the factor F for different numbers of letters on the menu showing that the number decreased very rapidly as the number of letters increased. (It is worth noting that without the diagonal board the number of random stops entirely depended on the number of loops.)

One particular entry from Turing's table shows that for a menu of 12 letters, $F = 0.0018$. This result can be used to illustrate the beneficial effect of the diagonal board.

Let the number of random stops obtained from a menu with 12 letters and c loops when using the diagonal board = N.

Then $N = 26^{4-c} \times 0.0018$

Suppose that another 'stronger' menu with 12 letters and k loops (where k is greater than c) would be required to produce the same number of random stops when the diagonal board is not connected:

Then $N = 26^{4-k}$
Hence $26^{4-c} \times 0.0018 = 26^{4-k}$

After some simplification this reduces to: $26^{k-c} = 500$

Hence $(k-c) = \log(500) \div \log(26) \; (\approx 1.90)$

Hence $k \approx c + 2$

This result shows that for a menu of 12 letters the effect of the diagonal board is approximately equivalent to the addition of 2 additional loops.

In order to identify the correct 'stop' from all the other 'random' ones, each had to be subjected to a process of hand testing. The first step in this task was to use the information provided by the 'stop' to determine the stecker partners for all of the letters appearing on the menu that were implied by it. These implied stecker partners were tested for their logical consistency by checking to see that for every letter on the menu the implied stecker partner was unique. All of the 'stops' that failed to satisfy this requirement were regarded as being due to chance and would be rejected.

The task of finding the implied stecker pairs was carried out with the aid of a small ancillary piece of equipment known as a 'checking machine', but sometimes there were additional difficulties. If a menu happened to be made up of two or more unconnected parts (known as 'webs') then often some of the implied stecker pairs could not be found directly in this way and in such cases some additional deductive work would be necessary to find them.

To come to an understanding of the function of the checking machine, consider again a menu previously given but now re-arranged into the equivalent form shown in the diagram below.

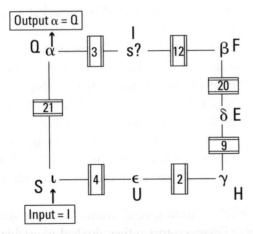

Suppose that a particular bombe stop found from this menu gave the rotor settings: H B L together with the stecker pair s/I. The validity of this stop would have been checked in the following way:

From the 'stop' it is known that letter s has letter I as its stecker partner, and so logically letter I should have letter s as its stecker partner. However the partners of the other letters Q, F, E, H and U are currently unknown. Let these unknown letters be represented by the Greek letters: α, β, γ, δ, and ε, so that Q/α, F/β, E/γ, H/δ and U/ε are the unknown stecker pairs.

From the stecker pair s/I given by the 'stop' it follows from the information in the diagram that if the letter I is used as the input to the scrambler system adjusted to 'position 21' that the output letter from this scrambler will be the implied stecker partner of letter Q on the menu. It is in fact found that α ≡ Q, indicating that letter Q must be 'self-steckered' i.e. Q/Q. (The standard German practice was to use six self-steckers in each Enigma key.)

In the same way by using this implied letter Q as the input to the next scrambler adjusted to 'position 3' the output letter obtained will be the implied stecker partner of letter I on the menu. For logical consistency this must be the letter s, otherwise there would be a contradiction with the stecker pair s/I given by the bombe 'stop'. So if a different letter were to be obtained then this would show that the 'stop' was a random one.

Supposing, however, that the letter s was obtained, then the testing procedure would be continued with letter s now being used as the input to the scrambler adjusted to 'position 12', so that the output β will be the implied stecker partner for letter F. This process could be continued for all the letters on the menu. If any logical inconsistency were to be discovered between the results then the 'stop' would be regarded as 'random' and would be rejected. This would happen if, for example, the two inconsistent implied stecker pairs T/F and U/T were to be obtained.

If no inconsistencies were found between any of the implied stecker partners for all of the letters on the menu then the stop was said to have provided a 'partial key'. If the partial key were set up on an Enigma machine then it would decrypt all the letters from the crib that had been used for the menu, but not usually the complete message because it was unlikely that the restricted number of letters on the menu would have enabled deductions to be made for all the ten stecker pairs that ultimately had to be found.

The checking machine used special drums that were similar in their design to the German Enigma rotors as they also had adjustable rings, unlike the drums used on the bombe. The machine had a fourth drum that was used in association with breaking the four-wheel naval Enigma. The machine also had 26 keys for the input letters and the same number of lamps to indicate the output letters. The selection of the drums and their ring settings was made to correspond to the information given by the 'stop' on the bombe. The set of drums on the checking machine would then be moved in turn to correspond to the positions given on the menu. As one stecker pair had already been given by the 'stop', the implied stecker partners for all of the other letters on the menu could then be found in turn.

Summary

After a menu had been set up on the bombe and a chosen set of drums had been installed, the machine would be systematically run through all of the possible starting positions, and at each of them tested for the condition that had to be satisfied to ensure that a unique stecker partner existed for a pre-selected letter on the menu. If at the end of a 'run' with a chosen rotor order all of the 'stops' that had been obtained were found to be false then another rotor order would have to be tried. The small number of partial keys obtained from the 'stops' that passed all the tests made by the checking machine were subjected to further examination. A brief account of how this was done will be given later.

If the unfortunate circumstances arose when none of the partial keys provided the complete key, then the validity of the menu had to be questioned, both with respect to its position relative to the letters in the original cipher text and also its literal accuracy.

Further Development of the Bombe

By the end of 1941 a more advanced version of the bombe (known as 'Jumbo') had been developed. This was fitted with additional circuitry that enabled a second test to be automatically carried out when the basic conditions for a 'stop' had occurred. The second test was designed to eliminate all those 'stops' that led to a 'legal contradiction', which the earlier versions of the machine were unable to detect. This second test checked the logical consistency of all the stecker pairs that could be directly deduced from the menu and if an inconsistency was detected then the new machine ignored the basic 'stop' condition that had occurred and continued with the 'run'. If, however, no inconsistencies were found then the machine did stop and automatically printed out all of the stecker pairs that could be directly deduced from the menu.

The introduction of Jumbo eliminated a major part of the hand-based work that had previously been necessary but, as only a few of these machines were actually made, the bulk of the work throughout the war was carried out on the spider bombes, of which over 200 were in service by the end of the war in Europe. This new version of the machine provided no more information about the stecker pairs than was intrinsically available on the original bombes, but by automatically eliminating all the inconsistent random 'stops' and printing out details of the remaining ones, Jumbo made it possible to run much weaker menus successfully. The few Jumbo machines that were made were reserved for work on important messages that had only provided very weak menus and were expected to generate large numbers of random stops when used with a spider bombe.

The following extract from an internal memorandum from Welchman to Travis (September 1941) is of interest:

> Dear Commander Travis,
>
> The problems which we have to deal with in HUT 6 fall into two main classes – those in which we have to try 17,576 positions per wheel order, and those in which we need only try a limited number of positions. Problems of the first class can only be dealt with by means of a bombe, and the possibility of dealing with a particular problem depends chiefly on the strength of the menus that can be prepared. For running on a standard bombe a menu must be strong enough to produce a small number of stops because the testing of a large number of stops would take too much time. Weaker menus can be run on Jumbo because the machine tests its own stops, but the menus that can be run are limited by two factors. When a menu is so weak that Jumbo has to stop hundreds of times in each run, the running time is too long. Also when Jumbo produces a large number of stories, which have to be examined, the time and labour required for this part of the work becomes excessive . . .
>
> At present we have eight bombes of which only one is a Jumbo.[3]

Difficulties Caused by Middle-Rotor Turnovers

A matter of vital importance that arose during the construction of the menus was the possibility that at some position within the span of the crib a middle-rotor turnover had occurred on the Enigma machine when the message had been encrypted. There was no prior way of knowing if this had happened, and if one had taken place and was not allowed for in the menu, then the 'stops' found in the subsequent bombe runs would all be wrong. Since a turnover on the middle rotor of an Enigma machine always occurred at some position during the encrypting of a sequence of 26 consecutive letters, it follows that for an menu to have more than an even chance of success its span could not exceed 12 consecutive positions of the cipher text.

During the war several procedures were devised to overcome this difficulty, for example from a crib spanning consecutive positions it was possible to derive two menus each spanning 13 of these positions so that if the middle-rotor turnover occurred in one of them then it could not have occurred in the other. However, this approach often resulted in two relatively 'weak' menus (i.e. containing less than 2 loops) which could result in an undesirable large number of random stops.

Other methods involved making a sequence of trial runs using different assumed positions for the middle-rotor turnover. As these runs had to be repeated for each of the rotor orders that were to be tested, these procedures were often very time-consuming.

The bombes were designed with three banks of 12 'scramblers', each scrambler consisting of three vertically aligned drums to emulate the three rotors in the Enigma machine. Then, provided that the menu used did not contain more than 12 letter pairs from the crib, this arrangement made it possible to try out three different menus or rotor orders simultaneously.

One remarkably innovative procedure was proposed by John Herivel, the originator of the 'Herivel Tip'. It appears in a BP research paper he wrote in the autumn of 1940 and required only one bombe run for each of the rotor orders to be tested.[4] However, during this single run on the bombe the machine had to be manually halted by the operator several times to enable changes to be made to the offsets of some of the middle drums.

In his paper Herivel expressed his understanding that there were plans to modify the electrical design of the first bombes and 'to interchange the slow and fast wheel'. This change made it possible for the bombe operators to use this new procedure he proposed. (In more recent times this perhaps unexpected design feature of the standard British bombes has often been a source of confusion.)

With this modification, the slow bottom drums on the bombe (that now represented the 'fast' right-hand position Enigma rotor) only stepped on at infrequent intervals thus making it easy to anticipate their arrival at particular offset positions so that the operator could manually halt the machine. The special menus that required changes to be made to some of the offsets of the middle drums during the course of a single run became known as 'hoppity' menus.

To assist with an explanation of this 'hoppity procedure', a dummy message consisting of 22 characters was encrypted using the following Enigma key:

> Reflector: B
> Rotor order (L M R): 3, 2, 1
> Ring settings: Z Z J,
> Message settings: P S B
> Steckers: A/C, B/Z, E/L, D/T, F/M, G/S, J/X, K/N, R/H, U/W

As the turnover notch on the 'fast' Enigma rotor (rotor 1) is located between the letters Q and R on its ring, when this rotor steps on from positions Q to R a middle-rotor turnover will occur. The 'fast' rotor setting given in the key is B, and this is 2 places 'in front' of Z on the ring. Consequently when the plain text was encrypted, a turnover of the middle rotor (from position S to position T) occurred when the right-hand rotor stepped on after the fifteenth position in the message (the seventeenth position on the ring scale) as shown in the following table.

Ring	0	1	2	3	4	5	6	7	8	9	10	11	12	13	14	15	16	17	18	19	20	21	22	23
L rotor			P	P	P	P	P	P	P	P	P	P	P	P	P	P	P	P	P	P	P	P	P	P
M rotor			S	S	S	S	S	S	S	S	S	S	S	S	S	S	S	T	T	T	T	T	T	T
R rotor			B	C	D	E	F	G	H	I	J	K	L	M	N	O	P	Q	R	S	T	U	V	W
Plain			–	A	T	E	S	T	M	E	S	S	A	G	E	F	O	R	H	O	P	P	I	T
Cipher			–	Z	O	N	U	M	F	U	N	W	M	K	D	J	Y	U	I	H	A	S	C	O
Position				1	2	3	4	5	6	7	8	9	10	11	12	13	14	15	16	17	18	19	20	21

The menu shown below was constructed from this table which spans 22 consecutive positions, with a middle-rotor turnover occurring immediately after the seventeenth position.

```
              20      16      17      2
   C ———————— I —————— H —————— O ═══════ ZZB ═══ T ——— M ——— A ——— Z
      ZZT  \  ZZP     ZZQ     ═══ ZZU      5    ZZE 10 ZZJ 1 ZZA
            \ 22         14 /        21                 6           18
              ZZV          ZZN                         ZZF          ZZR
                \        /                        13                 19
                   Y                       J ——————— F              ZZS
                                              ZZM                    P

           G —————— K
              ZZK                          N ———— S ———— W
                                            8  ZZH 9 ZZI
        Menu with 22                        3           4
   consecutive offsets ZZA to ZZV          ZZC          ZZD

                                    12      7       15
                                D ——— E ————— U ——— R
                                   ZZL  ZZG   ZZO
```

Menu with 22 consecutive offsets ZZA to ZZV

If this menu is used on the bombe it will fail to find the correct 'stop' unless measures are used to take the Enigma middle-rotor turnover into account. This can be done by advancing the offsets of the middle drums in the links 16 to 22 from z to A. After the menu had been modified in this way a run on an emulation of a bombe gave the correct bombe stop P S R (the correct initial rotor settings relative to ring settings z z z).

Finding the Ring Settings

According to Welchman in *The Hut Six Story*: 'The ring settings had to be worked out by crypto-analytical techniques and that sometimes proved troublesome.'

By means of a menu based on a crib, the bombe provided part of the original Enigma key that had been used to encrypt the message. From this information it was then usually possible to derive the complete set of 10 stecker pairs so that the known parts of the key then consisted of the rotor order, 10 stecker pairs, and the starting positions of the three Enigma rotor cores based on the ring settings z z z.

The original German ring settings would almost certainly have been different from the assumed ring settings, and consequently if the latter were used in an attempt to decrypt the entire message, the turnover positions of the middle and left-hand rotors would be wrong. Frequently it was possible to decrypt a part of the message with these wrong ring settings, up to the position where the first middle-rotor turnover took place. This could happen before or after the position where it had originally occurred when the message was being encrypted, as determined by the unknown German ring settings.

Following on from this position the decryption of the cipher text would 'go wrong' producing only random characters. However, it was sometimes found that at some later position in the cipher text, an additional sequence of letters would be correctly decrypted.

2	3	4	5	6	7	8	9	10	11	12	13	14	15	16	17	18	19	20	21	22	23	24	25	26	27	28	29
L	K	M	Y	E	Q	N	L	U	N	M	W	L	N	B	H	R	F	Y	X	F	S	S	V	I	L	X	E
B	S	T	I	M	M	S	P	R	U	C	H	F	R	M	Q	V	P	S	B	H	N	E	X	S	I	N	N
B	S	T	I	M	M	S	P	R	U	C	H	Y	Y	R	E	S	T	X	O	H	N	E	X	S	I	N	N

A real example of this is given in the table above. The first row is the cipher text, and the second is the decrypt obtained using the key found by means of the bombe which gave the drum starting positions H T N (i.e.

Enigma settings H T M) relative to the assumed ring settings Z Z Z. The third row is the correct plain text from the message.

It will be seen that the decrypt does 'go wrong' at position 14 but 'comes right' again at position 22 (8 places further on). The reason for this is that during the decrypting process, a turnover of the middle rotor occurred 'too soon' at position 14 so that the assumed ring-setting Z for the right-hand rotor must be 'moved back' by 8 positions from Z to R.

When the ring settings are changed to Z Z R, to maintain the wiring cores of the rotors at their orientations the Enigma rotor starting position must also be changed from H T M to H T E. After making these adjustments the decrypt obtained is entirely correct. This is shown in the third row of the table.

As the ring settings Z Z R enable the entire message to be decrypted it follows that the right-hand ring setting R must be correct because the turnover of the middle rotor now occurs at the correct place. It is, however, very unlikely that the ring settings of the other two rotors are those originally used by the German operator, as there are numerous combinations of ring settings and rotor starting positions that could have been used.

To find the original ring settings of these two rotors used it is necessary to carry out a search procedure involving a sequence of trials carried out on emulations of the Enigma machine. These trials are based upon the two groups of three letters of the message 'indicators' that had been included with the cipher message in the original W/T transmission. Some additional information might have been available that reduced the number of possible ring settings (e.g. German Air Force 'Ringstellung rules'). However, a worst-case scenario will require up to 26×26 (= 676) trials.

The following straightforward example is based upon the wartime message given above with the provisional Enigma key: rotor order 1, 2, 5; message settings T H E; ring settings Z Z R.

When used with the correct set of steckers, the ring settings Z Z R and rotor settings H T E, the provisional key correctly decrypted the entire message. The intercepted indicator letter groups for the message (included in the original W/T transmission) were: M A F P K R.

Theory of the Procedure

Suppose that the true message settings and ring settings are respectively x
yz and α β δ. Then from the given indicator groups M A F and P K R it follows
that with:

Enigma rotor settings = M A F and ring settings = α β δ
xyz will be encrypted as P K R

The procedure begins by configuring an Enigma machine (or an emulation
of one) so that with:

Enigma rotor settings = M A F and ring settings = Z Z R
H T E will be encrypted as ? ? ?

As the two rotor configurations H T E/Z Z R and xyz/α β δ decrypt the
message correctly both of them must define the same set of orientations of
the rotor cores

It follows that, starting with the message indicator H T E and the ring
settings Z Z R, if both are progressively advanced by one position at a time,
the orientation of the rotor cores will remain the same and consequently
at some stage the rotor settings H T E will have been transformed to xyz
and the corresponding ring settings will have been transformed to α β δ.
When this stage is reached then the unknown letters xyz will be encrypted
to P K R.

So the procedure begins with the Enigma rings set to Z Z R and the letter
group H T E is encrypted to see if the outcome is indeed P K R. If this is not
the case then the ring setting is advanced from Z Z R to Z A R and likewise
the middle letter of the letter group H T E advanced by one position from T
to U and the resulting letter group H U E is encrypted and the outcome
checked as before.

This procedure may have to be repeated many times. However,
eventually, at some stage in this process, the outcome will be P K R, at which
point the true ring settings α β δ and the original message settings xyz will
both be given by the current configuration of the machine.

The ring settings and letter groups for the first four trials are as follows:

1st (M A F) H T E 2nd (M A F) H U E 3rd (M A F) H V E 4th (M A F) H W E
   (Z Z R)   (Z A R)   (Z B R)   (Z C R)

At some stage the required combination as shown below is bound to arise:

Enigma rotor settings   M A F and ring settings X N R
                                    F H E will be encrypted as P K R

Thus it is evident that the original ring settings and message settings were respectively X N R and F H E.

The Rotor Turnovers

The turnover notches on the Enigma rotors are located at particular positions on their rings. For the first five rotors the positions of the single notch were as follows:

Rotor I	Rotor II	Rotor III	Rotor IV	Rotor V	Rotors VI–VIII
Q–R	E–F	V–W	J–K	Z–A	Z–A & M–N

The extra rotors VI–VIII used by the German Navy had 2 turnover notches on their rings and this could result in a considerable reduction in the length of the Enigma rotor cycle. For example if Navy rotors were used in the middle and right-hand position of the Enigma machine then the rotor cycle length was reduced to 4,056 ($26 \times 12 \times 13$). This shows that, although the use of rotors with more than one notch gave some advantages, it also had the effect of reducing the length of the Enigma rotor cycle. (The number given can be obtained by an analysis similar to that given above.)

Using 'Cillies' to Reduce the Possible Number of Rotor Orders

The fact that rotors I–V have distinctive notch positions on their rings made the Enigma machine less secure than it would have otherwise been. Indeed in 1940 one of the repeated lapses in security made by the Enigma operators made it possible to use the distinctive turnover positions of these rotors to reduce the number of rotor orders that had to be checked when recovering the keys. (The first success using the procedure now to be described was achieved with a German message in which the three letters C I L formed part of the indicator, hence the term 'cillies'.)

Cillies resulted from a lazy practice adopted by some Enigma operators when encrypting a multi-part message. After encrypting the first part of such a message, some operators often used the three letters of the current positions of the rotors (known at BP as the 'end positions') as the indicator settings for the second part of the message and would repeat this practice for any further parts.

As the number of letters in each part of the message was invariably included in its preface (transmitted in clear) it was then possible to reduce significantly the number of rotor orders that could have been used. Beginning with the known length of the first part of the message and 'working back' from the 'end positions' of the rotors (as disclosed by the first group of three letters in the indicator for the second part of the message), the possible message settings used for the first part of the message could be found.

Let the number of letters in the first part of the message be X. Suppose that at the completion of the process of encrypting the first part of the message the middle rotor had moved on by q positions and that the right-hand rotor had finished p positions from its starting position, then $X = 26q + p$ (where q and p are positive integers). Note also that, because of the limit the Germans set on their message lengths, for all the messages $X < 250$. Thus $26q + p < 250$, and hence $q < 10$.

For example, given that $X = 247$ then the only possible values for p and q are $p = 13$ and $q = 9$ $(247 = 26 \times 9 + 13)$

The rotor order that had been used would have been unknown and hence so would the positions of the turnover notches on the rings of the three rotors. However, the charts below and overleaf give the procedures that were used for 'working backwards' to find the possible rotor starting positions to encrypt the first part of the message. This shows that there are 4 possibilities to consider, each based on different assumptions for the locations of the turnover notches on the middle and right-hand rotors.

Length of the message = X characters

$$X = 26q + p$$

(i.e. Rotor R makes q complete revolutions + p additional steps)

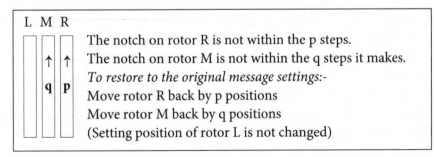

L M R

The notch on rotor R is not within the p steps.
The notch on rotor M is not within the q steps it makes.
To restore to the original message settings:-
Move rotor R back by p positions
Move rotor M back by q positions
(Setting position of rotor L is not changed)

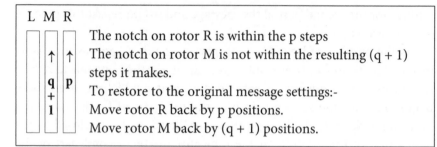

L M R

The notch on rotor R is within the p steps

The notch on rotor M is not within the resulting (q + 1) steps it makes.

To restore to the original message settings:-

Move rotor R back by p positions.

Move rotor M back by (q + 1) positions.

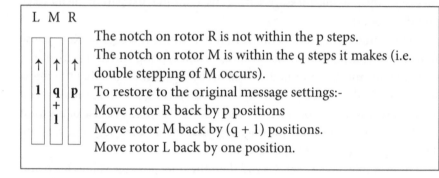

L M R

The notch on rotor R is not within the p steps.

The notch on rotor M is within the q steps it makes (i.e. double stepping of M occurs).

To restore to the original message settings:-

Move rotor R back by p positions

Move rotor M back by (q + 1) positions.

Move rotor L back by one position.

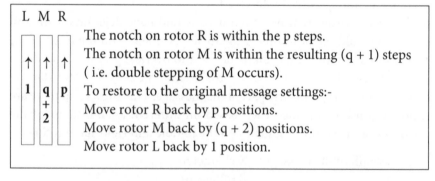

L M R

The notch on rotor R is within the p steps.

The notch on rotor M is within the resulting (q + 1) steps (i.e. double stepping of M occurs).

To restore to the original message settings:-

Move rotor R back by p positions.

Move rotor M back by (q + 2) positions.

Move rotor L back by 1 position.

So on the assumption that the German operator had used the lazy procedure previously described, it followed that one of only four possible message settings could have been used to encrypt the first part of a multi-part message.

Another procedural mistake was often made by the operators that enabled three of these possibilities to be eliminated. Some of them adopted the practice (contrary to instructions) of using 2 related groups of three letters for their indicators based on their own choice of 6-letter word or obtained by using letters that were in convenient (adjacent) positions on the German key-board.

When this practice had been adopted it was often fairly obvious from the first group of letters in the indicators that this had been done thus enabling the message settings to be inferred.

Indicator setting	Indicator	Likely message setting
LON	XJF	DON
QWE	GHT	RTZ
HIT	VZQ	LER
QAY	HMB	WSX
WER	RTG	ASD

Bearing this in mind, the 4 possible message settings derived for the first part of the message would be compared with those directly inferred from the indicators to see if there was a common three-letter group.

The occurrence of such a letter group provided strong evidence to support the conclusion that the common message settings thus identified were in fact correct. Once the message settings had been found they could be used to reduce the number of possible rotor orders that had to be tested.

For example suppose that the first part of a multi-part message consists of 247 letters and has the indicators L O N M R F, and that the second part of the message has the indicators E Z A F V Q.

Consider the first part of the message. From the indicator settings L O N it is feasible to assume that the message settings are possibly D O N.

Supposing that after the operator had encrypted the first part of the message he had used the 'end positions' of the rotors as the indicator settings for the second part of the message. Then by working back from the 'end positions' E Z A through the 247 letters of the first part of the message, using the procedures outlined in the above chart, 4 possible message settings are found: E Q N, E P N, D O N and D P N. (Readers may wish to confirm these results!). This new evidence now confirms the assumption that the message setting is likely to be D O N. This result can now be used to derive some information about the rotor order used.

When the 247 characters ($= 26 \times 9 + 13$) of the first part of the message were encrypted the positions of the three rotors changed from D O N to E Z A, showing that the left-hand rotor had moved on by one place.

This implies that the notch on the middle rotor must have been located between letters O and Z on its ring, so that only Rotors I or III could have occupied the middle position in the Enigma machine.

Since the position of the middle rotor changed from o to z, it must have stepped through 11 positions, while the right-hand wheel made 9 complete revolutions and an additional 13 steps.

In each revolution of the right-hand rotor the notch on its ring would have caused the middle rotor to move on by one place thus resulting in 9 places in all. However, when the notch on the middle rotor caused the left-hand rotor to step from d to e, the middle rotor would step on again by one place because of the 'double stepping' of this rotor that would occur. This brings the total number of steps of the middle rotor so far accounted for to 10 steps.

The fact that the middle rotor stepped on by a total of 11 places, implies that another step must have occurred at some point during the additional 13 steps of the right-hand rotor between letters n and a. Consequently the notch on the ring of the right-hand rotor must have been located at one of the 13 positions between these two letters.

Hence it has been deduced that the right-hand rotor must have been either rotors I or III or V. The following table shows all of the rotor orders that are possible when the above restrictive conditions are applied.

Left rotor	Middle rotor	Right rotor	Left rotor	Middle rotor	Right rotor
I	III	V	IV	III	V
II	III	V	IV	I	III
II	I	III	V	I	III
II	I	V	II	III	I
III	I	V	IV	III	I
IV	I	V	V	III	I

So by means of these empirical methods the number of possible rotor orders has been reduced from 60 to 12. (The above example was created by means of a computer emulation of an Enigma machine using the rotor order III, I, V). *Appendix 3* includes an authentic description of this method written by Dennis Babbage in correspondence with Welchman in 1982.

Appendix 3

A Comedy of Errors

M ost of the books that were published in the 1970s to tell the story of
Bletchley Park gave the impression that Enigma was a problem
which the British and American cryptanalysts had solved. It would seem
that both GCHQ and the NSA had no quarrel with this impression being
given. However, Welchman and most of his Hut 6 colleagues did not agree
and he explained why in *The Hut Six Story*:

> It is clear that, although the designers of the Enigma with which Hut
> 6 had to deal may be accused of not having done a perfect job, the
> real culprits were the people who laid down the operating pro-
> cedures, the people who were communicating with each other, and
> the cipher clerks who operated the machines. The machine as it was
> would have been impregnable if it had been used properly.

In his book, he went on to describe the comedy of errors committed by
the Germans. As with almost all of the technical detail in his book, Welchman had written this section from memory, without help from former
colleagues or official documents. Inevitably there were errors in his
manuscript and in early August 1982 he received a letter from Dennis
Babbage, one of the first recruits to BP, arriving just after Christmas 1939.
Once established in Hut 6, he had quickly become head of Hut 6's research
section and the chief cryptanalyst. Most colleagues regarded Babbage and
David Rees as Hut 6's technical wizards.

Babbage had read *The Hut Six Story* and had felt compelled to write to
Welchman, pointing out some of the errors in the book. He attached what
he described as a short monograph on the subject of cillies. As there does
not appear to be any account of Hut 6 activity in existing literature directly
attributable to Babbage, his monograph is included below in its entirety:

Sillies

I think that these were originally christened Cillies (perhaps by Dilly Knox?). They were not as described in pp. 99–103 [of *The Hut Six Story*]. If we had a 3-part message like that at the bottom of page 99 we should of course have guessed the text settings, but this wasn't a true cilli, and I don't remember anything quite so obvious occurring.

The essential thing about a cilli operator was that when he had encoded a message he would leave the wheels unaltered when he came to encode the text setting of his second message (or second part of the same message). If he had done this then by 'alphabetical subtraction' of the number of letters in the first message from the 3-letter indicator setting of the second we would get back to the text setting of the first message and thus have a 3-letter decode. The nature of this 'alphabetical subtraction' depended on the wheel-order. When a wheel advanced from one letter to the next, the wheel (if any) on its left would normally stay put, but when the first wheel passed through a certain 'critical position' it would take its left-hand neighbour with it. The critical positions for wheels 1, 2, 3, 4, 5 were Q/R, E/F, V/W, J/K, Z/A respectively.

Suppose we had a 5-part message whose indicator settings and indicators were as follows, where the figures in brackets give the number of letters in the text:

AVS MBU (161)

QGD LRT (166)

XZH FJK (167)

EKN YTL (171)

RMK BHC (150)

If we subtract 161 (or $6 \times 26 + 5$) 'alphabetically' from QGD we get QAY. 166 (or $6 \times 26 + 10$) from XZH gives *XTX*. 167 (or $6 \times 26 + 11$) from EKN gives EEC and 171 (or $6 \times 26 + 15$) from RMK gives *RGV*. QAY, XTX, EEC, RGV are very nearly the four consecutive 'keyboard diagonals' QAY, WSX, EDC, RFV, and we can in fact get back to these by 'alphabetical subtraction' if we make certain assumptions about the wheel order. Let us assume that we are dealing with a cilli operator and that the text settings of the first four parts are QAY, WSX, EDC, RFV. We get from QAY to QGD in $6 \times 26 + 5$ steps provided the right-hand wheel does *not* pass through a critical position in going from Y to D. If it does pass through such a position we arrive at QHD (or at RHD if also the middle wheel passes through a critical position in going from A to H). If the middle wheel has a critical position between A and G and the right-hand one does not have one between Y and D, we arrive at RGD. We deduce that the middle wheel is not 2 and that the right wheel is not 5. In order to get from WSX to XZH in $6 \times 26 + 10$ steps the middle wheel must have a critical position between S and Z, and the right-hand wheel must have one between X and H. Hence the middle wheel must be 3 and the right-hand one 5 or 2. The above assumptions lead us to the conclusion that the wheel order is 132 or 432 or 532, and it may be verified that with any of these wheel orders one does get from EDC to EKN in 167 steps, and from RFV to RMK in 171 steps.

Thus we have a 12-letter decode, or rather a 15-letter one, because we may assume with some confidence that the text setting of the fifth part is TGB, which is the fifth in the sequence of 'keyboard diagonals'. In searching for the stecker pairings we have only 3 wheel orders to consider instead of 60, and a strong Herivel tip might reduce the number of ringstellungs to be considered from $26 \times 26 \times 26$ to 1, at any rate as a first shot. I distinctly remember just such a situation occurring one day and my working out the machine setting by myself well before 7 a.m.

Apart from triads of letters forming recognizable patterns on the keyboard, some lazy cilli operators chose text settings three steps ahead of the indicator, not so much JAB JAB as JAB JAE, the point being that, after the text setting had been encoded, the wheels would be in the correct position for encoding the main text.

Other popular text settings were pronounceable 3-letter groups. One was SAK, which I suspect means something rather rude.

In searching for cillies of all these kinds one examined a sequence of messages from the same operator and carried out what I have described as alphabetical subtraction combined with intelligent guesswork about the wheel order. Perhaps Dilly Knox found a pronounceable sequence including CIL, short for CILLI, a girl's name?

German Air Force/Army Keys
Identified and Broken*

German Air Force Keys

Name	German Unit	First seen	Last intercept
Brown I	IV L.N. Versuchs Regiment	Start	To end
Red	General operational key	9/39	To end
Blue	Practice key	10/39	To end
Celery	Western weather key	Spring 40	2/45
Purple	[no unit given]	5/40	2/41
Light Blue	Mediterranean operational key	1/41	12/41
Mauve	Probably GAF key	2/41	3/41
Pink	Führungsnetz subcribers	2/41	To end
Onion	Navigational beam key	3/41	7/41
Beetroot	Western weather key	6/41	12/41
Leek	Eastern weather key	6/41	To end
Lily	Luftgau Belgien-Nordfrankreich	6/41	4/45
Mustard	German Y Service	6/41	To end
Speedwell	Luftgau Süd Ost	6/41	1/42
Tulip	Luftgau Holland	6/41	2/44
Heather	Luftgau Norwegen	Summer 41	12/41
Cowslip	Lufygau XI	8/41	8/41
Brown II	IV L.N. Versuchs Regiment	12/41	3/43
Beetle	Luftflotte 6	1/42	To end
Cockroach	Jagdkorps I	1/42	2/45
Firefly	Fliegerkorps XI	1/42	12/44
Gadfly	Luftwaffen Kommando Süd Ost	1/42	To end
Hornet	Fliegerkorps IV	1/42	12/43
Locust	Fliegerkorps II	1/42	To end
Mosquito	Luftflotte 1	1/42	To end
Primrose	Luftgau XXVIII	1/42	9/44
Wasp	Fliegerkorps IX	1/42	To end
Garlic	South Europe weather key	4/42	To end

* *Source:* The History of Hut 6 Volume II, HW 43/71. Some obvious literal errors in the original have been corrected.

Name	German Unit	First seen	Last intercept
Scorpion I	Fliegerführer Afrika	4/42	7/42
Snowdrop	Luftgau Westfrankreich	4.42	To end
Daffodil	Luftgau XI	5/42	To end
Polecat	3/Fernaufklärungsgruppe 122	5/42	5/42
Skunk	Fliegerkorps VIII	5/42	To end
Lion	Luftflotte 5	6/42	To end
Scorpion II	Fliegerführer Afrika	6/42	2/43
Narcissus	Luftgau Norwegen	7/42	11/44
Weasel	Flakkorps I	7/42	4/45
Crab	Fliegerführer Luftflotte 1	8/42	10/42
Ermine	Fliegerkorps I	9/42	To end
Civet	Kampfgeschwader 4	11/42	7/43
Dingo	Kampfgeschwader 76	11/42	10/43
Rabbit	Kampfgeschwader 55	11/42	4/43
Ferret	Kampfgeschwader 53	12/42	12/42
Lemming	Jafü Süd (Norway)	1/43	3/43
Porcupine	South Russian Front	1/43	3/43
Stoat	Night fighter groups	1/43	2/43
Dragonfly	Fliegerkorps Tunis	2/43	5/43
Hedgehog	Fliegerkorps I, IV, VIII	2/43	7/43
Clover	Luftgau I	3/43	4/45
Daisy	Luftgau Moskau	3/43	5/44
Foxglove	Luftgau XVII	3/43	To end
Gorse	Luftgau XXVI	3/43	11/44
Mouse	Geschwader key	3/43	4/43
Orchid	Luftgau XXV	3/43	11/44
Shamrock	Reserve Blue for March	3/43	3/43
Aster	Luftgau VII	5/43	To end
Mole	Geschwader key, S. Russia	5/43	6/43
Rat	Reserve Red for May	5/43	5/43
Mayfly	Fliegerkorps XIV	6/43	1/45
Squirrel	Fernkampfführer Luftflotte 2	7/43	11/43
Puma	Luftflotte 2	8/43	To end
Sheep	Jagdgeschwader 53	8/43	8/43
Beaver	Schlachtgeschwader 1	9/43	12/43
Brown III	IV L.N. Versuchs Regiment	9/43	To end
Gentian	Luftgau III	9/43	To end
Poppy	Luftgau XII/XIII	9/43	4/44
Indigo	General teleprinter key	10/43	To end
Endive	Central weather key	11/43	To end
Leveret	L.N. Regt. 200	11/43	1/45
Yak	Fliegerführer Kroatien	11/43	To end
Cricket	Jagdkorps II	12/43	11/44
Jaguar	Luftflotte 3	12/43	To end
Llama	Fliegerführer Albanien	12/43	9/44
Chipmunk	Versuchsverband O.B.d.L.	1/44	3/45

Name	German Unit	First seen	Last intercept
Hyena	Luftflotte Reich	2/44	To end
Leopard	Luftflotte 2	2/44	To end
Puce	Robinson Ost/Luftflotte 4	2/44	10/44
Armadillo	Flugsicherungs Regt. West	5/44	8/44
Cress	Y Service, Western Europe	5/44	8/44
Gnat	Fliegerkorps X	5/44	8/44
Ocelot	Luftflotte 3	5/44	To end
Platypus	Flakkorps III	5/44	1/45
Glowworm	Fallschirm AOK 1	6/44	9/44
Opossum	Kampfgeschwader 100	6/44	8/44
Racoon	I Kampfgeschwader 66	6/44	6/44
Gibbon	Zerstörergeschwader 1	7/44	8/44
Jerboa	Flak Regt. 155	7/44	2/45
Gorilla	Luftflotte 4	9/44	To end
Marmoset	Flakkorps IV	9/44	4/45
Chimpanzee	Luftflotte 10	11/44	To end
Wallflower	Luftgau VI	12/44	3/45
Monkey	Flakkorps II	2/45	4/45
Chamois	Flakkorps V	3/45	To end
Moth	Fliegerkorps II	3/45	5/45
Violet	Luftgau VIII	3/45	4/45
Termite	Fliegerdivision 9	3/45	4/45
Goat	Flakkorps VI	4/45	To end
Otter	Kampfgeschwader 200	4/45	4/45

German Army Keys

Greenshank A & B	Wehrkreise	1939	5/45
Orange	SS Stabs M/S	1939	5/45
T.G.D. [sic]	Reichssicherungsdienst	1939	5/45
Yellow	Norwegian campaign key	4/40	7/40
Rocket	Reichsbahn M/S	6/40	5/45
Azure	N.W. Europe	8/40	1/41
Lemon	Vienna	12/40	3/41
Gannet I	Armee M/S AOK Norwegen	1/41	[n.d.]
Magenta	Berlin–Romania	1/41	4/41
Chaffinch I	OKH Stabs M/S I	2/41	5/43
Chaffinch II	Sonder M/S Rome–Panzer Armee	2/41	5/43
Chaffinch III	OKH M/S I	2/41	5/43
Linnet	Forward operational key, Libya	3/41	8/41
Cuckoo	Balkan campaign key	4/41	5/41
Jay	OKH M/S B	4/41	6/44
Vulture I	OKH M/S II	4/41	Spring 44
Falcon	Wehrmarcht M/S Heimatkriegsgebiet	6/41	4/45
Kestrel	Rundspruch M/S	6/41	9/42
Hawk	D/F Lithuanian border	12/6/41	12/6/41

Name	German Unit	First seen	Last intercept
Kite	O. Qu. M/S A	7/41	4/45
Crow	Yugoslavia campaign	9/41	10/41
Raven	M/S Ägäisches Süd	9/41	4/45
Rook I	Eastern Front	9/41	10/42
Rook II	Y key between Finland/OKH (Goldap)	9/41	3/44
Jackdaw	D/F Russian Front	22/9/41	22/9/41
Apple	Police in Norway, N. Germany	11/41	8/42
Phoenix	Panzer Armee M/S Afrika	11.41	5/43
Seagull	Crete campaign	11/41	12/41
Gannet II	Armee M/S Gebs AOK 20	4/42	4/45
Skylark	Comms Channel Isles/France	4/42	5/42
Goose	Armee M/S Holland	4/42	5/43
Blackbird	Western Front	5/42	8/44
Osprey	M/S Organisation Todt	6/42	4/45
Merlin	Heeresetabs M/S	7/42	11/43
Robin	Railway system key	7/42	10/44
Thrush	Sonder M/S Rome–Maleme	7/42	11/42
Mallard	Heeres M/S	8/42	4/45
Pullet	Rundspruch M/S West	8/42	3/45
Quince I	SS Feldnachschub M.S.	8/42	5/45
Blunderbuss	Eisenbahn Truppen M/S	9/42	5/45
Heron	Norway campaign	10/42	12/42
Bittern	Rumanian Army	11/42	4/43
Bullfinch	Rome–Tunis (Special key)	11/42	5/43
Dodo	Armee M.S. Pz. AOK 5	11/42	4/45
Starling	Bucharest to Rostov-on-Don	11/42	12/42
Goldfinch	Bullfinch for Nov. 1942	12/42	12/42
Hawfinch	Same as Chaffinch I	1/43	2/43
Sparrow	Mediterranean Y key	3/43	3/45
Bantam	Wehrmacht M/S West	4/43	5/45
Buzzard	S.E. Europe campaign	4/43	6/43
Chicken	Armee M/S AOK 15 key	4/43	4/45
Cormorant	Sonder M/S for Rome–Sardinia	4/43	6/43
Drake	Armee M/S in Holland	4/43	5/43
Duck	Armee M/S AOK 7 key	4/43	5/45
Turkey	Western Front railway key	4/43	5/43
Albatross	Armee M/S AOK 10 key	5/43	4/45
Gosling	Armee M/S AOK 19 key	5/43	4/45
Swan	Armee M/S AOK 1 key	5/43	4/45
Hen	N.W. France campaign	6/43	7/43
Peregrine	V SS Geb. Korps/Prinz Eugen	6/43	9/43
Pigeon	Western Front key	7/43	[n.d.]
	Not in continuity with 7/43 key	8/44	3/45
Fowl	French campaign	8/43	12/43
Hobby	Übungs M/S von Wehrkreis VI	8/43	10/43

Name	German Unit	First seen	Last intercept
Nuthatch	Berlin–Vienna–Belgrade	Mid 43	2/45
Puffin	OKH M/S B	8/43	5/45
Shrike	Armee M/S Liguria	8/43	4/44
Wryneck	Armee M/S Pz. AOK 2 key	8/43	3/45
Goshawk	Wrongly named. Really Kite	9/43	9/43
Curlew	Wehrkreis II	10/43	6/44
Magpie	Dodecanese campaign	10/43	1/44
Stork	Hungarian Army key	10/43	11/43
Woodpecker	S.E. Europe teleprinter key	10/43	3/44
Owl	Armee M/S AOK 17 key	11/43	3/44
Toucan	Supply key in Italy	11/43	3/44
Bullfinch	OKH–AOK 10 (special key)	12/43	2/44
Quince II	SS Chef Sonder M/S	End 43	5/45
Coot	Supply key on Eastern Front	1/44	5/44
Fulmar	Armee M/S AOK 8 key	1/44	5/44
Corncrake	Sonder M/S P.W.Kdo. II (V2s)	2/44	4/45
Nightjar	Militär Befehlshaber M/S	2/44	8/44
Roulette I	Polchi M/S, Senior Police key	2/44	5/45
Wagtail	Wehrkreis VIII practice key	2/44	10/44
Pelican	Armee M/S Pz. AOK 1 key	3/43	6/44
Moorhen	Supply key in Italy	4/44	5/44
Pumpkin	SS propaganda key	4/44	4/45
Grapefruit	SS concentration camp key	5/44	4/45
Kingfisher	Armee M/S AOK 14 key	5/44	4/45
Medlar	SS Querverkehr M/S	5/44	5/45
Avocet	OKH M/S Eastern Front/Norway	6/44	5.45
Diver	Sonder M/S Channel Islands	6/44	4/45
Flamingo	Armee M/S Pz. AOK 3 key	6/44	8/44
Grouse	Wehrkreis XVII	6/44	5/45
Peewit	O.Qu. M/S B	6/44	5/45
Penguin	12 SS Pz. Div. Western Front	6/44	7/44
Erget	OKH Special Western Front	8/44	10/44
Emu I	Heeres M/S Süd	[no dates given]	
Emu II	Heeresstabs M/S Süd	8/44	5/45
Lorient	Sonder M/S	9/44	4/45
Culverin	Railway Western Europe	10/44	11/44
Flycatcher	Sonder M/S OKH–Crete	10/44	4/45
Guillemot	Kommander der Festungsbereich West	10/44	11/44
Ibis	V2 launches in Holland	10/44	4/45
Oriole	Y key between OKH/H.Gr. G	10/44	4/45
Quail	Armee M/S	10/44	5/45
Wheatear	Sonder M/S	10/44	12/44
Whinchat	Rundspruch M/S H.Gr.G	10/44	5/45
Tomtit	S.E. Germany campaign	11/44	2/45
Bunting	Supply key of H.Gr. E and F	12/44	1/45
Cassowary	Bev. Gen. Ungarn	1/45	4/45

Name	German Unit	First seen	Last intercept
Hummingbird	Rundspruch M/S H.Gr. B	1/45	4/45
Whimbrel	Armee M/S SS Pz. AOK 6	1/45	2/45
Plum	SS M/S Sondersatz C	3/45	4/45
Grebe	Armee M/S AOK 25 key	4/45	4/45

First Seen by Year

	Air Force	Army	Total
1939	3	3	6
1940	2	4	6
1941	13	19	32
1942	25	18	43
1943	30	30	60
1944	18	32	50
1945	7	5	12
Total	98	111	209

Last Seen by Year

	Air Force	Army	Total
1939	0	0	0
1940	0	1	1
1941	7	9	16
1942	5	8	13
1943	18	19	37
1944	18	24	42
1945	50	50	100
Total	98	111	209

Key Breaks

	Breaks
1939	16
1940	426
1941	991
1942	3,637
1943	5,296
1944	8,801
1945	2,804
Total	21,971

Letter from Sir Peter Marychurch

From the Director: Sir Peter Marychurch KCMG

Government Communications Headquarters
Oakley Cheltenham Glos GL52 5AJ
Telephone Cheltenham 21491 ext

D/2731DQ/1601/21
12 July 1985

G Welchman Esq
167 Water Street
NEWBURYPORT
Ma 01950
USA

Dear Mr Welchman,

It has come to my notice that Dr Christopher Andrew is proposing to publish an article of yours in a journal called "Intelligence and National Security". The article, entitled "From Polish Bomba to British Bombe: The Birth of Ultra", appears to have been conceived as a corrective addendum to your book published in 1982, "The Hut Six Story".

2.   Dr Andrew has submitted this article to the Secretary of the Defence Press and Broadcasting Committee for consideration under the D Notice system, stating that he does this at your request. I understand the Secretary to have replied that there are no deletions which he can usefully suggest and that the proper course was for you to submit any proposed publication to your former department, in accordance with your obligations under the Official Secrets Acts and with the guidelines issued by the Foreign Secretary in 1978 (endorsed by the Prime Minister in 1979) of which a copy is attached to this letter.

3.   I can only endorse the Secretary's response. It was (as I believe you know) a great shock to my predecessor and to the US authorities when you published you book in 1982, without consulting us and in defiance of undertakings which thousands of others have faithfully observed; I am disappointed to find you following a similar path again in 1985. These words may seem somewhat harsh, but I ask you to consider not only the direct damage to security but also the knock-on effect of your actions: each time a person like yourself, of obviously deep knowledge and high repute, publishes inside information about the inner secrets of our work, there is more temptation and more excuse for others to follow suit. The ultimate result must be as obvious to you as it is to me. We do not expect outsiders to show any great sense of responsibility in what they publish, but you can perhaps understand that it is a bitter blow to us, as well as a disastrous example to others, when valued ex-colleagues decide to let us down.

Yours sincerely,

Peter Marychurch.

P H MARYCHURCH

Appendix 6

Welchman's Publications

Academic Works

'The Number of Contact Primes of the Canonical Curve of Genus p', *Proceedings of the Cambridge Philosophical Society*, Vol. XXVI, Part 4, 1930, pp. 453–7

'On Elliptic Quartic Curves with Assigned Points and Chords', *Proceedings of the Cambridge Philosophical Society*, Vol. XXVII, Part 1, 1931, pp. 20–3

'Some Enumerative Results for Curves', *Proceedings of the Cambridge Philosophical Society*, Vol. XXVIII, Part 1, 1932, pp. 18–2

'Note on the Trisecants and Quadrisecants of a Space Curve', *Proceedings of the Cambridge Philosophical Society*, Vol. XXVIII, Part 2, 1932, pp. 206–8

'Plane Congruences of the Second Order in Space of Four Dimensions and Fifth Incidence Theorems', *Proceedings of the Cambridge Philosophical Society*, Vol. XXVIII, Part 3, 1932, pp. 276–84

'Additional Note on Plane Congruences and Fifth Incidence Theorems', *Proceedings of the Cambridge Philosophical Society*, Vol. XXVIII, Part 4, 1932, pp. 416–20

'Foci of Systems of Space', *Journal of the London Mathematical Society*, Vol. 7, Part 3, 1932, pp. 175–9

'Planar Threefolds in Space of Four Dimensions', *Proceedings of the Cambridge Philosophical Society*, Vol. XXIX, Part 1, 1933, pp. 103–15

' Incidence Scrolls', *Proceedings of the Cambridge Philosophical Society*, Vol. XXIX, Part 2, 1933, pp. 235–44

'Bisecant Curves of Ruled Surfaces', *Proceedings of the Cambridge Philosophical Society*, Vol. XXIX, Part 3, 1933, pp. 382–8

'Special Scrolls and Involutions on Canonical Curves', *Proceedings of the London Mathematical Society*, Vol. 40, Ser. 2, 1936, pp. 143–88

Introduction to Algebraic Geometry, Cambridge University Press, 1950

Technical Papers

Gordon Welchman wrote many detailed technical reports while working for the MITRE Corporation, many of which were classified. The following is a selection of such publications which were eventually approved for public release.

'Characteristics of Air Offense Missions Against Ground Targets in Two Broad Categories of Limited War', WP-5, 19 August 1965

'Mission and Military Value of the Airborne Tactical Air Support Team (ATAST)', WP-673, 14 June 1966

'A Concept for the Employment of Unit Digital Messages in a Tactical Command, Control, and Communications System', WP-858, 10 October 1966

'ESD/MITRE Interest in Computer-Managed Integration of Avionics Systems', WP-1312, 20 February 1967

'Selective Access to Tactical Information', M70-74, August 1970. Subsequently published in *Signal* magazine.

'A Concept of Selective Access to Tactical Information', M70-97, December 1970

'Latent Capabilities for Decision Making in a Dynamic Environment', M70-101, December 1970

'An Integrated Approach to the Defence of West Germany, an Information Paper', February 1974. Subsequently published in the *RUSI Journal* (Royal United Services Institute for Defence Studies)

'Alternatives in Air Strategy in Central Europe – A Background Study', M73-103, 5 March 1974

'A Soviet Master Plan and Its Prelude', M74-242, 15 October 1974

'A Five-Level Structure of NATO Ground Forces', June 1975

Works on Bletchley Park and Enigma

The Hut Six Story, Breaking the Enigma Codes, McGraw-Hill Book Company, United States, 1982

The Hut Six Story, Breaking the Enigma Codes, Allen Lane, Great Britain, 1982

The Hut Six Story, Breaking the Enigma Codes, Penguin, Great Britain, 1984

The Hut Six Story, Breaking the Enigma Codes, M. & M. Baldwin, 1997

'From Polish Bomba to British Bombe: The Birth of Ultra', *Intelligence and National Security*, Vol. 1, No. 1, January 1986

Notes

Abbreviations: GW – Gordon Welchman; NW – Nick Welchman;
SW – Susanna Welchman; RW – Rosamond Welchman

Prologue

1. Letter to the editor, *Guardian*, 29 November 1985.

Chapter 1: Origins: From Algebraic Geometry to Cryptography

1. NW provided the author with a written account of memories of his father's life from his childhood to December 1954.
2. Obituary, Sidney Sussex College Annual 1986.
3. Cambridge University Madrigal Society programmes – e.g. a performance of motets, King's College Chapel, Sunday, 16 February 1935.
4. A Cambridge friend recalled visiting him in Newburyport in 1981 when Welchman had remembered that it was Schubert's birthday and had suitable tapes to play in the car during a long journey.
5. Interview with Diana Lucy and Bunny Westcott.
6. When it was eventually published in 1950, it looked like a book out of its time as the subject had undergone considerable changes in the 1940s.
7. This had risen to 62 per cent in 2007.
8. Betty Huntley-Wright went on to have a long career on stage, chiefly in comedy and pantomime, as well as film, radio and television. She memorably played Mrs Twitchen in the fifth episode of the legendary British television series *Fawlty Towers*. In 1955, Welchman took his son and one of his daughters to see a Christmas pantomime in which Betty was appearing with her daughter and they all met after the show. They remained friends and corresponded regularly for the rest of GW's life.
9. Copy provided by RW.
10. Note on 'control of interception', n.d. [*c.* 1924] (TNA, WO 32/4897).
11. See Keith Jeffrey's official history *MI6: The History of the Secret Intelligence Service 1909–1949*, pp. 213–14. His source is referenced as 'Denniston, "Government and Code Cypher School", 49'.
12. TNA, HW 62/21.
13. Strachey had been born in 1874 and, after being educated at Oxford, had worked in Military (Army) Intelligence, MI 1, during the First World War and in GC&CS between the wars. In 1934, Strachey and Hugh Foss, another GC&CS veteran, broke the Japanese naval attaché machine cipher. He would go on to head the ISOS (Illicit/Intelligence Services Oliver Strachey) section at BP, decrypting messages on the Abwehr (German secret police) network and was involved with turned German agents as part of the Double Cross system.

In January 1942, Strachey went to Ottawa, Canada, where he was chief cryptographer in the Examination Unit, and remained there until July. This ambiguously named, top secret cipher department was the Canadian version of BP. His predecessor at the unit was the notorious Herbert Osborne Yardley, who had written a sensational exposé of American and British cryptography in the First World War, *The American Black Chamber*, in 1931. Yardley's contract was not renewed under pressure from Washington and Strachey refused to go to Ottawa until Yardley had left the city. Strachey brought with him from England keys to high-level Vichy French and Japanese diplomatic codes, which helped initiate closer co-operation between Washington and London. Although he did not speak or read Japanese, he helped break the Japanese encryption, which was very complex, since it used variations of *kanji*, *hiragana*, and romanization. See David Kahn's biography of Yardley for more detail on Strachey.

14. John Tiltman could lay claim to being one of the greatest cryptologists of his generation. Born in 1894, he was offered a place at Oxford when he was thirteen but did not take it up as his father had recently died. He left school at the end of 1911 to become a teacher. Following a distinguished career in the First World War, he was sent on an elementary Russian language course which would change his life. On 1 August 1920 he was seconded for two weeks to GC&CS to help with a backlog of translation work. He took to decryption work so well that the War Office posted him to GC&CS, initially for a year, and he never returned to conventional regimental duties. A biography of Tiltman is long overdue and his accomplishments are too numerous to cover here. He continued working for GCHQ after the war until his retirement in 1964. He was immediately asked to join the NSA as he was living in the USA and served until 1980 when he was eighty-six! He was honoured by the Directors of GCHQ and NSA for his 'uncountable contributions and successes in cryptology' and for setting 'exemplary standards of professionalism and performance in cryptology'.

15. See *Collected Writings of John Maynard Keynes* (Cambridge University Press).

Chapter 2: Bletchley Park: The First Four Months

1. TNA, HW 62/21.

2. There remains some question about whether or not Sinclair purchased BP with his own money. Jeffrey's official history of MI 6 is not explicit on the matter. In any event, an HM Land Registry document exists dated 13 June 1938 showing the first part of the transfer of BP from Faulkner to Sinclair for £6,000. The transfer is signed by Hubert Faulkner of 112 Simpson Road, Bletchley, Bucks, and Admiral Sir Hugh Sinclair of 21 Queen Anne's Gate, Westminster, London SW1. This Westminster address was the Passport Control Office and Hugh Sinclair had a flat within the premises that backed onto 54 Broadway, the headquarters of both his SIS & GC&CS. Sinclair had a connecting passage built between the two buildings leading to his offices on its fourth floor.

3. The British patent was specification no. 267,472 and was accepted on 11 August 1927. It provided exact details of the workings of an electrical encrypting machine.

4. The origins of this story appear to be Hugh Foss's 'Reminiscences on Enigma', written in 1949. In her biography of Knox, Mavis Batey confirms that GC&CS was in possession of a machine in 1929 after Foss completed his work on it. However, as an Enigma machine cost around £3,000 in today's values in the mid-1920s it seems unlikely that Knox would have purchased one with his own money. According to GCHQ Director Iain Lobban, in a speech given at the University of Leeds on 4 October 2012: 'In 1926, the Deputy Director of GC&CS, Edward Travis – who later became Director of GCHQ – went to Berlin and secured an Enigma machine by the simple expedient of going to the manufacturing company and buying one.'

5. Kendrick was a very talented cryptanalyst in his own right and he would go on to be a

founder member of Hut 8 before spending the rest of the war in Ottawa, as GC&CS's
representative to the Canadian sigint organization.

6. TNA, HW43/1 Chapter VI, 'Y' Versus 'Cryptography', p. 184.
7. TNA, HW43/1 Chapter VI, 'Y' Versus 'Cryptography', p. 185.
8. TNA, HW 3/83 Post-War Notes by Josh Cooper, Head of AI 4(f), p. 27.
9. In April 2000 an Abwehr Enigma G312 was stolen from BP. Police divers duly searched the lake but no wartime crockery was found.
10. He told his friend and former intercept operator Diana Lucy many years later that as far as he knew at this stage, they could have been falling from the sky.
11. The log-readers would eventually move to BP in 1942 at Welchman's instigation.
12. The *Beaumanor Staff Magazine* appeared from October 1941 until the end of the war. It was illustrated throughout by a distinguished cartoonist and full of poetry, essays, jokes and limericks, all presented with great wit and humour.
13. Perhaps even more remarkable is that while writing *The Hut Six Story*, Welchman did not have access to any documentation about the Polish methods. So in effect, he had to reinvent the idea of using perforated sheets (which became known as the Zygalski sheets or 'Netz' at BP) forty years later.
14. In correspondence with colleagues while researching his book, GW claimed that he did not feel slighted at all and was pleased that his idea had merit and was already under development. Furthermore, there was now a real chance that they would be able to read encrypted German messages.
15. It was hardly surprising that the Polish ambassador to Britain was outraged when the storyline of the 2001 film *Enigma* was revealed to him. Based on a novel by Robert Harris and set in BP, the plot describes how a cryptanalyst at BP is about to reveal its secrets to the Germans. His nationality – Polish! The Poles had been the first to work out the circuitry of the German military Enigma and read messages encrypted on it. Yet early accounts of the Enigma story by British and American authors mostly understated their pioneering work. Even Hinsley's official history of British intelligence in the Second World War was inaccurate and incomplete on the subject. Today, a striking monument to that contribution stands at BP, fittingly, adjacent to 'The Cottage' where Knox and his team were able to exploit the technical breakthrough made by the Poles in the 1930s.
16. The story was repeated by Tadeusz Lisicki in an episode of the 1977 BBC series *The Silent War* which told the story of Enigma and Ultra.
17. In researching his book, *Enigma: The Battle for the Code*, Hugh Sebag- Montefiore interviewed Paul Paillole in 1998. Paillole became head of French Counter-Intelligence during WW2 and provided details of Schmidt's involvement with the French. Montefiore also interviewed Hans Thilo Schmidt's daughter, Gisela.
18. A number of authors who wrote about this meeting years later mistakenly believed that it was not Sandwith who attended the meeting, but the future head of MI6, Stewart Menzies, in disguise as a distinguished British professor.
19. Rejewski's description is taken from his 1981 paper in the *Annals of the History of Computing*. He wrote several other papers around the same time and in 2005, the city of his birth, Bydgoszcz, published a book dedicated to him (see Bibliography).
20. TNA, HW 25/12.
21. TNA, HW 25/12.
22. TNA, HW 25/12.
23. GW corresponded with Winterbotham between 22 January 1975 and 15 March 1977.
24. GW corresponded with Robin Denniston from 19 January 1978 until his death in 1985.
25. GW corresponded with Twinn between 5 August 1975 and 12 March 1985.
26. TNA, HW14/3.

Chapter 3: The Ultra Architect

1. Interview in 2002.
2. TNA, HW 14/2, HW14/22.
3. Milner-Barry's only account of his wartime activities appears in Hinsley and Stripp's *The Codebreakers.*
4. GW engaged John Cushman of John Cushman Associates Inc. as his agent at the beginning of 1976 on the recommendation of Peter Calvocoressi. Cushman remained GW's agent until his death in 1984. His colleague, Jane Wilson took over the role until GW's death.
5. TNA HW14/4.
6. Kozaczuk, *Enigma*, p. 97 describes the farewell dinner and claims that Rejewski told him about it with 'photographic precision' in 1975. Guido Langer, in his unpublished memoir: 'Report on the work of Lieutenant-Colonel Langer's team during the French Campaign from 1 October 1939 to 24 June 1940' says that a British codebreaker, presumably Turing, was staying with the Poles in France when the first wartime Enigma message was broken on 17 January 1940.
7. The History of Hut 6 Volume I, TNA, HW 43/71–2.
8. Interview in *Station X*, a four-part documentary series. Darlow/Smithson production. Tx. Channel 4. 19 January 1999–9 February 1999.
9. Herivel describes this in his own memoir published in 2008 (see Bibliography).
10. TNA, HW 14/11.
11. TNA, HW 14/17.
12. According to the official history of MI6, Denniston's removal from BP by Menzies was a demotion. GW always believed that his removal was due to ill health. However, Harold Fletcher told him in a letter dated 26 October 1979 that: 'I have a clear recollection that you told me that Travis had had to tell C "Either he goes or I go".'
13. Ralph Erskine, 'The Development of Typex', *The Enigma Bulletin*, No. 2, May 1997; Kruh, Louis, and C. A. Deavours, 'The Typex Cryptograph', *Cryptologia*, 7: 2, 1983, pp. 145–66.
14. TNA, HW 43/72.
15. TNA, HW 43/71–3.
16. GW corresponded with R. V. Jones between 1 May and 7 September 1979.
17. Jones sent GW a complete transcript of the report in September 1979.
18. TNA, HW 43/73.

Chapter 4: Turing, the Bombe and the Diagonal Board

1. See Bibliography for details of Rejewski's papers.
2. TNA, HW 14/1.
3. Twinn made a point of this in a letter to GW in 1985.
4. See Bibliography for details of a short book about Keen and the work of BTM by his son John.
5. The document was given a classification of 'Top Secret Umbra', the highest level security for an intelligence-related document in the US and, remarkably, was only declassified on 30 October 2001. See Bibliography.
6. An entry in GW's diary for 15 July 1941 reads: 'With Turing, Alexander to London. 3.15 at H.Q. Cadogan'.
7. Extracts from Cadogan's unpublished diaries were passed on by the historian Christopher Andrew in a letter to GW in 1985.

Chapter 5: Expansion and Consolidation

1. The bombe would 'stop' when it found a wheel configuration which did not contradict any of the electrical connections described by the menu. It would provide part of the key:

the rotor order, the wheel settings relative to the starting position of the bombe drums (usually zzz) and one of the plug letter pairs. Further hand testing would either produce the rest of the key (a valid stop was called a story) or it would reveal contradictions such as one letter being plugged to two others (this type of stop was called a random stop), in which case further bombe runs were required.

When a key was broken at BP (all the settings of the Enigma machine for a twenty-four-hour period on a particular network were known), the key was said to be 'out'.

Each bombe run was called a 'job' at BP and when a run was successful, the members of the WRNS who operated them were told that the job 'was up'.

2. TNA, HW 43/71, HW 43/72, HW 43/73.
3. TNA, HW25/27.
4. C. H. O'D. Alexander, 'Cryptographic History of Work on the German Naval Enigma', TNA, HW 25/1.
5. GW corresponded with Fletcher between 19 August 1974 and 2 December 1984. The Welchmans often stayed with the Fletchers when they were in the UK. They remained close friends from the end of the war until Fletcher's death, a year before GW's.
6. TNA, HW 14/77.
7. BP was not alone in exploiting Hollerith technology. During WW2 Germany deployed more than 2,000 IBM punch-card and card-sorting systems throughout Europe. The equipment was used to help identify and destroy the Jewish people of Germany and Europe. IBM's collusion with Nazi Germany and its part in the Holocaust is a startling story. (See Bibliography for details of book on the subject by Edwin Black.)
8. Google has made a generous donation to the BP Trust to help restore Block C which housed the Hollerith operation. This was in part, in recognition of the importance of BP's early 'data search' technology.
9. Ronald Whelan, 'The Use of Hollerith Equipment in Bletchley Park', personal paper, 1994, BP Archive.
10. TNA, HW 3/164.
11. TNA, HW 25/27.
12. GW corresponded with Lewis between 21 September and 4 December 1984. As Head of the Central Party at BP, Lewis had fond memories of Katherine Welchman and her skill at log reading. For another view of the 'Fusion Room' see the Bibliography for Neil Webster's account, prepared by his daughter Joss Pearson in 2011. In late 1943 Lewis was asked to join Mountbatten at SEAC to take command of the No. 6 Intelligence School in Delhi. Instead, he ended up in America at Arlington Hall and attended the important British/US conference there in 1944 along with key BP people such as Travis and Tiltman.

The comments on the term 'Fusion Room' may explain why, in correspondence in July 1984 with Jean Howard (née Alington) who had worked in Hut 3, Welchman said that he had no recollection of the expression. GW corresponded with Howard between 12 July 1984 and 10 August 1985. She was researching a prospective BBC programme about the 'Y' Service, which, in the end, was not produced.
13. Fish was the name used at BP for the high-level encryption system used by the German Armed Forces High Command. It used teleprinters and was used for transmitting much longer messages than the Enigma systems.

Chapter 6: The Americans

1. Friedman signed the visitor's book in Hut 11 on 7 May 1943. The book is held in the BP Archive.
2. When Denniston died in 1961, Friedman had written a moving letter to his daughter. Friedman subsequently sent GW copies of the letter along with several other documents. Friedman went on to say:

'Your father was a great man, in whose debt all English-speaking people will remain for a very long time, if not for ever. That so very few of them should know exactly what he did towards achievement of victory in World War I and II is the sad part of the untold story of his life and of his great contribution to that victory. His devotion to the supremely important activities to which he gave so much of himself unstintingly, and with no thought to his own frail strength and physical welfare will not be forgotten by those of us who had the pleasure of knowing, admiring and loving him.'

Friedman's papers are held in the Marshall Library, Lexington Vermont.

3. See Bibliography for Yardley's account of the Black Chamber.
4. Friedman's work has been documented in a number of books. See Bibliography for books by Kahn and Clark.
5. Prescott Currier, 'My Purple Trip to England in 1941', *Cryptologia*, 20:3 (1996), pp. 193–201.
6. *Pearl Harbor: Warning and Decision*, Stanford University Press, 1962.
7. This myth gained such strength that even GW believed it, telling friends in the 1980s that he thought it had probably happened.
8. Denniston's reception by the US Navy's OP-20-G group was not so cordial. He met one of their top codebreakers, Agnes Driscoll, fifty-three years old and a twenty-year veteran of cryptanalysis. Her approach bore startling similarities to that of Dilly Knox. She rejected BP's automated solutions based on mathematics and claimed to have developed a much better hand method based on intuition. Her influence waned considerably following Pearl Harbor.
9. Turing's visit to Dayton was confirmed in 1999 with the release of a document written by him and titled: 'Visit to the National Cash Register Corporation of Dayton Ohio'. See Bibliography.
10. Bundy left Harvard Law School early in the war to join the US Army Signal Corps. After the war, he went on to a distinguished career in American politics and was foreign affairs advisor to Presidents Kennedy and Johnson. Welchman and Bundy renewed their friendship in the early 1980s and finally met again at the 1982 convention of the American Cryptogram Association at which Welchman was guest of honour.
11. 6812th Signal Security Detachment (Prov) APO 413 US Army, 15 June 1945.
12. Interview in *Station X*, a four-part documentary series. Darlow/Smithson production. Tx. Channel 4. 1999/01/19-1999/02/09.
13. William Bundy, 'The Literature of Spies and Codebreaking in the Second World War, A Layman's Guide', paper presented at Princeton Library, 1 November 1981. In the paper Bundy was very critical of the early books by Cave Brown, Winterbotham and Stevenson but praised works by Ewen Montagu, R. V. Jones, Patrick Beesly and Ronald Lewin. He also mentions Calvocoressi's 'small jewel of a book'.
14. Interview with Vanaman by Thomas Parrish on 12 May 1982.
15. Description of the flight of No. 783 from an account by Air Marshal Sir Ronald Ivelaw-Chapman.

Chapter 7: Bletchley Park: The Last Two Years

1. TNA, HW 62/5.
2. TNA, HW 14/87.
3. TNA, HW 62/6.
4. TNA, HW 62/6.
5. GW corresponded with Wallace between 18 December 1978 and 19 August 1984. They remained good friends after the war and GW often stayed with Wallace and his sister Hope when he visited England in the 1950s and 1960s.
6. GW corresponded with Bayly between 19 May 1982 and 22 August 1984. He had lost

contact with him after the war but finally managed to track him down in mid-1982. Bayly typed most of his letters on a computer from the beginning of 1983 because 'I want to practice this gadget on my computer called a text editor.'

7. Many historians prefer the original biography by H. Montgomery Hyde. Fourteen years later, Stephenson commissioned William Stevenson to write a more colourful version of his life in which some quite outlandish claims are made about his wartime achievements.

8. In September 1983, frail and feeble at eighty-seven, Stephenson arrived in New York from his retirement home in Bermuda to accept the William Donovan Award, the intelligence community's highest honour. Stephenson died in 1989, aged ninety-three, in Paget, Bermuda. For his wartime work, he was knighted in 1945. In recommending Stephenson for knighthood, Churchill wrote: 'This one is dear to my heart.' In 1946 Stephenson received the Medal for Merit from President Truman, at that time the highest US civilian award. He was the first non-American to receive the medal and General Bill Donovan presented the award. The citation paid tribute to Stephenson's 'valuable assistance to America in the fields of intelligence and special operations'. The 'Quiet Canadian' was recognized by his native land later: he was made a Companion of the Order of Canada on 17 December 1979.

9. GW had lost contact with Bayly after the war and in 1982, tried to make contact through Maidment. Eventually, Welchman made contact with both Maidment and Bayly and in November 1982 Maidment wrote to Welchman and offered some fascinating insights into Stephenson.

10. Years later, Bayly sent Welchman a copy of the photograph with an attachment which identified everyone in it. On a handwritten note also attached to it, Bayly said that he had another copy and not surprisingly, given some of the people in it, he went on to say: 'Why this picture wasn't classified I do not know!' Philip Lewis told GW in a letter in 1984 that he also had a copy of the photograph. Rather surprisingly, it seems that all of the participants were given their own copy.

11. TNA, HW 43/71, HW 43/72, HW 43/73. Milner-Barry was subsequently refused access to it and, remarkably, it was not declassified until 2006, more than ten years after his death.

12. See Bibliography for details of Oakley's *Bletchley Park Diaries*.

13. One former Wren, Ruth Bourne (née Henry), remembers removing the wiring from bombes and putting it in baskets, colour by colour. She cheekily kept a few strands of wire and wrapped them around the handle of her coffee mug. The mug can be seen today in a display cabinet in the Museum at BP. Happily, standing adjacent to the display cabinet stands a fitting memorial, not only to Turing, Welchman and Keen, but also to the intercept operators, cryptanalysts, Wrens and all the others who made the bombe such an effective tool in the attack on the Enigma system. The only operational bombe in the world stands proudly behind a small wooden fence. This rebuild of an actual bombe took a team of dedicated volunteers twelve years of meticulous reconstruction to complete using wartime design documents. On 17 July 2007, to coincide with the fiftieth anniversary of the British Computer Society, the machine was switched on. It is now regularly demonstrated to BP Museum visitors by a team of volunteers.

14. TNA, HW 62/6.

15. TNA, HW 3/169.

16. TNA, HW 3/169.

Chapter 8: Post-War and the Birth of the Digital Age

1. GW confirmed this in a letter to Fletcher.

2. Kent C. Redmond and Thomas M. Smith visited GW in Newburyport to interview him for books about Project Whirlwind. See Bibliography for details.

3. GW published a number of reports on this subject, some of which were approved for

public release. See: http://dome.mit.edu/handle/1721.3/39766.

4. See Bibliography for Tomash and Cohen's account of CSAW.

5. This development should not be confused with the Atlas computer installed at Manchester University and officially commissioned in 1962. The British Atlas was one of the world's first supercomputers and considered to be the most powerful computer in the world at that time.

6. In 1986, Sperry merged with Burroughs to form Unisys which today is a major IT service provider worldwide.

7. Quex Park remains a family home to this day. It now houses the Powell-Cotton Museum, which primarily contains a taxidermy collection of mainly African wildlife and ethnographical exhibits, but with many other items, including cannon, weaponry, porcelain and fine furniture.

8. Delay-line memory was a form of computer memory used on some of the earliest digital computers. Like many modern forms of computer memory, delay-line memory was refreshable but offered only serial rather than random-access memory.

9. Everett would go on to a distinguished career at MITRE, serving as President for seventeen years. He was also the recipient of numerous prestigious awards.

10. See Bibliography for details of Redmond and Smith's account of the evolution of SAGE.

11. See Dyer and Dennis, p. 74.

12. JITIDS is the longest continuously running and most widely used command and control system in existence.

13. When former MITRE colleagues remember Welchman today, the words unassuming and gentleman are often used. One, having been approached to contribute to this book, decided to look Welchman up online. He was fascinated to read about his former colleague's pre and post-war exploits, of which he knew little. He said that he was not surprised!

14. Interview with Diana Lucy and Bunny Westcott. When he published his book in 1982, they couldn't resist playfully referring to it as 'The Hot Sex Story'.

Chapter 9: Writing *The Hut Six Story*

1. See 'Prologue', *The Hut Six Story*.

2. GW's discussions with Calvocoressi lasted five years and included many letters between 21 August 1974 and 24 February 1979. They also met several times both in Newburyport and London.

3. A complete list of Calvocoressi's publications can be found at www.librarything.com/author/calvocoressipeter.

4. GW corresponded with Winterbotham between 22 January 1975 and 15 March 1977.

5. See Bibliography for details of Muggeridge's personal memoir.

6. *Colditz* was a British television series co-produced by the BBC and Universal Studios and screened between 1972 and 1974.

7. Now 'The National Archives' (TNA).

8. See Bibliography for details of Denniston's account of his father's life and career.

9. A seven-part television series produced by the BBC in conjunction with the Imperial War Museum documenting various technical developments during the Second World War. It was aired during 1977 and presented by William Woollard.

10. GW corresponded with Lewin between 11 January 1977 and 9 June 1982. They became good friends and following Lewin's death in 1984, his wife Sylvia wrote to GW. She pointed out that Lewin had been 'truly distressed by what he considered gross injustice to you'.

11. GW corresponded with Monroe between mid-August 1979 and 6 April 1982.

12. 'The Literature of Spies and Codebreakers in the Second World War, A Layman's Guide', a paper and presentation by William Bundy.
13. *Annals of the History of Computing*, Volume 4, Number 4.
14. *Cryptologia*, Volume 6, Number 2.
15. See Bibliography for details of Stengers's paper.

Chapter 10: Persecution and Putting the Record Straight

1. See for example Bertrand, Kozaczuk, Garlinski and Stengers.
2. Brian Randell, 'The Colossus', paper presented at the International Research Conference on the History of Computing, Los Alamos Scientific Laboratory, University of California, 10–15 June 1976.
3. TNA HW14/13.
4. Peter Hilton, 'Reminiscences of Bletchley Park, 1942–1945', *A Century of Mathematics in America*, Part 1, *c.* 1985.
5. Many historians regard an earlier biography of Stephenson by H. Montgomery Hyde as a more accurate account of his wartime work.
6. A novelty song by Frank Silver and Irving Cohn from the 1922 Broadway revue *Make It Snappy*.
7. According to Bayly, Willy's real name was Watson and he aspired to Travis's job. BP staff lists show a Captain W. Watson working in the Office of Deputy Director (Service), Commander Travis.
8. See Bibliography for details of Randell's papers.
9. Brian Randell, 'Report on Colossus', Computing Laboratory, Newcastle University, 1976.
10. Apparently, amongst many of its staff, the letters NSA stood for 'Never Say Anything' or 'No Such Agency'.
11. *Body of Secrets* review, Bruce Schneier, 2001, http://www.schneier.com/essay-103.html.
12. William (Bill) Casey served as US Director of Central Intelligence from 1981 to 1987. In this capacity he oversaw the entire United States intelligence community and personally directed the Central Intelligence Agency (CIA).
13. This is close to the format of the second edition of *The Hut Six Story*, published in 1997. The publisher, Mark Baldwin, replaced Part Four with Welchman's last paper 'From Polish Bomba to British Bombe', without any knowledge of Welchman's letter to Denniston.
14. See Bibliography for details of Kozaczuk and Kasparek's book.
15. GW corresponded with Lisicki between 22 August 1982 and 14 March 1985.
16. Kozaczuk's 1979 book was published in English in 1984, translated by Christopher Kasparek. This 2004 edition by Kozaczuk and Jerzy Straszak, replaces the original appendices, including Rejewski's papers, with six new ones.
17. Captain Kenneth ('Pinky') MacFarlan was the British liaison officer at PC Bruno, the Polish–French intelligence station which operated at the Château de Vignolles in Gretz-Armainvilliers, some forty kilometres east of Paris, from October 1939 until 9 June 1940. According to MacFarlan's daughter, he remained in regular contact with Bertrand after the war until Bertrand's death in 1976.
18. Herivel subsequently published the letters in his own book about BP in 2008.
19. Jean Howard quotes Gadd in a paper she wrote for the proposed 'Preparations for D-Day' TV programme.
20. Webster subsequently rejected all approaches by others to tell his story and died in 1990. After his wife died in 2007 his children decided to ask GCHQ for permission to publish. In April 2010, permission was granted and a copyright license issued to enable it although GCHQ still retained copyright.
21. GW claimed it was to save time and money but Diana, now a sprightly ninety-year-old

said it felt a bit more cloak and dagger than that.

22. A copy of the Marychurch letter GW received can be found in Appendix 5.

Epilogue

1. The name seems to have originated in the American comic strip Li'l Abner and refers to the job no one wanted: to be the inside man at the Skunk Works.
2. CERN was conceived at the end of the Second World War when European science was no longer the *crème de la crème*. A research laboratory was created which would not only unite European scientists but would also allow them to share the increasing costs of nuclear physics facilities. It was at CERN that an independent contractor, in the second half of 1980, proposed a project based on the concept of hypertext, to facilitate sharing and updating information among researchers. The contractor's name was Tim Berners-Lee and, in 1989, his original CERN proposal resulted in the creation of the World Wide Web.
3. PARC, formerly Xerox PARC, is a research and development company in Palo Alto, California, with a distinguished reputation for its contributions to information technology and hardware systems. Founded in 1970 as a division of Xerox Corporation, PARC has been responsible for such well-known and important developments as laser printing, ethernet, the modern personal computer, graphical user interface (GUI), object-oriented programming, ubiquitous computing, amorphous silicon (a-Si) applications, and advancing very-large-scale-integration (VLSI) for semiconductors.
4. Hinsley and Stripp, see Bibliography.
5. Statement by Margaret Thatcher about *Their Trade is Treachery*, Hansard, March 1981, col. 1079 *et seq.*
6. TNA PREM 19/910.

Appendix 2: Enigma and the Bombe in Depth

1. TNA HW 25/3.
2. This summary of the rationale used in the development of the bombe was provided to the author by John Herivel.
3. TNA HW 25/27.
4. BP wartime handwritten report, BP Trust Archive.

Bibliography

Sources

Correspondence between Gordon Welchman and the following:

Christopher Andrew

Dennis Babbage

Benjamin de Forest (Pat) Bayly

Ralph Bennett

Joan Bright

William Bundy

Peter Calvocoressi

William Casey

Malcolm Chamberlain

Jim Cochrane

John Cushman

Cipher Deavours

Robin Denniston

Barbara Eachus

Ralph Erskine

Harold Fletcher

George Goodall

Michael Handel

John Herivel

Andrew Hodges

Leonard (Joe) Hooper

Jean Howard

R. V. Jones

David Kahn

Bruce Lee

Ronald Lewin

Philip Lewis

Tadeusz Lisicki

Mark Lynch

Kenneth Maidment

Sir Peter Marychurch

John McLaughlin

Stuart Milner-Barry

John Monroe

Thomas Parrish

Brian Randell

David Rees

Neill Rosenfeld

Frank Rowlett

Jean Stengers

Sir William Stephenson

William Stevenson

Sir Edward Travis

Peter Twinn

Houston Wallace

Frederick Winterbotham

Interviews

Lord Asa Briggs, former MITRE colleagues, Andrew Hodges, Oliver Lawn, Diana Lucy, Patricia Macneal (née MacFarlan), Brian Oakley, Nick and Linda Welchman, Susanna Welchman, Rosamond Welchman, Ross and Bunny Westcott, Michael Wimer

Secondary Works

Andrew, Christopher, *Defence of the Realm: The Authorized History of MI 5*, Penguin, 2009

Bamford, James, *The Puzzle Palace*, Houghton Mifflin, 1982

———, *Body of Secrets: Anatomy of the Ultra-Secret National Security Agency*, Anchor, 2002

Batey, Mavis, *Dilly: The Man Who Broke Enigmas*, Dialogue, 2009

Beesly, Patrick, *Very Special Intelligence*, Hamish Hamilton, London, 1977

Bertrand, Gustave, *Enigma, The Greatest Riddle of the Second World War*, Paris, 1973

Black, Edwin, *IBM and the Holocaust*, Crown Publishers, 2001

Calvocoressi, Peter, *Top Secret Ultra*, Cassell, 1980

Cave Brown, Anthony, *Bodyguard of Lies*, Harper & Row, 1975

Ciechanowski, Jan Stanislaw, Jaroslaw Garbowski, Eugenia Maresch, Halina Piechocka-Lipka, Hanka Sowin'ska, Janina Sylwestrzak (eds), *Marian Rejewski 1905–1980. Living with the Enigma Secret*, Bysgosczc City Council, 2005

Clark, Ronald, *The Man Who Broke Purple*, Little, Brown, 1977

Copeland, B. Jack, *The Essential Turing*, Oxford University Press, 2004

———, and others, *Colossus*, Oxford University Press, 2006

DeBrosse, Jim, and Colin Burke, *The Secret in Building 26*, Random House, 2004

Denniston, Robin, *Thirty Secret Years*, Polperro Heritage Press, 2007

Dyer, Davis, and Michael Aaron Dennis, *Architects of Information Advantage, The MITRE Corporation since 1958*, Community Communications, 1998

Enever, Ted, *Britain's Best Kept Secret*, The History Press, 1994

Erskine, Ralph, 'The Development of Typex', *The Enigma Bulletin*, No. 2, May 1997

———, and Peter Freeman, 'Brigadier John Tiltman: One of Britain's Finest Cryptologists', *Cryptologia*, Vol. XXVII, No. 4, 2003

Fitzgerald, Penelope, *The Knox Brothers*, Macmillan, 1977

Garlinski, Jozef, *The Enigma War*, Charles Scribner's Sons, 1980

Harris Bath, Alan, *Tracking the Axis Enemy*, University Press of Kansas, 1998

Herivel, John, *Herivelismus and The German Military Enigma*, M. & M. Baldwin, 2008

Hinsley, F. H., and others *British Intelligence in the Second World War*, HMSO, 1979–1990

Hinsley, F. H., and Alan Stripp, *The Codebreakers*, Oxford University Press, 1993

Hodges, Andrew, *Alan Turing: The Enigma*, Burnett Books, 1983

Hooper, David, *Official Secrets*, Martin Secker & Warburg, 1987

Howarth, T. E. B., *Cambridge Between Two Wars*, Collins, 1978

Hyde, H. Montgomery, *The Quiet Canadian*, Hamish Hamilton, 1962

Ivelow-Chapman, John, *High Endeavour: The Life of Air Chief Marshal Sir Ronald Ivelow-Chapman*, Leo Cooper, 1993

Jeffrey, Keith, *MI6 The History of the Secret Intelligence Service 1909–1949*, Bloomsbury, 2010

Johnson, Brian, *The Secret War*, BBC Publications, 1978

Johnson, Kerry, and John Gallehawk, *Figuring it out at Bletchley Park*, Book Tower Publishing, 2007

Jones, R. V., *Most Secret War*, Hamish Hamilton, 1978

Kahn, David, *The Codebreakers*, Weidenfeld & Nicolson, 1968

———, *Hitler's Spies*, Macmillan, 1978

———, *Seizing the Enigma*, Barnes & Noble, 1991

———, *The Reader of Gentlemen's Mail: Herbert O. Yardley and the Birth of American Codebreaking*, Yale University Press, 2004

Keen, John, *Harold 'Doc' Keen and the Bletchley Park Bombe*, M. & M. Baldwin, 2003

Kozaczuk, Władysław, *W Kręgu Enigmy*, Książka i Wiedza, Warsaw, 1979

———, *Enigma – How the German Machine Cipher was Broken and How it was Read by the Allies in World War Two, with Appendices A to F (edited and translated by Christopher Kasparek)*, Arms and Armour Press, 1984

Large, Christine, *Hijacking Enigma*, John Wiley & Sons, 2003

Lewin, Ronald, *Ultra Goes to War, The Secret Story*, Hutchinson, 1978

———, *The American Magic*, Farar Straus Giroux, 1982

Montague, Ewan, *Beyond Top Secret ULTRA*, Coward McGann and Geoghegan, 1977

Muggeridge, Malcolm, *Chronicles of Wasted Time, The Infernal Grove*, Purnell Book Services, 1973

Murray, Joan, 'A Personal Contribution to the Bombe Story', NSA Document, DocID: 3269230

Oakley, Brian, *The Bletchley Park War: Some of the Outstanding Individuals*, Wynne Press, 2006
———, *The Bletchley Park Diaries, July 1939–August 1945*, Wynne Press, 2009
Page, Gwendoline (ed.), *They Listened in Secret*, Geo. R. Reeve, 2003
Parrish, Thomas, *The Ultra Americans*, Stein and Day, 1986
Pearson, Joss, *Cribs for Victory*, Polperro Heritage Press, 2011
Pincher, Chapman, *Their Trade is Treachery*, Sidgwick and Jackson, 1981
———, *Treachery: Betrayals, Blunders, and Cover-ups – Six Decades of Espionage Against America and Great Britain*, Random House, 2009
———, *Treachery: Betrayals, Blunders, and Cover-ups: Six Decades of Espionage Against America and Great Britain*, 'Updated and uncensored UK edition', Mainstream Publishing, 2009
Randell, B., 'On Alan Turing and the origins of Digital Computers', in B. Meltzer and D. Michie (eds), *Machine Intelligence 7*, Edinburgh University Press, Edinburgh, 1972
Randell, B. (ed.), *The Origins of Digital Computers: Selected Papers*, Springer Verlag, 1982
Rankin, Nicholas, *Ian Fleming's Commandos*, Faber and Faber, 2011
Redmond, Kent C., and Thomas M. Smith, *Project Whirlwind, The History of a Pioneer Computer*, Digital Press, 1980
———, *From Whirlwind to MITRE, The R&D Story of the SAGE Air Defense Computer*, MIT Press, 2000
Rejewski, Marian, 'An Application of the Theory of Permutations in Breaking the Enigma Cipher', *Applicationes Mathematicae*, Vol. 16, No. 4, 1980
———, 'How Polish Mathematicians Deciphered the Enigma', *Annals of the History of Computing*, Vol. 3, No. 3, July 1981
———, 'Mathematical Solution of the Enigma Cipher', *Cryptologia*, January 1982
Rowlett, Frank, *The Story of Magic*, Aegean Park Press, 1998
Sebag-Montefiore, Hugh, *Enigma, The Battle for the Code*, Weidenfeld & Nicolson, 2000
Smith, Bradley F., *The Ultra–Magic Deals*, Airlife, 1993
Smith, Michael, and Ralph Erskine, *Action This Day*, Bantam Press, 2001
Stengers, Jean, 'La Guerre des Messages Codes (1930–1945)', *L'Histoire*, February 1981
———, 'Enigma, the French, the Poles and the British, 1931–1940', in C. Andrew & D. Dilks (eds), *The Missing Dimension: Governments and Intelligence Communities in the Twentieth Century*, Macmillan, 1984
Stevenson, William, *A Man Called Intrepid: The Secret War*, Harcourt Brace Jovanovich, 1976
Stubbington, John, *Kept in the Dark*, Pen and Sword Aviation, 2010
Thirsk, James, *Bletchley Park: An Inmate's Story*, Galago, 2008
Tomash, Erwin, and Arnold A. Cohen, 'The Birth of an ERA: Engineering Associates, Inc. 1946–1955', *Annals of the History of Computing*, Vol. 1, No. 2, Oct. 1979
Turing, Alan, NARA RG 38, Crane, CNSG Library, Box 183, 5750/441, Bombe Correspondence, 'Visit to National Cash Register Corporation of Dayton Ohio', December 1942
West, Nigel, *MI 5: British Security Service Operations, 1909–1945*, Stein and Day, 1982
———, *A Matter of Trust: MI 5, 1945–72*, Weidenfeld and Nicolson, 1982
———, *The SIGINT Secrets, The Signals Intelligence War, 1900 to Today*, Weidenfeld & Nicolson, 1986
———, *Mole Hunt*, Weidenfeld and Nicolson, 1987
Winterbotham, F. W., *The Ultra Secret*, Weidenfeld & Nicolson, 1974
Wohlstetter, Roberta, *Pearl Harbor: Warning and Decision*, Stanford University Press, 1962
Wright, Peter, *Spycatcher*, Viking Penguin, 1987
Yardley, Herbert O., *The American Black Chamber*, Bobbs-Merrill, 1931

Index